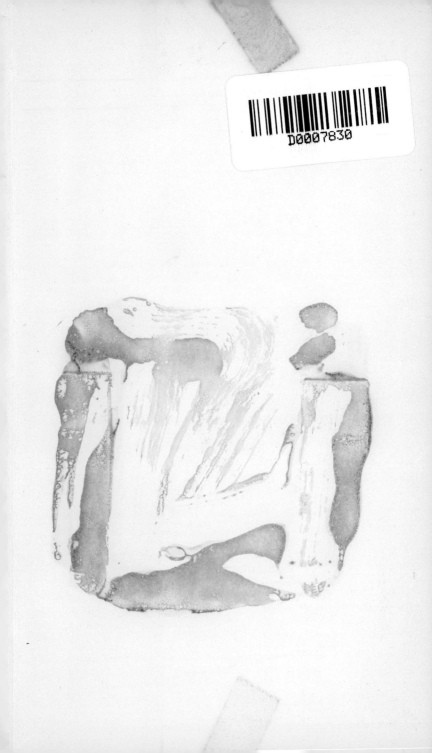

SPAIN IN AMERICA

VOLUME III OF THE AMERICAN NATION SERIES

EDITED BY ALBERT BUSHNELL HART

CHRISTOPHER COLUMBUS
(1451–1506)

DRAWN BY FRANK V. DU MOND, FROM A PHOTOGRAPH OF THE
ORIGINAL IN THE NAVAL MUSEUM OF THE SPANISH
GOVERNMENT IN MADRID

UNIVERSITY PAPERBACKS

SPAIN IN AMERICA

1450-1580

BY

EDWARD GAYLORD BOURNE, Ph.D.

LATE PROFESSOR OF HISTORY, YALE UNIVERSITY

*WITH NEW INTRODUCTION AND
SUPPLEMENTARY BIBLIOGRAPHY*

BY BENJAMIN KEEN

ASSOCIATE PROFESSOR OF HISTORY
JERSEY CITY STATE COLLEGE

BARNES & NOBLE, INC.

NEW YORK

Publishers · Booksellers

Since 1873

PUBLISHED IN 1904 BY HARPER & BROTHERS

REPRINTED BY BARNES & NOBLE, INC.
WITH NEW INTRODUCTION AND BIBLIOGRAPHY
COPYRIGHT, 1962, BY BARNES & NOBLE, INC.

L. C. CATALOGUE CARD NUMBER: 62-10840

Printed in the United States of America

20062

CONTENTS

INTRODUCTION

O F the many volumes published by Harper in the
American Nation series, under the general editor-
ship of Albert Bushnell Hart, between 1904 and 1908,
several have stood the tests of time and advancing historical scholarship. One of these durable works is
Spain in America, 1450–1580, by Edward Gaylord
Bourne (1860–1908). The book holds a seemingly
secure place in bibliographies of its field; authorities of
the stature of Samuel Eliot Morison continue to cite its
judgments with respect. Robert Ergang[1] observes that
it is "still the best concise work on the subject"; R. A.
Humphreys[2] calls it "admirable." These comments
typify modern scholarly opinion of Bourne's book.

What explains the enduring vitality of a survey written almost sixty years ago? Charles Gibson has written
that Bourne's merit "lay in the originality and acumen
with which he interpreted sources, in the objectivity of
his observation, and in the critical insights he applied
to Spanish colonization prior to 1580. He did not pursue his subject in detail beyond the sixteenth century,
but he did succeed, through an unequivocally scholarly
presentation, in laying a positive assessment of early

[1] *Europe From the Renaissance to Waterloo* (N. Y., 1939), xiii.
[2] *Latin American History. A Guide to the Literature in English*
(London, 1958), p. 21.

vii

Hispanic colonization before the American public. He may justifiably be termed the first scientific historian of the United States to view the Spanish colonial process dispassionately and thereby to escape the conventional Anglo-Protestant attitudes of outraged or tolerant disparagement."[3]

Bourne brought to his work a rare erudition and a mastery of the art of historical criticism perhaps unequaled by any of his contemporaries. To these sources of strength we may add a talent for synthesis that enabled Bourne to compress into a few pages the elements of a problem as complicated as the Vespucci controversy; and a clear, simple style, ideal in a work designed for the general reader.

The intellectual and political tendencies of his time unquestionably contributed to Bourne's achievement. The period in which he wrote saw the flowering of American scientific history, characterized by a strong emphasis on objectivity and critical use of sources. Not long before, Henry Adams had given a masterful example of the scientific method in his *History of the United States of America during the Administrations of Thomas Jefferson and James Madison*. On a much smaller scale, Bourne applied the same principles of personal detachment and meticulous critical method to his study of Spain in America.

Bourne's time also saw the rise, amid great public debate, of an American empire in the Caribbean and the Pacific, attended, in the case of the Philippines, by

[3] Charles Gibson and Benjamin Keen, "Trends of United States Studies in Latin American History," *American Historical Review,* LXII (July 1957), 857.

violent suppression by the United States of native rebels unwilling to accept her rule. It cannot be doubted that the new imperialist climate of opinion, America's new status as a colonial power, influenced Bourne's historical judgments and disposed him to view with greater sympathy the Spanish colonial process.

A book almost six decades old cannot entirely escape historical correction. Bourne's work contains some factual errors. Thus, in regard to Columbus's early life and his First Voyage, we can state with assurance that Columbus was not born "about 1446," but between August and the end of October, 1451; that the story of the presence of an Englishman and an Irishman on the First Voyage is a myth; and that the statement that at first "only the criminals in the jail were ready for the venture" rests on slight foundations. However, the few and relatively unimportant errors in Bourne's book do not materially diminish its value.

It is more important, perhaps, to note that two figures with whom Bourne dealt quite harshly, Sebastian Cabot and Amerigo Vespucci, have fared better at the hands of modern scholars. Particularly noteworthy is the recent effort to rehabilitate Vespucci, initiated by Alberto Magnaghi and pursued along varied lines by Frederick Pohl, Roberto Levillier, and others. I have indicated some recent writings on the Cabot and Vespucci problems in my supplementary bibliography.

The remarkable chapters on the Spanish colonial system are models of compression, organization, and lucidity; they continue to have great value as an outline sketch or introduction to the subject. Rereading these brilliant chapters, one is struck by the modernity of Bourne's thought, by his dispassionate tone, by his relativism, illustrated by his skillful comparisons of Spanish colonial experience with that of other nations to put Spanish policies and actions in a better light. Bourne has been criticized for excessive reliance on the *Recopilación de Leyes de las Indias,* for confusing Spanish legislation with colonial reality. However, Bourne used not only law codes but travel accounts and other sources, and he was well aware of the frequent divorce between the law and actual colonial practice. Thus, on the subject of the treatment of Negro slaves, Bourne wrote: "On the relative humanity of the Spanish laws in regard to slavery there can be no doubt; but whether Spanish slaves were more kindly treated than French or English is a different and more difficult question."

Bourne initiated a scholarly reaction in the United States against the *leyenda negra,* the "black legend" of Spanish cruelty and fanaticism. This reaction continues to gain strength. Indeed, one may rightly ask whether the wheel has not turned full circle, and whether a *leyenda blanca,* a "white legend" of Spanish altruism and tolerance, is not beginning to emerge from the writings of such scholars as Lewis Hanke. Bourne never made a statement so sweepingly favorable to Spain as Hanke's claim, in his *Aristotle and the American Indians* (1959), that "no other nation made so continuous or so passionate an attempt to discover what was the just treatment for the native peoples under its jurisdiction, as the Spaniards."

The past six decades have greatly extended our knowledge and understanding of the Spanish colonial world that Bourne sketched with such deft strokes. Scholars have investigated the themes of discovery and conquest in much detail; they have explored virtually every corner of the political structure of the Spanish Empire in America; and in recent decades they have made extremely fruitful researches into colonial economic, social, and intellectual history. In returning Bourne's book to active service, it seemed desirable to supplement his "Critical Essay on Authorities" with a bibliography that would introduce the general reader to the large literature that has accumulated since the first publication of *Spain in America*. This bibliography is of course highly selective. Readers who wish to extend their acquaintance with the literature of the field are particularly directed to the guide of R. A. Humphreys and to the sections edited by H. F. Cline and C. E. Nowell in the new (1961) American Historical Association *Guide to Historical Literature*.

BENJAMIN KEEN.

EDITOR'S INTRODUCTION

IN this volume begins the detailed narrative of the founding and development of the communities now included within the United States of America; and the story necessarily goes back to the discovery of the American islands and continents. The volume, therefore, closely connects with those chapters of Cheyney's *European Background of American History* (volume I. of this series) which deal with the intellectual uprising in Europe and the determined efforts of the Portuguese to find a way to India. Professor Bourne in his earlier chapters summarizes and restates, with many original conclusions, the controverted points with regard to the discovery of America. He counts Columbus a genuine discoverer and a man of lofty spirit, although unequal to the task of organizing and administering a colony. Out of the accumulated details on the discovery of America this volume selects those which are essential for the understanding of the problem and its solution; and it makes especially clear the division between Spain and Portugal by the demarcation line, not only in the Atlantic, but later in the Indian Ocean.

The earliest interest of England in the New World is described in chapter v., and the myth of Sebastian Cabot's voyages is dissipated. The volume is especially clear on the early development of the northern coast by the English and the Portuguese, and in chapters vi. and x. brings out the often neglected Spanish voyages along the eastern coast of the present United States.

Chapter vii., on Amerigo Vespucci, reveals a truth which has been much obscured, that the name America, derived from the Florentine voyager, spread slowly, was long applied only to South America, and for nearly two centuries was not habitually used by Spanish geographers. The Vespucci controversy is also made intelligible, and the solution of the writer seems inevitable.

A feature of this volume is its careful treatment of the voyages succeeding Columbus, and especially of Magellan's wonderful achievement (chapter ix.); and the author seems to establish his thesis that the first circumnavigation of the globe was a more daring, difficult, and wonderful achievement than the first voyage of western discovery.

Chapters xi. and xii. are devoted to a summary account of the explorations north of the Gulf of Mexico and the attempts of the French to establish themselves in Florida. Except for the voyages of Verrazzano and Cartier, this is the first appearance of the French in America, and precedes, by about twenty years, the first efforts of the English to establish a footing on the continent in the New World.

The remainder of this volume (chapters xiii. to xx.) is devoted to an account of the system of Spanish colonization. It should be read in connection with chapters v. and vi. of Cheyney's *European Background*, which describes Spanish institutions at home. The result of Professor Bourne's investigations, a result which seems supported by his references, is to establish the existence of a Spanish culture in the colonies of an extent and degree not realized by previous writers. He shows that the first century of Spanish colonists produced larger results in relation to the natives, the building of towns and cities, the construction of roads and bridges, and the encouragement of learning than in the first century either of French or English colonization. Yet he points out the two fatal weaknesses of the Spanish system: the wretched restrictions of trade and the lack of initiative and self-government. Upon the whole, he thinks the Indian better off under Spanish rule than has generally been supposed and the institution of negro slavery milder and of less importance. On the other hand, he points out, what has escaped most writers, that the prosperity of the main-land led almost to the depopulation of the islands, which did not again become important until about the time of the American Revolution.

These original and suggestive conclusions are supported by copious foot-notes, and by a critical essay on authorities which furnishes the investigator and the chance reader with a key to the prime materials to the best general works bearing upon this important field of American history.

The place of the volume in the series is to emphasize the importance of the Spanish discovery and colonization, both as showing extraordinary skill and pertinacity in exploration and in serving as the medium for the transmission of European culture to America. To this day larger areas in America are dominated by the Latin civilization than by the Anglo-Saxon. Inasmuch as the later influence has overtaken the earlier, and our realm extends over lands which for three, and in some cases for four, centuries were Spanish, the volume has a most direct bearing on the founding of the American nation.

AUTHOR'S PREFACE

IT has been my design in preparing this volume to accomplish two objects, so far as was practicable within the limits imposed by the conditions of the series to which it belongs. The first object was to provide an account, succinct and readable and abreast of present scholarship, of the discovery and exploration of the New World, from the birth of Christopher Columbus to the beginning of continuous activity in colonization by the English, at which point the succeeding volume takes up the story. Anything like a detailed account of the conquest of Mexico has been omitted as not preparing the way for future Anglo-Saxon occupation. The second part of my plan is to present an outline sketch of the Spanish colonial system and of the first stage of the transmission of European culture to America. This latter purpose seemed to me to be justified both by the intrinsic importance of the subject, some knowledge of which is essential for an understanding of effect on European politics of American colonization; and also by the considerations that more than one-half of the present territory of the United States has at one time or another been under Spanish dominion; that our country has assumed the responsibility of shaping the destiny

xvii

of several millions of people whose total acquisitions of European culture have until very recently come through Spain; and that more and more, in the increasing contact of the United States with Spanish America, will an appreciative recognition of the work and purposes of Spain in America be of service in promoting friendly relations.

The foot-notes and the bibliography reveal the sources from which the material has been derived. It is, therefore, unnecessary to make individual acknowledgments here; yet the extent to which my work has been facilitated by certain of my predecessors in the practical matters of shaping the proportions of the narrative, of fixing upon the essentials, of discovering the primary sources without unnecessary loss of time, and of indicating the present conclusions of scholars upon doubtful questions, would make it seem ungrateful, to myself at least, not to single out for particular mention, among the older works, Peschel's *Das Zeitalter der Entdeckungen* and Winsor's *Narrative and Critical History;* and among the later ones, Ruge's *Columbus*, Errera's *L'Epoca delle Grandi Scoperte Geografiche*, Günther's *Das Zeitalter der Entdeckungen*, and Hugues's *Cronologia delle Scoperte e delle Esplorazioni Geografiche.*

I wish also gratefully to acknowledge the value of Professor Hart's editorial suggestions, which have improved the form of the book without imposing irksome restraints upon the writer.

EDWARD GAYLORD BOURNE.

SPAIN IN AMERICA

SPAIN IN AMERICA

CHAPTER I

PRELIMINARIES OF DISCOVERY

(867–1487)

THE historic life of the ancient world was grouped about the Mediterranean Sea, and that body of water invited the early spirit of adventure and exploration. Its broad bosom was the highway of arms and of commerce, and the channel by which the elements of culture were transmitted from one people to another. As the world of ancient civilization expanded, its activities radiated from this centre; and during the Middle Ages the life of Europe and western Asia was still grouped about the Mediterranean. Consequently, of all the changes which mark the transition from ancient and mediæval to modern history, none is so profound as that which has regrouped human life about the Atlantic as a new and grander central sea.

The initial steps in this great change must be indicated briefly before the main story is taken

3

up.[1] Prior to the invention of the mariner's compass, geographical discovery did not advance beyond the range of land travel and of coasting voyages. The nearest approach to the unlocking of the secrets of the sea of darkness that was made without the guiding needle was accomplished by the fearless sailors of the North, who found Iceland in 867, colonized Greenland in 985,[2] and reached the shores later to be known as America, at a time when western Europe had hardly begun to recover what had been lost by the collapse of the Roman Empire and the decay of ancient knowledge.

Yet the distance was so great, the voyage so precarious, and the returns so slight that these ventures were discontinued; and northern enterprise remained content with the establishment of scattered settlements on the western shores of Greenland, which for three centuries were the remote outposts of Christendom in the west, obscure precursors of the future expansion of Europe and of Christianity.[3]

Of more consequence were the later ventures in the south, which, beginning with the isolated attempt of the Vivaldi brothers, of Genoa, in 1291,[4] to reach

[1] Cf. Cheyney, *European Background of American History* (*American Nation*, I.).

[2] Errera, *L' Epoca delle Grandi Scoperte Geografiche*, 360.

[3] The best account of the Norse voyages is to be found in J. Fischer, *The Discoveries of the Norsemen in America*.

[4] Pertz, *Der Aelteste Versuch zur Entdeckung des Seeweges nach Ostindien im Jahre 1291*, p. 10; in English in Major, *The Life of Prince Henry the Navigator*, 99, 100.

India by sailing round Africa, were continued by other stray Italian voyages to the African islands; they culminate in the fifteenth century in the systematic promotion of geographical discovery by the Portuguese Prince Henry the Navigator. His career and its results, the indispensable preparation in Europe for the discovery of the New World, naturally belong to the opening volume of this series. All that can be done here is to emphasize the importance for American history of creating a body of fearless ocean navigators; of breaking down the old imaginary barrier of a flaming zone in the tropics; of setting in train a range of activities which in little more than a century revealed a new world, encompassed the globe, and opened to Europe not only a broad field for its expanding energies, but also a new and more spacious home for its people.[1]

Near the end of Prince Henry's life the results attained under his leadership were incorporated in a map by the Venetian geographer, Friar Mauro, which records, in the part devoted to Asia, all the additions made to geographical knowledge by Marco Polo, John of Pian de Carpine, William of Rubruk, and other mediæval travellers. In addition, Friar Mauro, by a bold conjecture, relying upon the indications afforded by the voyages down the east and west coasts, depicted South Africa as circumnavigable, and confidently affirmed his belief that

[1] Cheyney, *European Background*, chap. iv.

one could sail from the Atlantic to the Indian Ocean.[1]

After the death of Prince Henry, his nephew, Alfonso V., prosecuted the work of exploration only intermittently, yet with some significant results. His reign is signalized by the first project of exploring the Atlantic to the west. Alfonso V., in January, 1474, granted to Fernam Tellez, who had rendered distinguished services in the African voyages, any islands he might discover in the ocean sea not in the region of Guinea.[2] Not quite two years later this privilege was extended to cover inhabited as well as uninhabited islands, and the Seven Cities are mentioned by name as the object of his explorations. On the map of Graciosus Benincasa, 1482,[3] the island of Antilia, with the names of the Seven Cities inscribed, is placed about as far west of the Madeiras as they are distant from Spain. Of the results of Tellez's efforts nothing is known. The positive achievement of Alfonso's reign was the actual crossing of the equator, demonstrating that the torrid zone was not uninhabitable or uninhabited.

Alfonso's successor, John II., took up with energy the work of Prince Henry. During his brief reign of fourteen years (1481–1495) the western

---

[1] Zurla, *Il Mappamondo di Fra Mauro*, 63; Errera, *L'Epoca delle Grandi Scoperte Geografiche*, 200; see map, p. 14.

[2] Ramos-Coelho, *Alguns Documentos*, 38, 41.

[3] Kretschmer, *Atlas*, plate 4.

coast of Africa was explored, until in 1487 Bartholomew Diaz rounded the Cape of Storms, renamed by
the king Good Hope. Owing in part to ill health,
King John made no further effort in that direction.
To the possibilities in the west he had not been indifferent, although he rejected the proposals of
Columbus, for in 1486 he granted to Ferdinand
Dulmo, a captain of the island of Terceira, in the
Azores, any island or islands or main - land that he
might discover in the Atlantic. Dulmo sailed in
1487, equipped for a voyage of six months, but he
lighted neither upon the fabled Seven Cities nor the
hidden islands of the west.[1] This good - fortune was
not to crown a century of exploration by the hardy
seamen of the western kingdom of the peninsula,
but was to be won by a countryman of Doria and the
Vivaldi brothers, whose first venture had anticipated
Prince Henry by more than a century.

[1] Ramos-Coelho, *Alguns Documentos*, 58.

CHAPTER II

PREPARATIONS OF COLUMBUS

(1446–1492)

OF the youth of the discoverer of America little is known. Although a voluminous writer of letters, in which he reviews his struggles, in none of those which are extant did he ever mention the date of his birth; nor are there the materials for an authentic story of his early days in the papers which his son Ferdinand and his friend Las Casas utilized for their accounts of his life prior to his arrival in Spain.[1] The self-made men of to-day often fondly dwell upon their humble origin, but Columbus in after-life drew a veil over the lowly circumstances of his birth; adopted the form Colon[2] for his name, thereby making more plausible his claim of relationship with the French admirals Coulon and of descent from a Roman general

[1] Cf. Ruge, "Der Roman des Jugendlebens," in his *Columbus*, chap. i.

[2] Cf. Las Casas, *Historia de las Indias*, I., 42–43; and Ferdinand Columbus, *Historie*, chap. i. Apparently the Italian Peter Martyr did not know Columbus's family name, as he Latinizes Colon as Colonus, not as Columbus. Oviedo always calls him Colom.

Colon (Cilon according to the best texts of Tacitus);
and transformed the simple weavers from whom
he sprang into wealthy merchants and importers
who subsequently suffered reverses.

It is, however, the generally accepted view of
modern scholars, based upon a careful collation of
the notarial documents of Genoa relating to his
family and to their business transactions, that
he was born in Genoa about the year 1446,[1] although as late a date as 1451 is supported by the
fact that in 1470 his signature was appended to a
legal document with the formal statement that he
was upwards of nineteen years of age.[2]

His father, Domenico Colombo, was a woollen-
weaver, and as late as 1472 Columbus signed a
document in Genoa giving as his occupation "laner-
ius de Janua," wool-worker of Genoa.[3] His earliest
apprenticeship to the sea may have begun somewhat earlier, yet this signature precludes a long-
previous seafaring life and militates as well against
the earlier dates conjectured for his birth. A story
told of his studies at the University of Pavia cannot
be authenticated, and is rejected by most modern
scholars; yet in some way the wool-worker of Genoa
in a few years mastered not only the whole art of
navigation, but learned Latin and read voluminously
in the geographical literature accessible in that
language.

---

[1] Ruge, *Columbus*, 24.
[2] Vignaud, *Real Birth-Date of Columbus*, 74-101.   [3] *Ibid.*, 17.

Among the authors that he studiously examined and commented upon were the *General History and Geography* of Æneas Sylvius,[1] later Pope Pius II.; the *Image of the World*,[2] an encyclopædic compilation by Pierre d'Ailly written early in the fifteenth century; and, most important of all, a Latin copy of the travels of Marco Polo.[3] His comments upon these works are written in a Latin somewhat careless of grammatical rules. In these marginal notes are revealed a curiosity about the Orient and a critical disposition to rectify the geographical tradition by the light of his own experience and knowledge.

For example, when Æneas Sylvius records that the frigid and torrid zones are uninhabitable, Columbus notes that the contrary is proved in the south by the Portuguese, and in the north by the English and the North Germans who sail those regions. Again, when D'Ailly pronounces the torrid zone uninhabitable on account of the excessive heat, Columbus notes in the margin, "It is not uninhabitable, because the Portuguese sail through it; in fact, it is teeming with people, and near the equator is his Serene Highness the King of Portugal's castle of *Mine*, which we have seen." Of all the statements in Pierre d'Ailly none impressed Colum-

---

[1] *Historia Rerum Ubique Gestarum* (Venice, 1477).

[2] *Imago Mundi*, printed between 1480 and 1483; Lollis, *Vita di Cristoforo Colombo*, 63.

[3] Published at Antwerp or Gouda circa 1485; Thacher, *Columbus*, III., 462.

bus more profoundly than the quotation from
Aristotle that "between the end of Spain and the
beginning of India the sea was small and naviga-
ble in a few days." Again, the assertion of the
apocryphal book of Esdras that the earth is six
parts land and that only the seventh part is water,
seemed so striking that Columbus notes the opinion of Ambrose and Augustine that Esdras was a
prophet.[1]

In the case of no navigator of that age or earlier
is there such impressive evidence of protracted study
of all available sources of information in regard to
any specific problem of geographical exploration.
In addition to this investigation of literary sources,
Columbus carefully noted all the indications which
he observed or which were brought to his attention,
pointing to the existence of islands to the west of the
Azores, Canaries, and other groups already known.
Reported voyages of exploration were also carefully
recorded. This preparatory work was done while
he was living in Portugal, whither he had gone early
in his experience as a sailor. There he married
Felipa Moniz, a connection of Bartholomew Peres-
trello, one of Prince Henry's navigators. During
a part of his residence in Portugal he lived for a time
in the island of Porto Santo; and at other times he
sailed on the Portuguese ships to Guinea and to the
north, certainly as far as the British Isles.[2]

[1] *Raccolta Colombiana*, pt. i., vol. II., 291.
[2] *Ibid.*, pt. ii., vol. II., marginal note No. 10.

In such an environment a mind so boldly imaginative, at once so practical and so visionary, could not fail to be incited to independent activity in this stirring field of ever widening knowledge. It is quite impossible, however, to fix with certainty the date when, reaching beyond projects of western exploration, his mind grasped the great design of going to the East Indies by sailing west. According to the substantially identical narratives of Las Casas and of Ferdinand Columbus, the suggestion of this idea was derived from the letters of the Florentine physician and astronomer, Paolo del Pozzo Toscanelli, which they reproduce and of which they were the sole sources until 1871, when Harrisse identified the Latin original of the first Toscanelli letter.[1]

From the first of these documents, written in June, 1474, we learn that Toscanelli's friend, Fernam Martins, living in Lisbon and interested in the Portuguese efforts to reach the Indies by way of Africa, had brought before King Alfonso the opinion he had heard Toscanelli express that it would be a much shorter way to the Indies to sail due west. The king then desired to hear from Toscanelli the reasons for such a view. The astronomer's reply contained in the first letter could have afforded little assurance to Alfonso, for there is no reasoned argument in it, but merely a series of assertions un-

[1] See Vignaud, *Toscanelli and Columbus*, 9–13, for the story of the discovery.

supported by evidence, followed by an alluring description of the wealth of the Orient derived from Marco Polo. The text was accompanied by a chart divided into equal spaces which depicted the Atlantic as bounded on the west by the coast of Asia. This map is no longer extant, and almost all reproductions of it are merely reproductions of the Atlantic Ocean side of Behaim's globe, 1492, reduced to what is supposed to be the projection devised by Toscanelli.

This letter, it is supposed, was brought to the notice of Columbus some years later and suggested to him the realization of the project. He then wrote to Toscanelli of his desire to go to the land of spices, and received in reply a copy of the letter to Martins and a chart similar to the one sent with the first letter. Somewhat later Toscanelli wrote again to Columbus in reply to his letters, but without conveying any further information as to how to make the voyage.

In recent years the authenticity of this correspondence has been challenged, and the effort has been made to prove that the letters are a subsequent forgery designed to give to Columbus's voyage the character of a reasoned scientific experiment and the dignity of the patronage of a renowned scholar.[1] As yet the critical attack on these documents has won little assent among scholars. This, however, at least may be said with confidence, that, admitting the genuineness of Toscanelli's letter to Martins, it gave Colum-

[1] Vignaud, *Toscanelli and Columbus*, passim.

WORLD MAP OF FRA MAURO, 1457–1459

This map is oriented inversely, and is consequently upside down It is adapted from
C. R. Markham, *Christopher Columbus*

bus no information about the Orient or the distance
across the Atlantic that is not more fully given in
the passages in Pierre d'Ailly and Marco Polo that
he annotated in the margin or copied. So far as
making out a plausible case for seeking the east by
the west is concerned, Columbus accumulated in
the marked passages of his own books a far more
convincing body of facts than anything in Toscanelli's letters. The most, then, that in any case can
be attributed to Toscanelli is the direction of his
mind to the problem, and not the furnishing of evidence or facts otherwise inaccessible. So far as can be
determined by internal evidence, the date of the correspondence is to be placed between 1479 and 1482.[1]

The extant archives of Portugal are equally destitute of references to Toscanelli and to Columbus,
and for our knowledge of Columbus's attempt to
secure the support of King John of Portugal in
making his great experiment we are dependent upon
the narrative of the Portuguese historian, Barros,
whose work, though written two generations later,
was in general based upon contemporary material.
According to Barros, Christovão Colom, a Genoese
by birth, an experienced and eloquent man, a good
Latin scholar,[2] but very boastful, had convinced himself by his studies and by his reading of Marco Polo

---

[1] Vignaud, *Toscanelli and Columbus*, 32–35.
[2] Harrisse, *Christophe Colomb*, I., 84, thinks Barros borrowed
this personal description from Oviedo's "bien hablado, cauto
é de gran ingenio, é gentil latino."

that it would be practicable to reach the island of
Cipango and other unknown lands by sailing west.
He therefore appealed to King John for some ships
that he might seek for Cipango in the western ocean.
The king saw, however, that Colom was a great
talker and boastful of his abilities and very visionary
with his island of Cipango, and he placed little confidence in him. Yet, on account of his urgency,
he referred him to the bishop of Ceuta and two
physicians, expert cosmographers, who regarded his
words as empty talk because it all rested on fancy
and description of Marco Polo's Cipango.[1]

Columbus left Portugal for Spain in 1484 in se-
crecy and haste and there persistently advocated his
project for seven years. During this period of futile
effort, fearing for the outcome, he sent his brother
Bartholomew to England to enlist the interest and
assistance of King Henry VII. Of Bartholomew's
activities there no local record remains; but according to the assertion of Las Casas and Ferdinand he
succeeded in securing promises from Henry, and was
returning to Spain to inform Christopher, when he
was told in Paris that his brother had discovered
some great lands which were called the Indies.[2]

---

[1] Barros, *Da Asia*, dec. I., liv. III., chap. ix.; Feust's Barros,
102.

[2] Ferdinand Columbus, *Historie*, chap. ix.; Las Casas, *Historia
de las Indias*, II., 78, 79. Oviedo, *Historia General*, I., 19,
places the proposition to King Henry VII. before that made to
the king of Portugal and says it was rejected. See also Harrisse,
Christophe Colomb, II., 193, 194.

Of Columbus's occupations during these weary years we know little, but it is probable that in them he did much of the careful reading of which the marginal notes in his books bear testimony; for in his letter to the king and queen recounting his third voyage he says: "I gave to the subject six or seven years of great anxiety. At the same time I thought it desirable to bring to bear upon the subject the sayings and opinions of those who have written upon the geography of the world."[1]

Finally, through the powerful assistance of a former confessor of the queen, Father Juan Perez, and of Luis de Santangel, the treasurer of Aragon, Isabella decided to make the venture, and Columbus was hastily recalled just as he was leaving Spain for France.[2]

It is so frequently asserted that Columbus's exclusive purpose was to reach the East Indies by sailing west that it will not be out of place to indicate that he counted upon discovering islands and possibly main-land, which, though perhaps connected with the Asiatic continent, were not the wealthy and civilized countries of Cipango and of the Great Khan. In the contract drawn up April 17, 1492, Columbus demanded that in return for what he should discover in the Ocean Sea he should be made admiral of all those islands and main-lands which

[1] Major, *Select Letters of Columbus*, 109.
[2] Las Casas, *Historia de las Indias*, I., 241, 245; Lollis, *Vita di Cristoforo Colombo*, 105, 108.

should be discovered or acquired through his agency, with all the prerogatives belonging to the dignity of admiral of Castile; that he should be made viceroy and governor-general of all the said islands and main-lands; and that from all the trade within the limits of the said admiralship he should receive a royalty of ten per cent. of all the net proceeds.[1]

It is not proposed here that Columbus should be invested with the kingdom of the Great Khan or Cipango, which were known and which were his proposed destination; but rather with such unknown regions as he should discover in the ocean in the course of his voyage. Similarly, Columbus in the opening pages of his journal describes his enterprise as an embassy to see the countries of India, "to see the said princes, and the cities and lands, and their disposition, with a view that they might be converted to our holy faith. . . . For this they [the Catholic sovereigns] . . . ennobled me, so that henceforth I should be called Don, and should be chief admiral of the Ocean Sea, perpetual viceroy, and governor of all the islands and continents that I should discover and gain in the Ocean Sea." [2]

The son of the humble woollen-weaver of Genoa has gone far in twenty years. He is now a noble and a high official in an ancient monarchy, and intrusted with a unique mission. Yet all depends

[1] Navarrete, *Coleccion de los Viages*, II., 9.
[2] Markham, *Journal of Columbus*, 17.

upon the chances of the voyage whether these
honors shall fade away in the mists of the Sea of
Darkness, leaving the mere shadow of a name, like
Ugolino de Vivaldi, in some such record as this:
"Christopher Colonus, a Ligurian, proposed to pass
over to the Indies by way of the west. After he
left the Canary Islands no news was heard of him;" [1]
or whether his name shall have eternal celebrity as
the discoverer of the New World. No man ever
faced chances of fortune so extreme. On the other
hand, no sovereign ever secured imperial dominion
at so slight a sacrifice as Isabella of Castile. Her
venture was small — a few thousand dollars and
presumably empty honors to an importunate visionary whose utterances seemed mere "fables."

[1] A combination of Peter Martyr's first mention of Columbus
with what Jacobus Doria reported of the attempt of Vivaldi.
Pertz, *Der Aelteste Versuch zur Entdeckung des Seeweges*, 10.

CHAPTER III

COLUMBUS'S DISCOVERY AND THE PAPAL DEMARCATION LINE

(1492–1494)

IN the early dawn of August, 1492, the people of the little town of Palos, in western Andalusia, must have watched with strange feelings the departure of three small ships for unknown waters. Less than three months had elapsed since the royal order came to provide two vessels for twelve months, and wages for the crews for four months, as a penalty for some offence against the crown.[1] At first the hardy sailors of Palos shrank from the mysterious voyage, and only the criminals in the jail were ready for the venture, relying on the promise that all who volunteered were to be exempt from any criminal prosecution until two months after their return.[2] But, thanks to the powerful influence of the Pinzon family, there was no need to depend upon the jail-birds, and capable crews were secured from Palos and the surrounding towns.[3]

The full list of sailors and landsmen was ninety,

[1] Navarrete, *Viages*, II., 12.   [2] *Ibid.*, II., 15; III., 578.
[3] *Ibid.*, III., 578; Las Casas, *Historia*, I., 260.

according to Las Casas, and one hundred and twenty, according to Oviedo.[1] Among them were the three Pinzon brothers, Juan de la Cosa, the maker of the famous map of 1500, and Luis de Torres, a converted Jew, who was taken as an interpreter by reason of his knowledge of Arabic. Besides the Spaniards there were two representatives of that race which was later in no small measure to enter into the inheritance of Spain in the New World. William Ires [Harris?] of Galway, Ireland, and Tallarte de Lajes [Allard?].[2] Neither returned from the voyage. It is not a little strange, in view of the religious spirit of the age and of the enterprise, that no priest joined the company.

Of the three vessels only the *Santa Maria* was fully decked and large enough to be styled a ship (nao). Her tonnage has been variously estimated at one hundred tons,[3] and at two hundred and eighty tons.[4] The other two, the *Pinta* and the *Niña*, of the low-built, swifter type called caravels, are supposed to have measured fifty and forty; or one hundred and forty and one hundred tons.

The admiral directed his course towards the Canaries, Spain's only pre-Columbian colonial dependency, and to-day almost the only remnant of her oceanic empire. There he tarried for about a month

---

[1] Las Casas, *Historia*, I., 260; Oviedo, *Historia General*, I., 22.
[2] Markham, *Life of Columbus*, 69.
[3] *Ibid.*, 66.   [4] Ruge, *Columbus*, 102.

refitting the *Pinta*. The final start was made on Thursday, September 6.

It is the singular good-fortune of posterity to possess a detailed account of this momentous voyage from the hand of the protagonist in the drama. No other in the history of the world was more important, and of no voyage earlier than or during the age of discoveries have we so full and so trustworthy a narrative. In the form in which it has come down to us it is an abridgment by Las Casas, closely following the text of the original daily record prepared for the king and queen, and frequently preserving long passages in the exact words of the author. In its pages we are admitted into the very presence of the admiral to share his thoughts and impressions as the strange panorama of his experiences unfolded before him.

The voyage was not imperilled by storms, yet as the waves rolled by day after day, as the little vessels followed the setting sun, the strain proved too great for the common minds of the crew. First there was secret grumbling, then plotting to put the admiral out of the way or to throw him overboard.[1] At last, on the tenth day of October, they could stand it no longer; but the admiral soothed them and reminded them of the advantages which would come from success; "and he added that it was useless to complain, as he had come to go to the Indies

---

[1] Peter Martyr, *De Rebus Oceanicis* (ed. 1574), 3; in English, in Hakluyt, *Voyages*, V., 168.

and he would keep on till he found them with the aid of our Lord."

Fortunately, the strain was soon relaxed. The next evening a flickering light was observed, and on Friday they found themselves near a small coral island in the Bahamas, called by the natives Guanahani, which Columbus renamed San Salvador (Holy Saviour), and which is probably Watling Island.[1] That he had reached the Indies, Columbus had no doubt, and in his first mention of the natives he calls them "Indians,"[2] thus attaching the name forever to the aborigines of the New World.

When on October 21 he heard of Cuba for the first time, he believed it to be Cipango, and planned to go on " to the main-land and to the city of Guisay,[3] and to give the letters of your highness to the Gran Can." This belief soon became a fixed idea, immovable in face of the most telling evidence. The very qualities that had insured Columbus's success contributed to his failure to realize just what he had achieved. Gazing at the naked Indians paddling their canoes, he could write, " It is certain that this is the main-land, and that I am in front of Zayto and Guinsay, a hundred leagues—a little more or less—distant the one from the other "[4]—Guinsay with its Oriental splendor and twelve thousand

---

[1] On the landfall, see Markham, *Life of Columbus*, 89–107.
[2] Markham, *Journal of Columbus*, October 12.
[3] Kinsai or Quinsai in Marco Polo.
[4] Markham, *Journal of Columbus*, 65 (November 1).

stone bridges,[1] and Zaitun with its hundred pepper ships a year![2]

Not less ready was he to read into the vague gestures and signs of the natives more grotesque recollections of his reading of Marco Polo. As the Venetian traveller reported that the island of Lambri was inhabited by men with tails, so Columbus understands the Indians to tell him of the province of Avan, in Cuba, whose "inhabitants are born with tails."[3] Again he understands that the island of Matinino is "entirely peopled by women, without men,"[4] for had he not read in Marco Polo of the two islands of Masculia and Femenina?[5] Why, too, does he report that he found no people of "monstrous appearance," but for the reason that he had read in Pierre d'Ailly that in the ends of the earth were "monsters of such a horrid aspect that it were hard to say whether they were men or beasts?"[6]

From the smaller Bahamas his course was directed to Cuba, the eastern third of whose northern shore he explored. Believing that he was upon main-land not far from the realm of the Great Khan, on November 2 he despatched his Jewish interpreter, Luis de Torres, to that monarch. Instead of the Oriental prince they found a village of naked Indians.

[1] Noted by Columbus on the margin of his copy of Marco Polo. *Raccolta Colombiana*, pt. i., vol. II., 462.

[2] Cf. Toscanelli's letter to Fernam Martins.

[3] Major, *Select Letters of Columbus*, 10.

[4] Markham, *Journal of Columbus*, January 15.

[5] *Raccolta Colombiana*, pt. i., vol. II., 468.   [6] *Ibid.*, 380.

It was on this journey, however, that Europeans first saw men drawing the smoke from the leaves of a plant which were rolled in the form of a tube and lighted at one end. These tubes they learned were called *tobaccos*.[1]

From Cuba, Columbus went to Hayti, which from the similarity of its first appearance to that of Spain he named La Isla Española,[2] "the Spanish Island," whence comes the English Hispaniola. There, on Christmas Day, the *Santa Maria* ran aground and became a total wreck. All the cargo and provisions were saved through the ready help and kindly honesty of the Indians. In consequence of this disaster, and to prepare a way for Spanish colonization by learning the native language and by acquiring a more complete knowledge of the resources of the island, Columbus decided to leave such as were willing to stay till his return.[3]

Every provision was made for a safe sojourn and the successful establishment of the first white settlement in the New World. He left bread and wine for a year, seed for sowing, tools, and arms. Among the forty-four who remained were skilled artisans, a good gunner, a physician, and a tailor.[4] Las Casas reports for us, presumably from the unabridged journal, the solemn injunctions which Columbus

---

[1] Markham, *Journal of Columbus*, October 15; Las Casas, *Historia*, I., 322, translated in Thacher, *Columbus*, I., 561.

[2] Markham, *Journal of Columbus*, December 9; cf. Thacher, *Columbus*, I., 586.   [3] Las Casas, *Historia*, I., 406.

[4] Markham, *Journal of Columbus*, January 2.

bestowed upon them before he left: that they should obey their captain implicitly, cultivate friendly relations with the natives, and scrupulously avoid injuring man or woman, and that they should keep together.[1]

The return was far from the peaceful progress of the outward voyage, for two violent storms were encountered, one on February 14, just before reaching the Azores, and the other the night of March 3 as they approached the coast of Portugal. They were both safely weathered, however, and on March 4, 1493, Columbus dropped anchor within the mouth of the river Tagus.

For half a century from time to time little fleets had started southward in the hope of eventually reaching the Indies. Four years before Columbus's voyage Africa had been rounded, and the fruition of so many efforts seemed within reach. Now the news spread that the stranger in the caravel had returned from " the Indies," and soon the "crowd that swarmed to see the Indians and to hear the story of the voyage overran the little vessel; nor could the surrounding water be seen, so full was it of the boats and skiffs of the Portuguese." [2]

Four days later, on March 8, the admiral received a letter from the king of Portugal, inviting him to visit him at Valparaiso, some thirty miles

[1] Las Casas, *Historia*, I., 415, translated in Thacher, I., 632.
[2] Ferdinand Columbus, *Historie*, 122 (ed. 1867), in English in Pinkerton's *Voyages*, XII., 52.

from Lisbon. About nine years earlier the two had met, when the petition of the visionary sailor was rejected as mere prattle of the island of Cipango, an echo of Marco Polo.[1] Now the admiral of the Ocean Sea proudly announces that he has returned from the discovery of the islands of Cipango and of Antilia, and shows his Indians, gold, and other trophies, and reminds King John of his failure to accept the opportunity offered to him. In the king's opinion, however, the discoveries were embraced in his dominion of Guinea. The contemporary chronicler, Ruy de Pina, who describes the interview, says that the said admiral went beyond the bounds of truth, and made out the affair as regards gold and silver and riches much greater than it was. By-standing courtiers suggested that the intruder could be provoked into a quarrel and then killed without any suspicion of connivance on the part of the king. But the king, a God-fearing prince, forbade it, and showed honor to the admiral.[2]

On Friday, in the early afternoon of March 15, 1493, Columbus cast anchor in the harbor of Palos. The joy and pride of the villagers may be imagined. The whole population turned out to receive Columbus with a procession and to give "thanks to our Lord for so great favor and victory."[3]

[1] See above, p. 16.
[2] Ruy de Pina, *Chronica del Rey D. João II.; Collecção de Livros Ined.*, II., 178; translated in Prescott's *Ferdinand and Isabella*, II., 161, *n.*
[3] Ferdinand Columbus, *Historie*, 124.

The news of Columbus's voyage was disseminated
rapidly, first through private correspondence, and
later through the publication of his own narrative,
addressed in the form of letters to Luis de Santangel
and to Gabriel Sanchez. The most important accounts in private correspondence, although not the
earliest, are found in the letters of Peter Martyr of
Anghiera, an Italian resident at the court of Spain,
later the author of the first history of America.
On May 14 he wrote to Count Giovanni Borromeo
from Barcelona, where Columbus had appeared before the king and queen a month previous: "A few
days since, one Christopher Colon, a Genoese, returned from the antipodes in the west. From my
kings he had obtained three ships to visit this province, with some difficulty, indeed, for what he said
was esteemed fables." [1]

The knowledge which the world at large obtained
of the discovery was derived from the various editions of Columbus's own letter inscribed to Gabriel
Sanchez, which is merely a duplicate of the letter to
Luis de Santangel. The Sanchez letter was translated into Latin in April, 1493, and in that form it
was reprinted in different countries and passed
through nine editions within a year. There were,
besides, two Spanish editions of the Santangel letter,
and three editions of the Sanchez letter in Italian. [2]
Two of these were a quaint poetical rendering by

[1] Letter no. 131, in Thacher, *Columbus*, I., 54.
[2] Thacher, *Columbus*, II., 72.

the Florentine poet Giuliano Dati.[1] The earliest titles of the Latin letter read: "Letter of Christopher Colom; to whom our age owes much; on the islands of India lately found beyond the Ganges."[2]

The earliest European potentate to be informed of the discoveries was naturally the head of the church. Ferdinand and Isabella seem to have lost no time in announcing to Pope Alexander VI., himself a Spaniard, that some time since they had purposed to explore and discover islands and remote and unknown main-lands, but had been detained by the war in Granada; that having successfully completed that conquest, they had despatched Christopher Colon, at much labor and expense, to make search for such lands; and that with God's help, sailing in the west towards the Indians,[3] he had discovered some very remote islands not hitherto found; that gold, silver, and spices were produced in these islands, and that their inhabitants seemed fitted for Christianity.[4]

Two things in this announcement attract our attention: the assertion that the monarchs had planned such an exploration before 1492; and that the royal purposes of Columbus's voyage were as stated in their patent, discovery, and the extension of the

[1] Major, *Select Letters of Columbus*, pp. xc.–cviii.
[2] Fac-simile in Thacher, *Columbus*, II., 48.
[3] "Versus Indos," in bull of May 3, omitted in bull of May 4.
[4] Text of bull of May 4 and Eden's translation in Fiske, *Discovery of America*, II., 580 ff.; modern translation of both bulls in Blair and Robertson, *The Philippine Islands*, I.

Christian religion, and not a new route to the Indies. Apparently Ferdinand and Isabella were not altogether convinced that Columbus had reached the Indies of Marco Polo, and make no point of that in their communication. If this be true, they were not alone in such scepticism, for Peter Martyr entertained strong doubts whether Columbus had reached the Orient; for on October 1, 1493, after having had abundant opportunity to talk with Columbus, he wrote the archbishop of Braga that Columbus believed that he had reached the Indies; for himself he would not absolutely deny this, but he believed that the size of the globe seemed to suggest otherwise.[1] Similarly, John II. of Portugal believed that Columbus's voyage had been really in western waters, in the region covered by his dominion of Guinea.

Since the Portuguese lordship of Guinea rested upon a long series of discoveries, reinforced by papal bulls granting to the king of Portugal all that had been or should be discovered south of Cape Bojador towards Guinea and the southern shores; and since Spain had by the treaty of 1480 conceded to Portugal all the islands discovered or to be discovered from the Canaries southward in the region off Guinea, it was evident that, unless a compromise could be effected, some clash must arise between the sovereigns of Spain and Portugal over these new lands. It was for this reason that the matter was brought so promptly to the attention

[1] Thacher, *Columbus*, I., 59.

of the pope, and that he was requested to issue a
bull declaring the rights of Spain.[1]

For such a function of umpire the pope from his
international position was well fitted. Alexander
responded with equal promptness, and in his famous
bulls of May 3 and 4 he recognized the existing
rights of Portugal and established those of Spain,
by drawing an imaginary line from north to south,
one hundred leagues west of the Azores and Cape
Verd Islands. East of this line Portugal was to
retain the rights already assigned to her; and south
and west of it the Spanish monarchs were to have
the same exclusive rights of exploration, trade, and
colonization over all the lands that should be discovered that were not occupied by any Christian
prince. This award delimited, in modern phrase,
two spheres of influence. It did not divide the
world between Spain and Portugal, but rather
marked out the regions in which the right of discovery would give unquestioned and final title.

Still the phrasing was not altogether satisfactory
to Ferdinand and Isabella, apparently for the reason,
possibly urged by Columbus, that nothing was said
of the Indies. Hence, in September, 1493, Alexander
issued another bull granting the Spanish monarchs
full rights to hold such lands as they should discover to the south and west "and eastern regions
and to India." Thus if the Spaniards by going west
should eventually reach the East Indies, their right,

[1] Navarrete, *Viages*, II., 60, 77, 90.

by prior discovery and occupation, would hold against the Portuguese, who might feel that India was preempted to them by the earlier bulls. King John was not satisfied with the location of the demarcation line,[1] and he was still less satisfied with this amplification of the Spanish rights.

In consequence it was agreed by the treaty of Tordesillas, between Spain and Portugal, June 7, 1494, that the line of demarcation should be drawn three hundred and seventy leagues west of the Cape Verd Islands, or at a distance about half-way between the Cape Verd Islands and the new discoveries.[2] This shifting of the line to the west later secured Portugal's title to Brazil, and, after the immense distance of the Spice Islands beyond India was discovered, encouraged Spain to believe that these islands really fell within her demarcation.

[1] Navarrete, *Viages*, II., 96.

[2] Translations of the bull of September 25 and of the treaty of Tordesillas are given in Blair and Robertson, *The Philippine Islands*, I. Thacher gives fac-similes and translations of the bulls, *Columbus*, II., 124 ff., and a translation of the treaty, 175 ff.

CHAPTER IV

COLUMBUS AT THE ZENITH OF HIS FORTUNES
(1493–1500)

FOR Columbus the spring and summer of 1493 were the happiest period of his life. The scanty records of the time depict him as enjoying the admiration of the crowd and the grateful appreciation of his sovereign. Spain had never seen such a cavalcade as slowly wended its way from Seville to Barcelona in early April, 1493. "From all the neighboring places the people gathered along the highway to see him and the Indians and the other things so novel that he brought with him."[1] He was met by the dignitaries of Barcelona and the court and escorted to the place where the royal pair awaited him with all majesty and grandeur, on a richly decorated seat under a canopy of cloth of gold. And when he went to kiss their hands they rose as to a great lord and made him sit beside them, thus bestowing the highest distinction that could be shown to a subject in Spain.[2] Later he was

---

[1] Ferdinand Columbus, *Historie*, 125.
[2] Peter Martyr, *De Rebus Oceanicis*, 10; Ferdinand Columbus, *Historie*, 125.

accorded a coat of arms, which in after years bore the legend:

"For Castile and Leon
Colon found a New World." [1]

These summer months, however, were not mere holiday for the admiral, for preparations went on apace for his return to the Indies, with a colony and for further explorations. During the last week of May, Ferdinand and Isabella issued no less than twenty-five executive orders, commissions, and proclamations relating to the equipment of the expedition which, it was announced as early as May 23, 1493, was to be despatched to "the Indies," [2] the name henceforth adopted in Spain for the New World. Fifteen thousand ducats were appropriated for the expenses, or about five times the cost of the first voyage. Authority was conferred upon Columbus and Juan de Fonseca, archdeacon of Seville, to take charge of the preparations, and Columbus was appointed captain - general of the fleet. Finally everything was ready and the fleet set sail September 25, 1493.

These seventeen ships were freighted with the seeds of European life. Among the fifteen hundred men on board were the returning converted Indians, soldiers, missionaries, artisans of all kinds, field laborers, knights, and young courtiers. All but

[1] Oviedo, *Historia General*, I., 31.
[2] Navarrete, *Viages*, II., 41.

about two hundred volunteers were under pay.[1]
Besides a few horses for cavalry service, there were
carried for breeding purposes mares, sheep, heifers,
and other animals. Vegetables, wheat, barley, and
other cereals were not forgotten, nor the vine and
fruit trees. All kinds of tools, too, that would be
needed in a colony were included. At the Canary
Islands they added to their stock calves, she-goats,
ewes, pigs, chickens, seeds of oranges, lemons,
melons, and other garden-plants, and, most important of all, sugar-cane.[2] It is not strange that
no women were taken upon an expedition so
hazardous and so military. Yet to their absence
must be attributed some of the most serious causes
for the subsequent troubles with the natives, and
their presence would have lessened the terrible
homesickness and have been a consolation in illness.

Thus laden with the gifts of the Old to the New
World, this fleet pursued its way across the Atlantic
to lay the foundations of the Spanish colonial
empire. November 3 they reached one of the
smaller Antilles, which was named Dominica, as
it was Sunday. Sailing from one island to another
—among them was Porto Rico—it was the night of
November 27 before they arrived at the site of the
little garrison of Navidad. A salute from the
ships' cannon was followed by an ominous silence.

[1] Columbus in the *Torres Memorial*, Major, *Select Letters of
Columbus*, 100.
[2] Las Casas, *Historia*, I., 497, II., 3.

About midnight a canoe approached Columbus's
ship full of Indians crying out "Almirante! Almirante!" When the admiral appeared they came on
board to say that some of the Christians had died of
illness, and that others had gone into the country
with their wives and some with many wives. The
admiral felt they must all be dead.[1] The morning
revealed a scene of complete desolation. Not a
Spaniard had survived.

For his new station Columbus tried to select a
more favorable site, somewhat farther east, on the
north coast of Hayti. Here all disembarked, and
the foundations for a permanent settlement were
laid in December, 1493. Everything seemed full of
promise—a fertile soil, good building-stone, clay for
bricks and tiles. Columbus set his people at work
with energy on the new town of Isabella. Streets
and a plaza were laid out, and solid public buildings,
ever a characteristic feature of the Spanish colonies,
were planned—an arsenal and storehouse, a church,
a hospital, a fort, all built of stone. Private houses
were of wood and straw. But the men, worn by the
long and unaccustomed sea-voyage, especially the
laborers, put to such heavy work in a strange
climate, soon fell sick; even Columbus did not escape. For a time among all the hundreds of
colonists there was hardly a well man.[2]

Early in January, 1494, two young cavaliers, one
of them Alonso de Hojeda, a notable explorer and

[1] Las Casas, *Historia*, II., 11.　　　[2] *Ibid.*, II., 21, 22.

conquistador, led out reconnoitring parties to the reputed gold-bearing region of Cibao, in the interior. Their reports were glowing and stimulated Columbus to a more thorough exploration of the country.[1] In the mean time, however, reinforcements and supplies were urgently needed; and, consequently, about the middle of February Antonio de Torres was sent back to Spain with twelve ships. The memorial that Columbus despatched by him setting forth the needs of the new colony is devoid of visionary schemes; it shows to great advantage the practical side of Columbus's abilities, and forecasts some features of the later colonial system.

The prevalent sickness he correctly attributed to the change of air and water and the lack of fresh meat; he emphasized the need of fresh provisions, wine, raisins, sugar, honey, rice, and medicines, clothes, shoes, and leather, more domestic animals for work and for breeding. Gloriously rich in some aspects of nature, the New World was notably poor in food plants and domesticable animals, those two indispensable aids to advancing culture. He proposed, when the supply-vessels should return, to send to Spain some of the cannibals—men, women, and children—to learn Spanish, so that communication could be had with them, for their language was different from that of the Lucayans whom he had taken to Spain. Columbus reported hopefully

---

[1] *Torres Memorial*, Major, *Select Letters of Columbus*, 73, 74; Las Casas, *Historia*, II., 24 ff.

in regard to gold and spices, but sent little of the precious metal.[1]

To bridge over the costly and unprofitable years of laying the foundations of his colony, in case there should not be much gold, Columbus proposed that their majesties should authorize contractors every year to bring over cattle and beasts of burden, for which they might be paid with slaves taken from among these cannibals, "who are a wild people fit for any work, well proportioned, and very intelligent, and who, when they have got rid of their cruel habits to which they have been accustomed, will be better than any other kind of slaves." [2]   The proposition gave pause to Ferdinand and Isabella, and they reserved it for further consideration.

To characterize Columbus as ambitious to become a slave-driver, as a recent biographer has done,[3] reveals a lack of the historical spirit.   It is more reasonable to imagine him already haunted by the problem of keeping in progress the great movement he had started.   Already may he have had a premonition of the angry cries of impoverished and starving Spaniards accusing his spurious Indies of being their ruin.[4]   In any case, the suggestion proposed a means rather than an end, and a means sanctioned by the past,[5] however much to be

---

[1] Major, *Select Letters of Columbus*, 85.   [2] *Ibid.*, 88.
[3] Winsor, *Columbus*, 282.   [4] See below, p. 51.
[5] The slave-trade had been the economic basis of the Portuguese African voyages of exploration, although not their primary object.   Cf. Cheyney, *European Background*, chap. iv.

discredited in the future or questioned at the time.

After Torres' departure, the first serious trouble in the colony arose during the illness of Columbus. Unexpected hardships, disease, and homesickness, in place of a holiday adventure, undermined both courage and discipline. Still worse, one of the gold assayers, Fernin Cedo, scouted the idea of there being much gold in the island. In this time of trial one of the royal officials, Bernal de Pisa, headed a plot to seize the remaining ships and make for Spain. Columbus acted with promptitude and resolution. Bernal was confined in one of the ships, to be sent to Spain with a statement of his offence.[1] But even this exercise of authority galled the discontented colonists, and from their resentment Las Casas traces the beginning of Columbus's later troubles.

When the admiral felt fully recovered he selected from the well and strong about four hundred men, who, in full martial array, with banners and trumpets to dazzle and impress the islanders, followed him, March 12, in a southerly direction towards Cibao. After passing the first ridge they beheld a magnificent plain, affording, according to Las Casas, one of the most splendid prospects in the whole world.[2] About seventy miles south of Isabella, in the mountains of Cibao, nuggets were found and other indications of gold. For the security of miners and

[1] Las Casas, *Historia*, II., 27.   [2] *Ibid.*, 29.

prospectors, Columbus built a fort which he named St. Thomas, on account of the doubters, who there could see the precious metal with their eyes and handle it with their hands. It was garrisoned by Pedro Margarite and fifty-six men.[1]

Upon his return to Isabella the admiral found the settlers still more wasted, for the few who had escaped illness or death were much reduced in strength, owing to the scarcity of provisions. As most of the laborers were disabled, Columbus ordered the gentlemen to take hold and work, under threat of severe penalty. To add the degradation of labor with their hands to their suffering was too much for the Spanish hidalgos, and Columbus never escaped from the resentment engendered at this time.

Leaving the colony under a commission, Columbus, towards the end of April, undertook the exploration of Cuba. Sailing along the southern shore, he diverged to the south and discovered Jamaica, May 14, 1494. The next month was spent in cautiously threading his way along the Cuban coast towards the west through a bewildering number of islets. The vaguely understood signs of the natives were interpreted, now to indicate that Cuba was an island, and now the main-land. Its coast-line seemed interminable; and, provisions growing short, it was necessary to return, and apparently equally necessary to have some positive results to show for the exploration. So all the ship's officers and com-

[1] Las Casas, *Historia*, II., 35–39.

mon sailors and the expert map-maker, Juan de la Cosa, on whose famous map, six years later, Cuba was plainly depicted as an island, were required to take solemn oath that they had no doubt that this land was main-land, the beginning of the Indies and the terminus that whosoever desired to come from Spain overland to these parts would reach.[1]

It is a strange irony of fate that two more days' sailing would have brought Columbus to the western end of Cuba and possibly have led to the immediate discovery of Yucatan, or Mexico.[2] His illusion, however, gave rise to the first project of going round the world, for his son Ferdinand writes in a passage almost certainly derived from Columbus's journal of the second voyage, no longer extant, "that if he had had abundance of provisions he would not have returned to Spain except by way of the East."[3] This is confirmed by Bernaldez, the curate of Los Palacios, who derived the account of this voyage from Columbus himself. One notes with interest, however, that the circuit of the globe was not to involve the circumnavigation of Africa, but a land journey from the Arabian gulf to the Mediterranean.[4]

---

[1] Navarrete, *Viages*, II., 145. The affidavits are translated in Thacher, *Columbus*, II., 327. On this oath cf. Markham, *Columbus*, 166; Ruge, *Columbus*, 175; Lollis, *Colombo*, 235–237.

[2] Peschel, *Zeitalter der Entdeckungen*, 200.

[3] Ferdinand Columbus, *Historie*, 166.

[4] Bernaldez, *Historia de los Reyes Catolicos*, chap. cxxiii.; translated in Mass. Hist. Soc., *Collections*, series VIII., 42.

On the return the south shores of Jamaica and of Española were explored. Late in September, 1494, Columbus, worn out by labors and watchings, collapsed and remained insensible for a long time; and five months passed before he was fully recovered.[1]

During his absence his brother Bartholomew arrived at Isabella, having been sent from Spain by the sovereigns upon his return from England. Bartholomew was a most energetic man, thoroughly devoted to the interests of his brother, who immediately appointed him "adelantado of the Indies," that is, provincial military governor. Yet this appointment so natural under the circumstances, did not prove an unmixed advantage. Bartholomew ruled with more severity than Christopher, and in the eyes of the proud Spaniards he was even more of a foreigner and an upstart. His rigorous discipline did much to create the subsequent impression that the admiral was cruel.[2]

That a strong hand was needed at the helm was only too evident. During the admiral's absence the native population had grown more and more apprehensive and restless. The hunger of the Spaniards seemed insatiable,[3] and in the gratification of their lust they respected neither the rights nor feelings of husbands and parents. Under the cir-

---

[1] Ferdinand Columbus, *Historie*, 177.

[2] Las Casas, *Historia*, II., 80.

[3] Las Casas, with his usual exaggeration in numbers, says that "one Spaniard would eat more in a day than the whole household of a native in a month," *Historia*, II., 73.

cumstances these evils were inevitable, yet they
nearly wrecked the colony. In addition, the officials had proved false to their trust. Margarite
deserted his post at St. Thomas, and with Friar Boil,
accompanied by some priests and many others, took
the ships that Bartholomew brought and went back
to Spain, where they disparaged the Indies, declaring that there was no gold there nor any other
thing of profit.[1]

With the recovery of Columbus began a period
of open warfare with the various native kings, in
which the clumsy fire-arms of the period and the
cross-bows were frightfully effective. Even more
terrible were the centaur-like monsters, the cavalry-
men; and next the hounds that at the words "take
him," would each kill—so Las Casas reports—a
hundred Indians an hour.[2] These raids lasted nine
or ten months, until the islanders were thoroughly
terrorized and subjected to the payment of tribute.
Those who lived near the mines must furnish a
Flemish hawksbell (half to two-thirds of an ounce)[3]
full of gold every three months; while from those
not near the mines was exacted an arroba (twenty-
five pounds) of cotton.

These burdens Las Casas pronounces excessive,
and adds that in despair the Indians fled to the
mountains, preferring to starve to death by re-
nouncing all cultivation of the soil, if only they could
bring famine upon the Spaniards. The friendly

---

[1] Las Casas, *Historia*, II., 75.   [2] *Ibid.*, 96.   [3] *Ibid.*, 103.

cacique Guarionex offered to put an enormous tract
of land under cultivation for growing grain if the
admiral would only not demand gold, but Columbus
needed gold to demonstrate that the colony would be
profitable.   When he found that the tribute was too
high he commuted it to one-half, but even then it was
beyond the power of many of the unfortunate natives.[1] In these three years of conquest—a life-and-
death struggle between the invaders and the natives
—the population of Española was supposed to have
been reduced by at least two-thirds; such was the
opinion of Las Casas and Ferdinand Columbus, and
they no doubt represent the belief of the admiral.[2]

In March, 1496, Columbus having become convinced that the interests of the colony required his
return to Spain, set sail with two caravels containing
some two hundred and twenty homesick and enfeebled colonists and thirty Indians. His brother
Bartholomew was left in authority at Española.

When Columbus arrived in Spain, June, 1496,
three years had passed since the triumphal progress
from Seville to Barcelona. They had been years of
no small achievement compared with the initial
years of later English or French exploration and
colonization; but the results had been disappointing
to the expectations aroused by the announcement
that the Indies of Marco Polo had been reached and
the doors opened to fabulous wealth. As a con-

[1] Las Casas, *Historia*, II., 103, 104.
[2] Ferdinand Columbus, *Historie*, 183; Las Casas, II., 106.

sequence Columbus was thrown upon the defensive. He must vanquish his detractors and those who decried the vaunted Indies; the popular imagination must again be kindled and the sovereigns allured to further ventures.

Columbus assumed the garb of humility and religion, that of a Franciscan friar, presenting striking contrast to the Indian captive prince Don Diego, with a gold chain about his neck weighing six pounds. Gold dust and nuggets, crowns, masks, and girdles, and specimens of Indian workmanship were laid before Ferdinand and Isabella.[1] These picturesque arguments, reinforced by Columbus's persuasive eloquence, restored his fortunes. Yet, unfortunately for him, the foreign enterprises of the crown caused delays and diminished the funds available for the new colony; and, unfortunately for the colony, Columbus succeeded in securing the reversal of measures taken for its advantage because they clashed with his monopoly rights.

In particular, in April, 1495, the sovereigns adopted a plan of voluntary assisted emigration to Española, of free opportunity to any one to make explorations and to engage in trade,[2] a policy in marked contrast to that subsequently pursued. Promptly availing themselves of this opportunity, "different shipmasters set sail for different shores

---

[1] Bernaldez, *Historia de los Reyes Catolicos*, chap. cxxxi.
[2] Navarrete, *Viages*, II., 162; in English in *Memorials of Columbus*, 88.

of the otner hemisphere,"[1] but these private ventures resulted in no new discoveries of which we
have record. Such enterprises the admiral not un-
naturally regarded as an infringement upon his
rights, and he induced the king and queen to revoke
the privilege.

We cannot tell how the plan would have succeeded,
but it is melancholy to observe to what extremities
Columbus was reduced to get colonists beyond
those numbered on the royal pay - list. In June,
1497, a general order was issued to all the officers
of justice in Spain authorizing the transportation
to Española of criminals—excepting heretics, traitors, counterfeiters, and sodomites—in commutation
of death or prison sentences.[2] The three hundred
and thirty authorized to be on the royal pay-list
were to comprise forty esquires, one hundred foot-
soldiers, thirty able seamen, thirty common sailors,
twenty goldsmiths, fifty field laborers, ten gardeners,
twenty handicraftsmen of various kinds, and thirty
women. Their stipend was to be $4 a month, a
bushel of wheat every three months, and a further
allowance for food of eight cents a day.[3]

After most discouraging delays occasioned by the
lack of money, Columbus was able to despatch two
ships in January, 1498; and then to follow himself
with six ships and two hundred colonists on his

[1] Letter of Peter Martyr, June 11, 1495, quoted by Hugues,
Cronologia, 3.   [2] Navarrete, *Viages*, II., 207, 212.
[3] *Ibid.*, 204; *Memorials of Columbus*, 83.

third voyage, the last of May. At the Canaries the
fleet was divided, three ships being sent direct to
Española, while Columbus with three others turned
southward to take his westward course along the
equator. In these regions the suffering from the
heat was intense, and Columbus veered again to the
northward as soon as the wind permitted. Land
was sighted July 31, and the name Trinidad was
given to the island.

Far to the south, on August 1, the main-land of
South America was descried, and on the supposition
that it, too, was an island it was called "Isla Santa."
Two weeks later he perceived the truth in regard to
the land to the south and west and recorded in his
journal, "I am convinced that this is the main-land
and very large, of which no knowledge has been had
until now." [1] This continental region he declared to
his sovereigns to be an "otro mundo," "another
world." [2]

The tribulations of the last few years had deepened
the vein of religious mysticism in Columbus. Thrown
back upon himself in the strain of his ceaseless labors on the sea, of the racking contests with in-
subordinate and angry colonists, and of adverse
conditions in Spain, he came more and more to regard himself as the chosen messenger of God, the
instrument for the fulfilment of prophecy. "God
made me the messenger of the new heaven and the

[1] Las Casas, *Historia*, II., 264.
[2] Major, *Select Letters of Columbus*, 148.

new earth, of which he spoke in the Apocalypse of
St. John, after having spoken of it by the mouth of
Isaiah, and He showed me where to find it." [1]   His
hold on the shreds of scientific knowledge and
scientific spirit, that had filtered down from Aristotle through Roger Bacon to Pierre d'Ailly, relaxed;
and he yielded to the spell of the mythological geography of Sir John Mandeville. Cipango and the Indies fade away into visions of the earthly paradise,
forming the summit of a pear - shaped earth from
which flow the four great rivers of the world. [2]

The mass of fresh water emptying into the ocean
from the northern mouths of the Orinoco River, and
the fact that he was south of Cipango, led him to
the conclusion that he had reached "the end of the
East " and that he was near the earthly paradise. [3]
It is in the early glow of this conviction that he described his outgoing voyage and its results. Those
who disparage his work should remember that no
"princes of Spain ever acquired any land out of
their own country, save now that your highnesses
have here another world." "These lands," he concludes, "which I have recently discovered, and
where, I believe in my soul, the earthly paradise
is situated, will be immediately explored by the
adelantado "—*i.e.*, Bartholomew Columbus. [4]

From such dreams he was rudely awakened a few

[1] Major, *Select Letters of Columbus*, 153.
[2] *Book of Sir John Mandeville*, chap. xxx.
[3] Major, *Select Letters of Columbus*, 134.   [4] *Ibid.*, 148, 150.

days later, when he arrived at the new town on the south shore of Española, founded by Bartholomew and named Santo Domingo for their father, Dominico,[1] the oldest European settlement in the New World which still exists. Here he heard the disheartening tale of renewed revolts on the part of the Indians, and, more serious still, of civil war among the Spaniards. The Indian chiefs had found the tribute almost insupportable, and the lassitude and illnesses which afflicted so many of the Spaniards encouraged them to plan to exterminate the invaders. The design, however, proved beyond their strength, even with the Spaniards divided into two hostile parties.

The causes of this dissension lay in Columbus's prolonged absence of thirty months, the belief that his cause was waning, the desperation engendered by want and disease, and the severe discipline enforced by Bartholomew. Francis Roldan, a protégé of the admiral, who had appointed him alcalde, or chief-justice, raised the standard of revolt, planned the death of Bartholomew and Diego Columbus, and, failing of that, withdrew into the interior with about ninety men, where they preyed upon the Indians and gave themselves up to the indulgence of the passions of lust and cruelty.

Of the total number of Spaniards left on the island

---

[1] Ferdinand Columbus, *Historie*, 239; Las Casas, *Historia*, II., 136, says it received its name because the Spaniards arrived there on Sunday, "Domingo."

two years before a large proportion had died, and of the remainder over one hundred and sixty were afflicted with the "mal francese." [1] Columbus felt it expedient to come to terms with Roldan, and with many concessions he was granted immunity from punishment and restored to his official position.

In the mean time, Columbus had sent to Spain (October, 1498) for reinforcements, characterizing the insurgents as "abominable knaves and vilands, theeves and baudes, ruffians, adulterers, and ravishers of women, false-perjured vagabonndes, and such as had bin evther convict in prysons, or fledde for feare of judgement, etc." Not less passionate was the indictment preferred against him by the insurgents and despatched by the same ship, for they accused the admiral and his brother of being "unjust menne, cruell enemies, and shedders of Spanishe bloode," declaring that upon every light occasion they "would racke them, hang them, and head them, and that they tooke pleasure therein, and that they departed from them as from cruell tyrantes and wilde beastes rejoycing in bloode, also the kinges enemies, etc." [2]

Confronted by such charges and counter-charges, and shocked by the reports of the conditions in Española and by Columbus's reliance upon the slave-trade as the economic basis of the colony, not only

[1] Ferdinand Columbus, *Historie*, 240.
[2] Eden's translation of Peter Martyr, in Hakluyt, *Voyages*, V., 199.

advocated in his letters but exemplified by a cargo
of six hundred shipped on this return voyage,[1] the
monarchs felt the gravest misgivings of Columbus's
capacity as a ruler.   Nor was the constant railing
clamor of impoverished returned colonists without
weight.   Ferdinand Columbus, in his life of his
father, recalled the bitter experience of his boyhood,
when in the summer of 1500 fifty or more of these
vagabonds followed him and his brother in Granada,
shouting, "There go the sons of the admiral of the
mosquitoes who has found lands of vanity and de-
lusion, the grave and misery of Castilian gentlemen."[2]

Under the pressure of all these circumstances,
Ferdinand and Isabella, in the spring of 1499, appointed as judge and governor of the islands and
main-land Francisco de Bobadilla; but owing to lack
of money he did not sail till July, 1500. He was
ordered to take back some of the Indians whom
Columbus had shipped.[3]   Bobadilla was a knight-
commander of the military order of Calatrava, and
is described by Oviedo as an old servant of the royal
house, very honest and religious.[4]   Yet he evidently
started strongly prejudiced against Columbus, and
this prejudice seems to have been turned upon his
arrival to violent animosity by the sight of seven

[1] Las Casas, *Historia*, II., 323, 340.
[2] Ferdinand Columbus, *Historie*, 276.
[3] Navarrete, *Viages*, II., 237, 239, 246.
[4] Oviedo, *Historia General*, I., 69.

Spaniards hanging on the gallows and the report that five more were to be executed on the morrow.[1] After a one-sided hearing of accusations he acted with military promptness and put the admiral and his brothers in irons.

Early in October, 1500, Columbus sailed for Spain, his fortunes apparently sunken to their lowest ebb. His feelings found expression in pathetic eloquence in a letter to a noble lady, formerly the nurse of Prince John. In this he reviews his career, and protests against the unjust standard by which he is judged in Spain. Instead of being treated like a provincial governor in Spain accused of malfeasance, he "ought to be judged as a commander sent from Spain to the Indies . . . by the Divine will I have subdued another world to the dominion of the king and queen." Bobadilla, he wrote, had treated him worse than a pirate treats the merchant.[2]

That Bobadilla proceeded with undue haste and relentless severity cannot be denied. Yet if he earlier bore the character ascribed to him by Oviedo, we must believe that he was impelled by a feeling of remorseless indignation aroused by the accumulation of charges preferred against the Columbus brothers. Las Casas summarizes them, and in their aggregate they recall those preferred against the iron rule of Governor Dale in Virginia.[3] Some of the

---

[1] Las Casas, *Historia*, II., 478.
[2] Major, *Select Letters of Columbus*, 169, 170.
[3] Eggleston, *Beginners of a Nation*, 46, 66.

accusations Las Casas pronounces false, but that the majority of the colonists were "discontented and very indignant against the admiral and his brothers"[1] is only too clear; and the friendly Las Casas writes that he has "no doubt that they did not show the modesty and discretion in governing Spaniards which they should have done, and that they were much at fault, particularly in the severity and parsimony with which they allotted provisions, not distributing them according to each one's need, when the monarchs designed them for the support of all."[2]

As soon as the monarchs heard of Columbus's arrival they ordered his release, and requested that he should appear at court at Granada. The meeting was an affecting one, and the monarchs assured Columbus that Bobadilla had exceeded his instructions, that they had not intended his imprisonment, and that his property and rights should be restored to him. In two respects, however, Columbus was never to recover his former position: he was not promised nor was he ever afterwards intrusted with political authority; and his monopolistic control over the whole field of western exploration was more and more invaded.

[1] Las Casas, *Historia*, II., 492.   [2] *Ibid.*, 495.

CHAPTER V

VOYAGES OF THE CABOTS AND CORTE-REALS

(1496–1502)

THE relation which England bore to early Atlantic exploration offers some striking points of similarity to the position of Portugal. Situated like the peninsular kingdom upon the western verge of Europe, facing the sea of darkness, her hardy sailors had ventured into the northern waters just as those of Portugal pushed their way into the tropics. The exact date at which Bristol seamen began to resort to Iceland for trade and fishing cannot be ascertained; but such voyages were common in the fifteenth century,[1] and, it is probable, even earlier, at a time when more or less regular communication was still maintained between Iceland and Greenland.[2] That the seafaring men of

[1] See Anderson, *History of Commerce*, year 1415, who quotes Rymer, *Fœdera*, IX., 322.

[2] The Greenland colony survived into the fifteenth century, and the pope had news of the conditions there, after 1418. See the letter of Pope Nicholas V., September 20, 1448, in *Documenta Selecta e Tabulario Secreto Vaticano*, Rome, 1893, translated in *The American Hist. Mag.*, April, July, and October, 1902. The letter of Nicholas V. is in the July number, 288. Cf. also the facts recited in the letter of Alexander VI., *ibid.*, 290.

Bristol knew by tradition of Greenland is possible, and even probable. Through their commercial intercourse with Portugal they were also familiar with the Azores, and may have known some of the early Portuguese ventures or projects to discover the islands of Antilia and Brazil.

Hence it is not altogether surprising that we find recorded similar attempts at western voyages by Bristol sailors several years before Columbus undertook his great experiment. In the contemporary chronicle of William de Wyrcestre is the entry: "In 1480, on July 15, the ships of . . . and John Jay, junior, of eighty tons burden, began a voyage at the port of Bristol, from King road to the island of Brasylle in the region west of Ireland faring over the sea, and Thlyde [i.e., perhaps, Th. Lyde] is master of the ship, the scientific seaman of all England, and news came to Bristol on Monday, September 18, that the ships sailed the seas for about nine months [weeks?] and did not find the island, but were turned back by the storms of the sea to a port in Ireland for the protection of the ship and sailors." [1]

But England's first great achievement in oceanic exploration, like Spain's, was to be under the leadership of an Italian sailor, who first appears in the English records on March 5, 1496, requesting a patent authorizing him to make discoveries in the eastern, western, or northern seas, and granting him dominion over any islands so discovered.

[1] Weare, *Cabot's Discovery of North America*, 59.

The wording of the patent, framed in accordance with the suggestions of this John Cabotto, indicates familiarity with the grants accorded to Columbus, and the omission from the charter of the words "Southern Seas" reflects, no doubt, his intention or that of Henry VII. not to intrude upon the fields of discovery already occupied by Spain and Portugal.[1]   Indeed, during Cabotto's negotiations at court the Spanish ambassador Puebla informed his sovereigns that "one like Colon had come to engage the king in another enterprise like that of the Indies, yet without prejudice to Spain and Portugal."[2]

Of the earlier career of John Cabot very little is known directly. He is described by the Spanish minister as a Genoese who had been in Seville and in Lisbon endeavoring to secure aid for this discovery.[3] In 1476 he received full citizenship in Venice after a residence of fifteen years.[4] All that we know of the genesis of his project is derived from a letter of the Milanese agent, Raimondo de Soncino, written in December, 1497, from which we learn that as Cabot had seen the kings of Portugal and of Spain occupy unknown islands, he planned to do the same for King Henry. Soncino adds that Cabot had a map of the world and a globe; and that earlier in life when in Mecca he had learned that the spices came from the remote east, and reasoned that as the

---

[1] Weare, *Cabot's Discovery*, 96.
[2] *Ibid.*, 110, 111.   [3] *Ibid.*, 160.   [4] *Ibid.*, 70.

earth is round their source could be reached by sailing westward. In another voyage he expected to reach Cipango, where all the spices in the world grow. If success crowned these efforts he hoped to make London a greater market for spices than Alexandria [1]—a striking forecast of the shifting of the centre of the world's commerce that was to be a consequence of the discoveries.

Early in May, 1497, over a year after the granting of the patent, John Cabot set sail from Bristol with one small ship and eighteen men. After passing the western extremity of Ireland he ascended towards the north and then began to sail to the eastern regions, leaving the north on his right hand.[2] After sailing some four hundred leagues [3] he reached main-land, which he reported to be the land of the Gran Cam. Signs of inhabitants were found, but no people. He followed the coast for three hundred leagues, and then started upon the return voyage, which he did not interrupt to explore two fertile-looking islands which appeared on his right. Early in August he reached Bristol, having been absent about three months.[4]

The safe return and the successful paralleling for

---

[1] Weare, *Cabot's Discovery*, 144 ff.

[2] "*Ale parte orientale.*" It refers not to the direction, but to his destination, the Orient.

[3] Weare, *Cabot's Discovery*, 143, 159. The letter of Pasqualigo gives the distance as 700 leagues. *Ibid.*, 138.

[4] Letters of Pasqualigo and Raimondo de Soncino, in *ibid.*, 138, 144.

England of Columbus's work for Spain aroused great enthusiasm in Bristol and London, and Cabot was called "the great admiral." Frugal Henry VII. kept his own feelings within moderate bounds, if we may judge from the entry among the privy-purse accounts, August 10: "To hym that found the New Isle, £10." [1] In the December following the king granted him a pension of £20 per year, to be paid from customs' receipts at Bristol. [2]

Such, in brief, are the principal facts of the voyage on which England's rights to America were originally based. Even for this scanty narrative it is only within the last forty years that the slender details have been known. Few characters in history owe more to modern research than John Cabot. Not a writer himself like his great compatriot, he left his fame a legacy to his son, who, instead of devoting to it a pious memorial, like Ferdinand Columbus, deftly clothed himself with it and secured for over three centuries the principal credit of an expedition in which there is no direct evidence to show that he even participated.

In such accounts of the Cabot voyages as were derived from Sebastian Cabot in Spain he is always the principal actor; in some, his father is not mentioned; and in one he is described as already dead. [3] In not one is the true relation of his father to the enterprise correctly given. The intricacies of the

---

[1] Weare, *Cabot's Discovery*, 124.　　　[2] *Ibid.*, 128.
[3] See the documents, *ibid.*, 169–209.

Cabot problem yield only to a careful classification of our sources of information: first, into English state documents; second, contemporary reports by Italian and Spanish envoys in England derived in part from John Cabot himself; and third, narratives in the Spanish and Italian writers derived fifteen or twenty years later from Sebastian Cabot. The first two classes agree with each other and are at variance with the third, which, in accordance with sound principles of historical criticism, must therefore be rejected.

The date of the land-fall, June 24, does not appear earlier than the so-called Cabot map of 1544. It was probably derived from Sebastian Cabot. In regard to the land-fall, controversy has been as busy as with the identity of the San Salvador of Columbus, but the results are not so satisfactory. The Canadian scholars Dawson and Prowse advocate respectively Cape Breton and Newfoundland. Harrisse has been insistent for Labrador, but with slight assent from those familiar with the region, and he now inclines to a more southern region.[1] In view of this uncertainty, it has been questioned whether John Cabot's report that he found the main-land should be accepted as final. He may have been as much mistaken as was Columbus about Cuba.

As a daring navigator, John Cabot must rank with the greatest of that age; his crew numbered eighteen,

[1] Weare, *Cabot's Discovery*, 278 ff.; Harrisse, *Découverte et Évolution Cartographique de Terre-Neuve et des Pays Circonvoisins.*

the exact equipment of the *Niña*, the smallest of Columbus's little fleet, and hence it may be assumed that the two vessels were about the same size— that is, about forty tons burden. Of a second Cabot voyage, in 1498, we have little unquestioned knowledge. A new patent was granted to John Cabot alone on February 3, authorizing him to take as many as six ships and such masters, mariners, or other subjects as should volunteer.[1] In the early spring the fleet of five vessels set sail for the Spice Islands, if we may accept Soncino's report of Cabot's intentions.[2] In the despatch of the Spanish ambassador Puebla,[3] it is still the island of Brazil that is the goal; while the other Spanish envoy, Ayala, writes that the purpose was to visit the discoveries of the previous year.[4] We are left strangely in the dark as to the results of this voyage, and this scarcity of information about the first attempt to found an English colony reflects how far England was behind Spain in appreciating such enterprises at that time, and reminds us of what we have lost from England's having had no Peter Martyr or Oviedo.

. It is unknown whether John Cabot came back alive or whether Sebastian Cabot went on the voyage. There is no record of the return of the expedition, yet as John Cabot, for lack of time, could not have explored in 1497 all the region marked on the La Cosa map, including the "sea discovered by the

[1] Weare, *Cabot's Discovery*, 156.
[2] *Ibid.*, 146.   [3] *Ibid.*, 159.   [4] *Ibid.*, 160.

English," corresponding roughly to the waters from Long Island to North Carolina; and as the account of the one Cabot voyage described to Peter Martyr about 1515 by Sebastian Cabot [1] cannot apply to the first voyage for the same reason, this narrative has generally been accepted as a loose and inaccurate account of the voyage of 1498. On the basis of these two sources it would appear that in his second voyage Cabot followed the coast of North America down to the latitude of South Carolina, if not somewhat farther. This conclusion is confirmed by the injunctions of the Spanish monarchs to Hojeda in 1501 when about to set sail for the Caribbean Sea, to put a stop to the discoveries of the English in that quarter,[2] clearly implying a report to the monarchs that the English had either been met with in West Indian waters or that their English envoys had reported such an intrusion.

Additional evidence of an exploration of the southeastern shores of North America before 1502 is afforded by the Cantino map prepared in Lisbon in that year, which clearly depicts the peninsula of Florida and a considerable stretch of coast to the north, and applies some twenty names to it. Again we have the recollection in Robert Thorne's tract of an English voyage on which, "if the mariners would then have been ruled and followed their

---

[1] Weare, *Cabot's Discovery*, 169.
[2] Navarrete, *Viages*, III., 86.

pilot's minde, the landes of the West Indies (from whence all the gold commeth) had been ours." [1]

Three years later, on March 19, 1501, King Henry granted to Richard Warde, Thomas Asshehurste, merchants of Bristol, and to John Farnandez and Francis Farnandez, a very detailed and elaborate charter covering discoveries, trade, and colonization in all seas east, west, south, and north, excepting where the king of Portugal or some other Christian prince had made a settlement.[2] In 1502 the company, if such it may be called, was reorganized, the names of Richard Warde and John Farnandez dropping out, and that of Hugh Elyot, of Bristol, taking first place.

Of their enterprises we have no record, but voyages seem to have been made under these charters. On December 6, 1503, an order of King Henry's to his treasurer recalls that on September 26, 1502, he "gaf and graunted unto our trusty and well-beloved subjectts ffraunceys ffernandus and John Guidisalvus squiers in consideracion of the true service which they have doon unto us to our singler pleasur as capitaignes unto the newe founde lande." [3] That voyages were made under the second charter seems to be indicated by the grant of the king, September 30, 1503, of £20, " to the merchants of Bristol that have bene in the Newe founde Launde." [4] More-

[1] Winship, *Cabot Bibliography*, 98.
[2] Biddle, *Sebastian Cabot*, 306.
[3] Harrisse, *John and Sebastian Cabot*, 397, 398.
[4] Harrisse, *Discovery of North America*, 692.

over, there is in Hakluyt a brief report of a voyage made presumably in 1503 by Nicholas Thorne with "a merchant of Bristowe named Hugh Elliott." [1]

It is worthy of remark, in connection with the activities of this company, that there is no reference to Sebastian Cabot; if he was a capable mariner at this period, and had been on either of his father's voyages, this complete silence is noteworthy.

The shadowy history of the work of these Bristol merchants and Azorean navigators must not be dismissed without noting that their organization was the pioneer English colonial company, the forerunner of the East India Company and of the Hudson's Bay Company; and that their charter stands at the head of the long procession of colonial charters which are the foundation-stones in the noble fabric of American written constitutions. For the development of the New World, however, England was not ready; her rulers found continental politics too alluring; it was a region where sooner or later they must clash with a friendly state whose alliance was sought and valued; and the country itself was uninviting. Therefore, after these early ventures, inspired by "another Genoese like Columbus," English connections with the New World fade away into the obscurity of unrecorded fishing voyages.

At the beginning of this chapter attention was directed to the similarity between the first English and the first Portuguese attempts to explore the

[1] Harrisse, *Discovery of North America*, 692.

Atlantic. This similarity is especially striking when we notice how closely parallel with the Cabot voyages are the undertakings of the Corte-Real brothers. In pursuance of a charter issued May 12, 1500, granting to him any islands or main-land that he should discover,[1] Gaspar Corte-Real set sail early in the summer and reached "a land which was very cool and with great woods."[2] This is identified with much probability by Harrisse as the eastern shore of Newfoundland.

The next spring, 1501, with three vessels equipped in collaboration with his brother Miguel, he made another voyage, from which he never returned. Most of our information in regard to this second voyage is derived from the correspondence of Pietro Pasqualigo and Alberto Cantino, Italians living in Lisbon. In 1502 Cantino had a map made in Lisbon for the duke of Ferrara, and the testimony of this map points unmistakably to the conclusion that Corte-Real on this voyage reached the southern end of Greenland and then veered off towards Labrador and more thoroughly explored Newfoundland.[3] Cantino's report, however, of a coast where many large rivers flowed into the sea, and where, upon landing, they found delicious fruits of various kinds, trees and pines of marvellous

---

[1] Harrisse, *Discovery of North America*, 59.

[2] Goes, *Chronica*, translated in Markham, *Journal of Columbus*, 230.

[3] Such, at least, is Harrisse's view, *Discovery of North America*, 63.

height and girth, would point rather to the north-eastern shores of the present United States.[1]

On the other hand, the two caravels that returned brought between fifty and sixty captives who are described sufficiently closely to identify them as Eskimos. "They have brought from thence a piece of a broken sword, gilded, which was certainly made in Italy. A native boy had two silver rings in his ears, which, without doubt, seem to have been manufactured in Venice." [2] Even more interesting than these relics of the Cabot voyages was the conjecture of those that returned that this land "is joined to the Andilie,[3] which were discovered by the sovereign of Spain, and with the land of Papagá lately discovered by the ship of this king when on its way to Calicut." [4] This is the earliest conjecture of a great continental region extending from the arctic circle to the tropics.

Of Gaspar Corte-Real nothing more was ever heard. His brother Miguel went out to search for him with three ships in May, 1502; two of these returned, but Miguel Corte-Real followed his brother to an unknown fate. King Emmanuel "felt the loss of these two brothers very much, and of his own royal and pious motion, in the year 1503, he ordered two armed ships to be fitted out at his own cost to go in

[1] Markham, *Journal of Columbus*, l., li.   [2] *Ibid.*, 237.
[3] Antilles. Antillia was the current Portuguese name for the West Indies.
[4] Markham, *Journal of Columbus*, 235. The reference is to Cabral's discovery of Brazil.

search of them. But it could never be ascertained
how either the one or the other was lost." [1] Gaspar
and Miguel Corte-Real, and perhaps John Cabot,
too, head the long and sad procession of daring navigators who have perished in these northern waters.
Yet the Corte-Reals were more fortunate than John
Cabot, of whom no memorial was erected for four
hundred years; for to Newfoundland and the neighboring main-land was given on Portuguese maps and
their derivatives the name of "Land of the Corte-
Reals." [2]

[1] Goes, in Markham, *Journal of Columbus*, 231.

[2] For the evidence that the Gulf of St. Lawrence was explored
by the Portuguese Fagundes in 1520, see Hugues, *Cronologia*,
27, 28, and Harrisse, *Discovery of North America*, 182.

CHAPTER VI

DEVELOPMENT OF THE COAST-LINE

(1499–1506)

WHILE Columbus was contending with rebellious Spaniards and revolting caciques in Española, others were exploring the confines of the "earthly paradise." The glowing account of this region and the map sent to the monarchs were shown by Bishop Fonseca,[1] who had charge of Indian affairs in Spain, to the adventurous Hojeda, who had so brilliantly distinguished himself by his resource and daring in the conflicts with the natives in Española. Hojeda, although no sailor, shrank from nothing; and, attracted more by the pearls than by the "earthly paradise," promptly got up an expedition through the assistance of the Seville merchants.

Upon this expedition he was accompanied by two very remarkable men, Juan de la Cosa, the famous pilot and map-maker, who had been with Columbus on his second voyage (and probably also on his first voyage),[2] and Amerigo Vespucci, a Florentine

[1] Las Casas, *Historia*, II., 269, 389; Navarrete, *Viages*, III., 539; Markham, *Letters of Amerigo Vespucci*. 70.

[2] Markham, *Columbus*, index art. "Cosa," and list of sailors, 69.

business-man of scientific tastes and some literary gifts, who was destined to have his name attached to the New World, through the impression conveyed by his descriptions that he was the first to discover a continental region south of the equator unknown to the ancients. The little fleet of four vessels set sail in May, 1499, following the route of Columbus in his third voyage.

Hojeda reached the continent of South America somewhere near Paramaribo, in Surinam, and then coasted northward and westward the whole breadth of British Guiana and of Venezuela (Little Venice), whose name dates from Hojeda's finding a village built on piles in the Gulf of Maracaibo which reminded him—somewhat remotely, it must be supposed — of the Queen of the Adriatic.[1] The new ground covered in this voyage was the coast-line first southeast and then west of the strip seen by Columbus. Its geographical results are depicted on Juan de la Cosa's map of 1500. Hojeda then turned north and spent some two months in Española. Sailing thence for Spain, he raided two of the lesser Antilles, capturing some two hundred and twenty natives to be sold as slaves. These with the pearls and gold from the coast of terra firma formed the returns for the venturers. For Vespucci the voyage yielded the principal materials for his descriptions of his first voyage,

[1] Markham, *Vespucci*, x. Markham gives translations of Las Casas's accounts of Hojeda's voyage, 68.

which he boldly antedated as having taken place in 1497.

Not long after Hojeda left Cadiz, Alonso Niño, of Moguer, an expert pilot who had accompanied Columbus in his second and third voyages, set sail from Palos with one caravel of fifty tons burden and thirty-three men for the pearl coast, which he reached a few days before Hojeda.[1] This voyage was the most profitable made up to this time, and its success greatly promoted the exploration of northern South America.[2]

The first approach to that part of the continent south of the equator which was later to fall to Portugal in accordance with the demarcation line established by the treaty of Tordesillas in 1494, was made almost simultaneously by the Spaniards and Portuguese. In November, 1499, while Columbus was still in Española, his old companion of the first voyage, Vicente Yañez Pinzon, equipped four vessels and secured a permit from the sovereigns to make discoveries in the Indies.[3] Leaving Palos on November 18, Pinzon boldly struck out a new route, first going south to the Cape Verd Islands and then bearing off to the southwest. A violent storm drove him farther south than he intended to go, and he lost sight of the north star. January 20 he sighted land on the eastern shore of Brazil.

---

[1] Peschel, *Zeitalter der Entdeckungen*, 251, *n.*
[2] *Ibid.*, 254; Navarrete. *Viages*, III., 540.
[3] Navarrete, *Viages*, III., 82.

No inhabitants were found at first, but later they appeared, and the Spaniards were astonished at their size. After futile attempts at peaceful trade they turned northward and followed the coast about two thousand miles, discovering on the way the mouth of the Amazon. Sharing the view of Columbus, they believed this region to be an extension of the India of the Ganges.[1] Of the three vessels, only that of the leader weathered the storm encountered on the return, and it reached Palos September 30, 1500. Unfortunately for his later fame Pinzon was not a writer, and our knowledge is mainly derived from Peter Martyr's interviews with those who went on the voyage.[2] Yet Pinzon's title to be the first who explored South America below the equator is at present unchallenged, and was explicitly recorded by Juan de la Cosa on his map.

Pinzon's course was closely followed a few weeks later by Diego de Lepe, who also started from Palos, and whose distinctive achievement was attaining a more southern point below Cape St. Augustine, on the Brazilian coast, before he returned north.[3] He reported his discoveries earlier than Pinzon, having reached home in June, 1500. These parallel voy-

[1] Peter Martyr, *De Rebus Oceanicis*, 99, 101.

[2] *Ibid.*, 95; Hakluyt, *Voyages*, V., 206; Thacher, *Columbus*, II., 510 (a translation of Martyr's account as it first appeared in the *Libretto de Tutta la Navigazione, etc.*, 1504).

[3] Peschel, *Zeitalter der Entdeckungen*, 258; Las Casas, *Historia*, II., 453, 454.

ages of Pinzon and Lepe in all probability afforded Amerigo Vespucci the materials for the narrative of his second voyage. That he went on one of them is the conclusion of most investigators, and it is the general trend of opinion that he accompanied Lepe.[1]

The next Spanish voyage was made by Rodrigo de Bastidas, a notary of Seville, with the co-operation of Juan de la Cosa. They set sail in October, 1500, from Cadiz, and devoted themselves to the exploration of the northern coast of South America west of Cape de la Vela (where Cosa and Hojeda turned homeward), which they completed as far as the later Nombre de Dios on the isthmus. After a variety of fortunes they reached Cadiz in September, 1502.[2]

Thus, between the arrival in Spain of Columbus's letter announcing the discovery of the main-land and pearl region in 1498 and his departure on his fourth voyage, the coast of South America from Cape St. Augustine, eight degrees south latitude, to the Isthmus of Panama had been explored, a distance of three thousand miles. In the mean time, the activity and success of the Spaniards in exploring the western Indies now led King Emmanuel, who succeeded to the throne of Portugal in 1495, to

---

[1] Hugues, *Cronologia*, 7; Günther, *Zeitalter der Entdeckungen*, 93.

[2] Navarrete, *Viages*, III., 545. On these minor voyages, see also Irving, *Companions of Columbus*, chaps. i.–v.

take up again with energy the pursuit of the long-sought goal of an ocean route to the eastern Indies, which had been intermitted after Diaz had rounded the Cape of Good Hope in 1486, owing in part to the ill health of King John II. In midsummer, 1497, Vasco da Gama, a young man of unwavering courage and iron resolution, sailed from Lisbon with a small fleet of four ships. From the Cape Verd Islands he struck off boldly through the mid-south Atlantic, the first to venture in that vast waste of waters, until he reached the parallel of thirty degrees south; when, availing himself of the westerly trades, he turned towards Africa, where he made the first landing in St. Helena Bay, about one hundred miles north of the cape. For ninety-three days he had been out of sight of land, as compared with Columbus's thirty-five days on his first voyage.[1] Thus before his work was half done Da Gama made the longest unbroken sea-voyage up to this time.

The details of the remainder of the expedition around the Cape of Good Hope and then to India lie outside the scope of this work, for it is with its bearing on American history only that we are concerned. The first news of his success reached Lisbon July 10, 1499, through the arrival of his associate Coelho, almost exactly two years after their departure. Da Gama's return, a few weeks later, was followed early in September by a triumphal entry into Lisbon.

[1] Ravenstein, *Vasco da Gama's First Voyage*, xviii., 186–190.

Six years earlier Columbus had proudly announced to King John that he had discovered the Indies by sailing west; but every year had piled up perplexities and doubts, and even the intense convictions of the admiral were sometimes shaken. Now, while his fortunes were sinking because Spanish expectations were not realized, King Emmanuel was able with a courteously veiled exultation to report to Ferdinand and Isabella that the real Indies had been reached by "Vasco da Gama, a nobleman of our household, and his brother Paulo da Gama"; that they found "large cities, large edifices, and rivers, and great populations, among whom is carried on all the trade in spices and precious stones. . . . Of spices they have brought a quantity, including cinnamon, cloves, ginger, nutmeg, and pepper, . . . also many fine stones of all sorts, such as rubies and others." The great trade which now enriches the Moors in those parts he hopes will be diverted " to the natives and ships of our own kingdom, so that henceforth all Christendom in this part of Europe shall be able, in a large measure, to provide itself with these spices and precious stones." [1] Every detail of contrast between the real Indies and the West Indies appears upon the comparison of this letter of July, 1499, with the descriptions of the voyages of Columbus.

Early in the following year a large fleet of twelve big ships and one caravel, under the command of

[1] Ravenstein, *Vasco da Gama's First Voyage*, xviii., 113, 114.

Pedralvarez Cabral, sailed from Lisbon for India.
After leaving the Cape Verd Islands Cabral followed Vasco da Gama's course, and probably his
advice,[1] in striking out into the Atlantic in a southwesterly direction. In so doing he was perhaps
carried farther by the westerly equatorial current[2]
than he planned, for on April 21 land was sighted. It was the eastern coast of Brazil, near the
modern Porto Seguro, in about eighteen degrees
south latitude. Cabral named the country Santa
Cruz ("Holy Cross"), despatched a ship to report
his discovery, and resumed his way to India. Ever
since the time of the Portuguese historian Osorio it
has commonly been stated that Cabral was blown
out of his course by a storm.[3] There is no mention
of this storm in the contemporary accounts,[4] and
Osorio evidently misplaced the violent storm which
befell Cabral after he left Brazil, and sank four of
his ships with all on board before his eyes.[5]

That Cabral was not consciously much out of his
way is clear from King Emmanuel's announcement
to Ferdinand and Isabella after his return that the
newly discovered land "was very convenient and
necessary for the voyage to India." [6]   That the

---

[1] Ravenstein, *Vasco da Gama's First Voyage*, xviii., 190.

[2] Peschel, *Zeitalter der Entdeckungen*, 263.

[3] Osorio, *De Rebus Emmanuelis*, etc., pub. 1571 (ed. of 1791),
I., 177.

[4] *Alguns Documentos*, 108. Barros describes the storm that
fell upon them before reaching the Cape Verd Islands, *Da
Asia*, dec. I., liv. V., chap. ii.

[5] Navarrete, *Viages*, iii., 95.   [6] *Ibid.*

Portuguese should have lighted on Brazil in their second expedition sent out to the East Indies as a consequence of natural conditions is one of the most singular incidents in history, for it shows with almost complete certainty that if Christopher Columbus had never lived, the New World would have been discovered within a few years of the time of its actual discovery, as an inevitable sequel of the activities of Prince Henry the Navigator in promoting geographical exploration.

This fact, of course, does not detract from the genius and courage of Columbus or diminish the immense impetus which he gave to Spanish exploration and colonization; yet it is true, and as strange as true, that one of the most universally celebrated men in all history could have been spared without affecting materially the occurrence of the great event inseparably associated with his career. The loss would have been spiritual rather than material. The western hemisphere would have been found and reported in the natural colors of its virgin life, not clothed in the raiment of the gorgeous East. Such is the potency of the genius of man in its sway over us that the illusions of the great Genoese are so in-wrought into the very texture of early American history that one feels it impossible to reconstruct it as it would have unfolded without his touch.

Just what impression the voyages of Vasco da Gama made upon the mind of Columbus is not recorded in any of his writings, but that it reawakened within him the desire to demonstrate that the real Indies could be reached by going west is clear from the preparations for his fourth and last voyage. Yet, on the other hand, while King Emmanuel and Vasco da Gama were ushering in the modern era of world-ocean commerce, Columbus, still feeling the appeal of mediæval ideals, had day-dreams of the recovery of the Holy Sepulchre. He faces both ways, now to the future with its enormous development of scientific knowledge of the world, now to the past with its mysticism. He is at once ahead of and behind his age. In the months that followed his return from his third voyage he devoted much time to the compilation of his *Book of Prophecies*, one of the most curious of his literary remains. It is a medley of Scripture passages supposed to foretell the recovery of the Holy City and Mount Zion, and "the discovery and conversion of the islands of India and of all peoples and nations." [1]

In February, 1502, Columbus wrote Pope Alexander VI. a short account of his voyages, in which he identifies Española with the Tarshish and Ophir of the Bible and with Cipango, and concludes with his hopes for his next voyage, the fourth. "This undertaking is made with a view to expend what is derived from it in guarding the Holy Sepulchre for Holy Church. After I was there and had seen the

---

[1] See the extracts in Navarrete, *Viages*, II., 260; in English in Thacher, *Columbus*, III., 660–664. The whole is reproduced in the *Raccolta Colombiana*.

land I wrote the king and queen my lords that in seven years I would pay for fifty thousand foot and five thousand horse for the conquest of it, and in five more years fifty thousand more foot and five thousand horse, making ten thousand horse and one hundred thousand foot—Satan has disturbed all this." [1]

The more immediate purpose, however, of Columbus in his fourth and last voyage was to find a strait that would take him beyond the terra firma revealed by the voyages of Hojeda, Pinzon, and Bastidas into the Indian Ocean.[2] The sovereigns readily gave him the permission, and by the spring of 1502 he had four ships ready. Besides his brother Bartholomew and his younger son Ferdinand he requested the privilege to take two or three men familiar with Arabic to serve as interpreters in case the strait was found.[3]

On May 9, 1502, he set sail and was so favored by the weather that he made the run from the Grand Canary to Martinique in twenty-one days, arriving there June 15. The sovereigns, for fear of trouble,[4] had given Columbus permission to land in Española only on the return voyage; yet one of his ships was in such bad condition that he went thither to despatch letters to Spain requesting another ship.

---

[1] Navarrete, *Viages*, II., 280–282; *Raccolta Colombiana*, pt. i., II., 164.

[2] Las Casas, *Historia*, III., 22; Ferdinand Columbus, *Historie*, 293; Navarrete, *Viages*, III., 556.

[3] Las Casas, *Historia*, III., 25.   [4] *Ibid.*, 29.

The governor, Ovando, however, was firm in abiding by the letter of his instructions, and the former viceroy of the Indies was denied access to his recent dominion.

This humiliation occurred when there was assembled in the harbor of Santo Domingo a great fleet of twenty-eight ships, in which were embarked for Spain his relentless judge, Bobadilla, his rebellious protégé, Roldan, and the captive cacique, Guarionex, and some two hundred thousand castellanos of gold, half for the king and half belonging to the passengers, including a famous nugget weighing six hundred ounces, worth to-day about $11,000. According to Ferdinand Columbus and Las Casas, Columbus urged Ovando to delay their sailing for a week because he foresaw a storm, but he was not heeded, and must needs himself seek shelter elsewhere. The great fleet started, but only to have swoop down upon it a West-Indian hurricane which overwhelmed twenty of the ships, not a soul escaping, and on land swept clean all the houses in the older part of Santo Domingo.[1] Columbus escaped without loss. No wonder such a visitation seemed to the filial Ferdinand a signal instance of divine retribution.[2]

For Columbus, however, it was the beginning of a series of gales which made this his last voyage the

[1] Santo Domingo was rebuilt on the other side of the river on a less exposed site.

[2] Ferdinand Columbus, *Historie*, 286; Las Casas, *Historia*, III., ; there were thirty or thirty-one ships.

most arduous of his life. Of these terrors he gives a vivid picture in his letter to the sovereigns. For eighty-eight days was he buffeted by one continuous storm without sight of sun or stars. At length towards the middle of September land was descried, and gratefully named "Thanks be to God" (Gracias á Dios).[1] In this neighborhood, off the coast of Honduras, he met a large canoe with an awning over it, loaded with men, women, and children and various articles of merchandise. The people were partly clothed and their fabrics showed fine workmanship. Here was something different from the naked simplicity of Española. These Indians had attained a relatively high stage of culture. But Columbus had his mind too firmly fixed upon the strait to follow up such indications with unbiassed eyes, and from these natives and others to the south he got only confirmations of his own illusions.

Nothing can so well illustrate the spell which this man's imagination and his prepossessions cast over his eyes and ears than to read what he believed he learned from the aborigines of Honduras and Costa Rica—although neither he nor any of his followers knew a word of their various languages[2]—in regard to the up-country inhabitants of those regions. "They are all likewise acquainted with the pepper-plant; according to the account of these people the inhabitants of Ciguare are accustomed to hold fairs and markets for carrying on their commerce; . . .

[1] Major, *Select Letters of Columbus*, 178.   [2] *Ibid.*, 201.

others assert that their ships carry guns, and that
the men go clothed and use bows and arrows, swords
and cuirasses, and that on shore they have horses,
which they use in battle, and that they wear rich
clothes and have most excellent houses. They say
also that the sea surrounds Ciguare, and that at ten
days' journey from thence is the river Ganges." [1]
That he had at last found the Malay Peninsula, the
Golden Chersonese of the ancients, he had no doubt.
From Honduras he followed the coast till he reached
the narrowest part of the Isthmus of Panama, continually reinforced in these convictions. What he
had really done was to complete the proof that from
sixteen degrees north to eight degrees south latitude there was an unbroken coast - line. Henceforth the search for the strait must be made in
higher latitudes.

This fourth voyage was filled with many romantic
episodes, such as the canoe voyage of Diego Mendez
to Española for help, when the ships, riddled with
borers, had to be beached on the Jamaica shore; [2]
and the intimidation of the Indians by foretelling a
darkening of the moon as evidence that God was
angry with them for their hostility to His servants,
the Spaniards, a stroke that has more than once
served to thrill the readers of the fiction of modern
adventure. [3] Yet these incidents belong more prop-

---

[1] Major, *Select Letters of Columbus*, 181, 182.
  is narrative is in Major, *Select Letters of Columbus*, 212–243.
  rdinand Columbus, *Historie*, 346.

erly to the biography of Columbus. After waiting
nearly a year in Jamaica, amid perils from treacherous followers and hostile natives, he was rescued by
the caravels despatched by Mendez.

It was November, 1504, when he arrived in Seville,
a broken man, something over twelve years from
the time he first set sail from Palos. Each successive voyage since his first had left him at a lower
point. On his return from his second he was on the
defensive; after his third he was deprived of his
viceroyalty; on his fourth he was shipwrecked, in
addition to his previous misfortunes. The last
blow, the death of his patron Isabella, soon followed.
It was months before he was able to attend court.
His strength gradually failed, he sank from the public view, and on the eve of Ascension Day, May 20,
1506, he passed away in obscurity in the city of
Valladolid.[1]

The busy correspondent, Peter Martyr, was in
Valladolid that spring from February 10 to April
26, and then again from June 30, and wrote several letters from there in June and July; but the
death of the "certain Ligurian" whose strange voyage he had reported thirteen years before found no

[1] The date of Columbus's death was settled by Duro, who found
this entry in the MS. chronicle of José de Vargas Ponce: "El
Almirante Colon, que descubrió las Indias y otras muchas tierras,
Morio en esta Villa [Valladolid] Miercoles vispera de la Ascension, 20 de Mayo de 506." Ruge, *Columbus*, 205. The first
printed notice of his death appeared ten years later, in the
first chapter of the second decade of Peter Martyr (Alcala,
1516); Thacher, *Columbus*, III., 506.

mention in them.[1] The first historian to moralize upon the career of Columbus was Oviedo, who, a generation later, wrote: " Besides his services to the sovereigns of Castile, all Spaniards owe him much, for although many of them suffered and died in the conquest of these Indies, many others became rich and otherwise advantaged. Yet what is greater is that in lands so remote from Europe, and where the devil was served and worshipped, he has been driven out by the Christians, and our holy Catholic faith and the church of God established and carried on in this far country, where there are such great kingdoms and dominions by the means and efforts of Christoval Colom. And more than this, such great treasures of gold, silver, and pearls, and many other riches and merchandise, have been brought and will be brought hence to Spain that no virtuous Spaniard will forget the benefits bestowed upon his country with God's help by this first admiral of the Indies." [2]

Upon Columbus the man the most diverse judgments have been pronounced. His great contemporaries whose achievements challenge comparison with his own, Vasco da Gama and Magellan, are silent figures, iron rulers of men, whom we see only through the eyes of those whom they dominated. Columbus, on the other hand, has revealed himself in his writings as few men of action have been revealed. His hopes, his illusions, his vanity and love

[1] Thacher, *Columbus*, III., 504, 505.
[2] Oviedo, *Historia General*, I., 81.

of money, his devotion to by-gone ideals, his keen
and sensitive observation of the natural world, his
credulity and utter lack of critical power in dealing
with literary evidence, his practical abilities as a
navigator, his tenacity of purpose and boldness of
execution, his lack of fidelity as a husband and a
lover, his family pride, all stand out in clear relief.

Columbus is a living personality with all its baffling
mystery. No one of the many portraits that have
come down to us is surely authentic, and they differ
from one another as widely as the characterizations
of the historians. The attempt to portray him either
in words or colors has resulted quite as much in the
self-revelation of artist or historian as in the restoration of this vanished personality.

In the career of its discoverer there is the prophetic intimation that America would mean opportunity. Of all the self-made men that America
has produced, none has had a more dazzling success, a more pathetic sinking to obscurity, or achieved
a more universal celebrity. Born a plebeian, his
descendants are hereditary nobles; the son of a
woollen-weaver of Genoa, he becomes the viceroy
of the Indies; "loosing the barriers of the Ocean Sea
which had been closed with such strong chains," [1]
"he gave to Castile and Leon a new world," and
then, after all, he left the stage almost unnoticed.

[1] Major, *Select Letters of Columbus*, 191. The words Columbus
heard in a trance on his fourth voyage.

CHAPTER VII

AMERIGO VESPUCCI AND THE NAMING OF AMERICA

(1499–1507)

THE voyages of the Florentine Amerigo Vespucci belong rather to the literary than to the
geographical history of the New World. An acute
observer of things new and strange and a clever
writer, he became, through the publication of his
letters in the countries beyond the Pyrenees, the
principal source of information about the western
Indies. In these narratives he made himself the
central personality; in not one of them did he mention the name of the commander under whom he
sailed, and consequently the impression easily gained
ground that he was a discoverer. His place in the
history of the discoveries is the most remarkable
illustration of eternal celebrity won through a happy
combination of the literary gift and self-advertise-
ment, with the co-operation of the printing-press.

Amerigo Vespucci, generally known to the English
world under a Latinized form of his name, Americus Vesputius, was born in Florence March 9, 1452,
where he lived until some forty years of age.[1] He

[1] Hugues, *Raccolta Colombiana*, pt. v., II., 115.

entered business life, became connected with the mercantile house of the Medici, and in 1492 went to Seville, in Spain, as its foreign agent. He first appears in the Spanish documents as employed in carrying out the contracts of an Italian merchant, Berardi, engaged in equipping vessels for the government for the service to the Indies. He apparently continued in this business as a contractor till 1499,[1] when the vicissitudes of business life finally led him to desire something more " praiseworthy and stable." He then resolved to " see the world," and availed himself of the opportunity to join an expedition of four ships which was going out to discover new lands towards the west.[2]

It is at this point that the first puzzle in Vespucci's career or his character is met with. He says explicitly that the expedition sailed from Cadiz May 10, 1497; but there is no record, official or unofficial, outside of his letter, of such a voyage in 1497. Further, Columbus's monopoly privileges were solemnly renewed April 23 of this year, and the earlier authorization of independent voyages was officially revoked June 2.[3] That these formal recognitions of Columbus's privileges should be flagrantly violated by the crown while the admiral was in Spain is hardly conceivable.

It is, then, the accepted conclusion of very nearly

[1] Hugues, *Raccolta Colombiana*, pt. v., II., 117.
[2] Vespucci's letter to Soderini in Markham, *Letters of Amerigo Vespucci*, 3.   [3] Navarrete, *Viages*, II., 214, 219.

all competent scholars that Vespucci's first voyage was made in 1499 with Hojeda. We have Hojeda's own statement under oath, in the suit of Diego Columbus for his privileges, that Vespucci was with him;[1] and we also have sworn statements that Hojeda's was the first exploration of the northern coast of South America, which was the region visited by Vespucci in his first voyage.[2] Vespucci's narrative harmonizes in a number of minor details with what we know of the voyage of Hojeda.

The attempt was made by the Brazilian scholar Varnhagen, whose views are familiar to English readers from John Fiske's enthusiastic adoption of them,[3] to show that Vespucci's voyage was really directed to the coast of Honduras and the shores of the Gulf of Mexico. In the Latin translation of the Soderini letter describing the four voyages, the first is said to have been along the coast of Parias, the region where Columbus approached the continent of South America on his third voyage in 1498; while in the original Italian the name "Lariab" is given to the region, a name not elsewhere found. This is ordinarily explained as a misprint, but Varnhagen argued that it was correct and that it meant Hon-

[1] Navarrete, *Viages,* III., 544; in English in Markham, *Letters of Amerigo Vespucci,* 30.

[2] Hojeda's testimony as above; also Navarrete, *Viages,* III., 558, 586, 590. In part reprinted in Markham, *Letters of Amerigo Vespucci,* 109.

[3] Varnhagen's view is also presented by Thacher, *The Continent of America,* and by Gaffarel, *Histoire de la Découverte de l'Amérique,* II., 163.

duras. This conjecture he based on the statements of the historians Gomara and Oviedo, who, writing, one a generation, the other two generations later, asserted that Vicente Yañez Pinzon discovered Honduras before the fourth voyage of Columbus.[1] The most probable year for this voyage of Pinzon, Varnhagen thought to be 1497, which would harmonize then with Vespucci's narrative of an expedition in that year. But the historian Herrera states that Pinzon's voyage to Honduras was in 1506.[2] This assertion Mr. Fiske tried to break down by characterizing it "as the single unsupported statement of Antonio de Herrera, whose great work was published in 1601." Unfortunately for this argument, Herrera copied this assertion from Las Casas, who was a contemporary and who was living in the Indies at the time. Las Casas does not give the year, but explicitly asserts that Pinzon's voyage was undertaken when the news came of what Columbus had discovered on his fourth voyage.[3] Not less explicit is the assertion of Ferdinand Columbus that the voyage of Pinzon and Solis took place in 1508.[4] Still again, Peter Martyr dates the voyage the year before that of Nicuesa (1509).[5]

---

[1] See Fiske, *Discovery of America*, II., 70.
[2] Herrera, *Historia General de los Hechos de los Castellanos, etc.*, dec. I., lib. VI., chap. xvii.; the passage is given in Fiske, *Discovery of America*, II., 66.   [3] Las Casas, III., 200, 201.
[4] Ferdinand Columbus, *Historie*, 290 (chap. 89 in original ed.).
[5] Peter Martyr, *De Rebus Oceanicis*, dec. II., chap. vii. (p. 181 of the ed. of 1574).

In view, then, of the restoration of Columbus's monopoly privileges, of the absence of any recorded voyage in 1497, and of the evidence that the Pinzon-Solis voyage occurred later than 1504, the conclusion is wellnigh as positive and confident as it is almost universally accepted to-day that Vespucci made no voyage in 1497 such as he ascribes to himself; and that consequently he was not the first discoverer of the main-land of South America, as he appeared to be from the widely circulated Latin edition of the Soderini letter, nor of the coast of Honduras as was first suggested by Varnhagen not forty years ago.

Vespucci's first voyage, then, was made in 1499 under Hojeda. His second, so far as can be ascertained, was made immediately upon his return from the first (it being supposed that he did not tarry in Española, as did Hojeda) with Diego de Lepe in 1500, when the westward trend of the coast of South America below eight degrees south latitude was discovered.[1]

Vespucci's third voyage was made with a Portuguese captain in 1501, who was despatched to explore the lands just discovered by Cabral. This expedition ran down the coast of Brazil to the thirty-second degree parallel, then veered off through the south Atlantic until the fifty-second degree was reached, the highest southern latitude attained up to this time.[2] After a fierce storm land was dis-

[1] Hugues, *Cronologia*, 7.   [2] *Ibid.* 9.

covered, which is identified with the island of South Georgia.

Vespucci's fourth voyage in 1503 was undertaken with "the intention of discovering an island in the East called Melaccha, of which it was reported that it was very rich, and that it was the mart of all the ships that navigate the Gangetic and Indian seas."[1] This project of the king of Portugal was based on the reports brought back by Cabral from Calicut in 1501. It was, therefore, a renewed effort to carry out the original design of Columbus, which was not destined to be actually accomplished until the time of Magellan. The details of the history of this expedition correspond to what the historian Goes tells us of the voyage of Coelho, who went over in part the same ground as that of 1501 without, however, going beyond sixteen degrees south latitude.[2]

Of neither of these voyages was Vespucci the initiator, but according to his own account the first expedition on the return was intrusted to his command and in the second he was a captain. His name, however, is not to be found in the contemporary Portuguese histories nor in the vast mass of documents in the archives of Portugal relating to the discoveries.[3] If his two private

[1] Markham, *Letters of Amerigo Vespucci*, 53.

[2] Hugues, *Cronologia*, 12. Yet cf. Markham, *Letters of Amerigo Vespucci*, xliii.

[3] Santarem, in Navarrete, *Viages*, III., 310; also Santarem, *Researches*, 13.

letters to friends had not been published in Latin, instead of having the New World called after him, his name would have been known to us only as that of a map-maker and as the official examiner of pilots in Spain.[1]

Turning now to the products of his pen which wrought the seeming miracle, those whose authenticity is accepted consist of a letter written to Lorenzo Piero Francesco de' Medici from Lisbon, in March or April, 1503, describing his third voyage, of 1501; and of a longer letter written equally from Lisbon, in September, 1504, to his old school friend Pietro Soderini, of Florence, at that time gonfaloniere of the republic, in which he described all four of the voyages. The original of the first or Medici letter is lost, but it was translated into Latin and published late in 1503 or early in 1504 under the title "Mundus Novus."[2] The longer letter to Soderini was published at Florence in 1505. It dropped out of sight, and only five copies are known to be extant. A French version of it, prepared for René II., duke of Lorraine, was translated into Latin and published in 1507 as an appendix to the *Cosmographiae Introductio* of Martin Waldseemüller, a professor of geography in the College of St. Dié, in Lorraine.

These letters are full of details of the strange aspects of nature and of man in the new regions.

[1] Cf. the documents, Navarrete, *Viages*, III., 291–309.
[2] Quaritch, *The First Four Voyages of Amerigo Vespucci*, v.

They have a confidential and personal note, perhaps not unnatural in a private correspondence, which at times rises from self-importance to self-exaltation. In variety of matter they surpass Columbus's letters about his first voyage and relate of course to a different field of exploration. In considering their extraordinary popularity it is to be remembered that Columbus's own account of his third voyage, when he discovered the main-land of South America, was not printed till the nineteenth century; nor was any description of it printed until 1504, when one appeared in the little Venetian collection of voyages entitled *Libretto de Tutta la Navigatione de Re de Spagna de le Isole et Terreni Novamente Trovati*, translated from the manuscript of Peter Martyr's unpublished *Oceani Decas*. The matter in this *Libretto* was taken over into the *Paesi Novamente Retrovati*, a larger collection published in 1507; and Peter Martyr published his *Oceani Decas* (Decade of the Ocean) in 1511.

If it is now remembered that Vespucci dated his first voyage 1497, and that his account of it was presented to the Latin-reading world in 1507, while Peter Martyr's brief account of Columbus's voyage of 1498 did not get before the Latin-reading world till 1508, in the Latin translation of the *Paesi Novamente Retrovati*, it is perfectly clear why the fame of Vespucci as the discoverer of continental South America eclipsed that of Columbus. Nor must it be forgotten that the Latin translation of the

Medici letter descriptive of equatorial South Ameri-
ica was being read all over Europe from 1503 on,
for it is to this narrative more than to the other
that the greatness of Vespucci's reputation was
owing.

An enumeration of the number of editions which
were published within the next few years will
illustrate this fact. There appeared in rapid succession fifteen editions of the Latin translation,
seven editions in German, and one in Flemish.[1]
Down to 1550 forty editions of this Medici letter
have been recorded.[2] Less numerous were the
Latin editions of the Soderini letter describing all
four voyages, yet, as they were appended to small
treatises or text-books on geography, their influence
on the rising generation was most marked.

Outside of Spain Vespucci decidedly eclipsed
Columbus. In the peninsula the case was different.
The people among whom he lived and on whose ships
he sailed knew little or nothing of him. No Portuguese translation of his letters was published until
1812, and no Spanish one until 1829. Peter Martyr
just mentions his Brazilian voyages; Oviedo knows
him not. Las Casas regards him as an impostor, and
his view is echoed by Herrera. Hardly less severe
are the moderns Muñoz and Navarrete. In Portugal, Goes, Barros, and Osorio pass him in silence,

[1] See Fumagalli's bibliography appended to Bandini's *Vita
di Amerigo Vespucci* (Uzielli's edition).
[2] Hugues, *Raccolta Colombiana*, pt. v., II., 139.

and in the nineteenth century Santarem devoted a book to exposing his pretensions.

The enormous circulation of the Medici letter under the title " Novus Mundus," etc., familiarized the European public outside of Spain with the association of Vespucci's name with the New World. Impressive, too, was his apparently clear conviction that it was a new part of the world and not simply the East Indies that had been found. In the very beginning he writes of the regions which "we found and which may be called a new world (novus mundus), since our ancestors had no knowledge of them, and the matter is most novel to all who hear of it. For it goes beyond the ideas of our ancients, most of whom said there was no continent below the equator and towards the south, or if any of them said there was one they declared it must be uninhabited for many reasons. But that this opinion is false and altogether contrary to the truth this last voyage of mine has made clear." [1] Here was a positive, clean-cut declaration of the most striking character, very different from Columbus's enthusiastic but not altogether convincing identifications of Cipango and Cathay in his first letter.

Yet that it was really in any sense original with Vespucci may be questioned. In the first place, the Portuguese had proved thirty years earlier that equatorial Africa was both habitable and inhabited;

[1] Varnhagen, *Amerigo Vespucci*, 13; Markham, *Letters of Amerigo Vespucci*, 42.

and opposite D'Ailly's assertion in his *Imago Mundi* that the torrid zone "is uninhabitable on account of excessive heat," Columbus had written in the margin at least a dozen years before: "It is not uninhabitable, because the Portuguese sail through it nowadays, and it is, indeed, very thickly inhabited; and under the equator is the king of Portugal's Castle of Mine, which we have seen." [1] Secondly, the letter of Columbus to Ferdinand and Isabella, describing his third voyage, on which he discovered the main-land of South America, was shown to Hojeda and inspired his voyage of 1499, [2] on which he was accompanied by Vespucci. That Vespucci was also familiar with the contents of the letter is altogether probable, particularly if he went on the voyage, as is supposed, as a government agent. In this letter Columbus said of the mainland: "Of this half part (of the world) Ptolemy had no knowledge"; [3] "if this river does not flow from the earthly paradise, it comes and flows from a boundless land to the south of which hitherto there has been no knowledge"; [4] "now when your highnesses have here [*i.e.*, across the Atlantic] another world" (otro mundo). [5] In the letter to the nurse of Prince Juan, Columbus wrote of his third voyage: "I undertook a new voyage to the new heaven and new world (nuevo cielo e mundo), which

---

[1] Hugues, *Raccolta Colombiana*, pt. ii., II., 375.
[2] See above, p. 66.   [3] Major, *Select Letters of Columbus*, 136.
[4] *Ibid.*, 147.   [5] *Ibid.*, 148.

up to that time was concealed ";[1] and again, "where by the divine will I have put under the dominion of the king and queen, our lords, another world."[2]

Further indication that this use of the name Novus Mundus did not originate with Vespucci is afforded by one of the sketch - maps prepared by Bartholomew Columbus in 1503, when on the fourth voyage, in which the land south of the Mar de Caribi is called "Mondo Novo." Some additional illustrations of the use and meaning of the terms "new world," "other world," "West Indies" may be given here in order to clear away in some measure the confusion in which the subject has been involved.[3]

The name West Indies was originated by Columbus himself and was used by him for the first time in document xliii., article iv., of his *Book of Privileges*, written before 1502, in which he refers to "la calidad de las dichas Yndias ocidentales á todo el mundo innotas" ("the character of the said West Indies unknown to all the world").[4]

As for the term New World, in one or another of its Latin equivalents it was used from the beginning by Peter Martyr to describe Columbus's discoveries. In reality it did not mean a region detached at all points from the hitherto known world, but a new part of the globe not hitherto within the

---

[1] Major, *Select Letters of Columbus*, 154. [2] *Ibid.*, 170.
[3] *E.g.*, in Fiske, *Discovery of America*, I., 444, *n.*, 515, II., passim.
[4] Spotorno, *Codice Diplomatico Colombo - Americano*, 286; *Memorials of Columbus*, 215; Thacher, *Columbus*, II., 530.

range of European knowledge. The use of it, therefore, implies of necessity nothing as to the physical connection or disconnection with Asia, but simply the fact of situation outside the bounds of previous knowledge, just as we say figuratively of a man in unfamiliar surroundings, "He found himself in a new world." Thus the Venetian Cadamosto, writing of his voyages down the hitherto unexplored coast of Africa in 1455 and 1456, says the regions he saw in comparison with Europe might well be called "un altro Mondo" ("another world").[1] Similarly, after the name had become familiar as applied to South America, Francis Serrão, in writing to Magellan of the Maluccas, refers to them as farther than the antipodes and as being "another new world" ("outro novo mundo").[2]

Peter Martyr uses the phrase "western antipodes" in his letter of May 14, 1493; "new hemisphere of the earth" in that of September 13, 1493; he calls Columbus "that discoverer of new world" ("ille novi orbis repertor") November 1, 1493; he writes of more wonders from the "New World" ("Orbe Novo") October 20, 1494; and in December of the same year he uses the phrase "Western Hemisphere" ("ab occidente hemisperio").[3] The Florentine Simone del Verde, in January, 1499, in

---

[1] Humboldt, *Kritische Untersuchungen*, III., 130, *n.*

[2] Barros, *Da Asia*, dec. III., liv. V., chap. viii.

[3] All these will be found in Thacher's extracts from Peter Martyr's *Opus Epistolarum*, in his *Christopher Columbus*, I., 55.

a letter from Cadiz, remarks that the admiral had had great courage and genius in having discovered the other world opposite our own ("l'altro mondo opposito al nostro").[1]   That Vespucci's letters first gave wide publicity to the discovery of a continental region south of the West Indian islands is undeniable; but that he was the first to recognize this discovery as such is not true.   In fact, his conviction may have been simply the fruit of the seed planted by Columbus.

That Columbus believed at the same time that he had found islands lying off the eastern coast of Asia and also a main-land to the south of these islands unknown to the ancients presents no difficulty, but rather offers a solution to old-standing perplexities.   Many writers have insisted that Columbus died in ignorance of his real achievement, believing that he had discovered the islands off the coast of Asia and part of the main-land of that continent.   Others with equal confidence maintain that he realized that he had discovered a new world.   His own language supports both views, and his position and that of his contemporaries becomes intelligible enough in the light of the interpretation given above of the phrase "new world," if we once realize the striking analogy between the relation of Australia to the Malay Peninsula and that of South America to the parts of North

[1] Harrisse, *Christophe Colomb*, II., 97; Thacher, *Columbus*, I., 63.

America that Columbus visited. To take an illustration from a map published after Columbus's death and after the publication of Vespucci's voyages: in Ruysch's map in the Ptolemy of 1508, Florida occupies the position of Borneo, Española of New Guinea, and Mundus Novus of Australia.[1] In other words, if America and the Pacific had not existed and Columbus had done just exactly what he supposed he did, he would have discovered Borneo, New Guinea, and Australia, and these regions would have been called "another world," and Australia, *par excellence*, "Mundus Novus." It was only after Magellan's voyage across the Pacific that antagonism appears between Columbus's different descriptions. He did not and could not, nor could any one else, divine that vast expanse of waters.

Returning now to the history of the narrative of Vespucci's voyages, with its widely published announcement of a hitherto unknown southern continental region, we come to the first suggestion to attach the Florentine's name to this "Mundus Novus." Martin Waldseemüller, the young professor of geography at the college in St. Dié, who published the Soderini letter or narrative of the four voyages as an appendix to his *Cosmographiae Introductio*, 1507, when he enumerated the different parts of the world, wrote: "In the sixth

---

[1] A sketch of Ruysch's map is given in Fiske, *Discovery of America*, II., 114. A comparison by means of any map on the Mercator projection will make clear the points made in the text.

climate towards the south pole are situated both
the farthest part of Africa recently discovered, and
Zanzibar, the islands of lesser Java and Ceylon,
and the fourth part of the globe which since Americus discovered it may be called Amerige—*i.e.*,
Americ's land or America."—"In sexto climate
Antarcticum versus, et pars extrema Africae nuper
reperta, et Zamzibar, Java minor et Seula insulae,
et quarta Orbis pars (quam quia Americus invenit
Amerigen, quasi Americi terram, sive Americam
nuncupare licet) sitae sunt."[1]

A little further on, when ready to take up the
parts of the world unknown to the ancients, he opens
his account: "Now, indeed, as these regions are
more widely explored, and another fourth part has
been discovered by Americus Vesputius, as may be
learned from the following letters, I do not see
why any one may justly forbid it to be named
Amerige—that is, Americ's Land, from Americus,
the discoverer, a man of sagacious mind, or America,
since both Europe and Asia derived their names
from women."—"Nunc vero et hae partes sunt
latius lustratae et alia quarta pars per Americum
Vesputium (ut in sequentibus audietur) inventa est,
quam non video cur quis jure vetet ab Americo in-
ventore sagacis ingenii viro Amerigen quasi Americi
terram sive Americam dicendam cum et Europa et
Asia a mulieribus sua sortita sint nomina."[2]

---

[1] Fol. 3 b, cited from Kretschmer, *Entdeckung Amerikas*, 364.
[2] Fol. 15 b, *ibid*.

It will be noted that this young scholar, who in the prevailing fashion of the Renaissance had dignified his cumbrous family name of Waldsee-müller into the Greco-Latin compound Hylaco-mylus (Gr. ὕλη, a wood; Lat. *lacus*, lake; Gr. μύλος, mill), which effectually concealed his identity in later days until it was revealed by Humboldt, pursued a similar process in devising the first of the two names which he proposed for the New World. Amerige is made up of Ameri(ci) and *ge*, the Greek γῆ, land. As an alternative the feminine of Americus is suggested by analogy with Asia, Europe, and Africa.

As between Amerige and America euphony soon gave the palm to America, and only a writer here and there adopts the former.[1] The same advantage and the apt analogy in form to Asia and Africa, effectively and indispensably seconded by the rapid multiplication of geographies and maps in Germany, soon gave America the lead over all its competitors, in spite of the recurring sense of the injustice done to the memory of Columbus.

From the time of Schöner, who first made the charge in his *Opusculum Geographicum*, 1533, to the time of Humboldt, who completely refuted it, the belief was not uncommon that Vespucci had a hand in giving his own name to the New World. An interesting side-light on this point is thrown by the

---

[1] *E. g.*, Nicolini del Sabio, in his edition of the *Cosmographiæ Introductio* (Venice, 1535); Marcou, *Nouvelles Recherches*, 44.

fact that his nephew, Giovanni Vespucci, did not adopt the name in the map he made in 1523.[1] Waldseemüller himself, when he became more thoroughly acquainted with the real history of the first discoveries, quietly dropped the name, and on his map of 1513 substituted for it on the mainland of South America "Terra Incognita," with the inscription, "This land, with the adjacent islands, was discovered by Columbus, a Genoese, under the authority of the King of Castile."[2]

The name America, notwithstanding the activity of the German press, made little or no headway in the Spanish peninsula, where "The Indies" was the prevalent official name and the one used by historians like Oviedo, Las Casas, and Herrera. The first Spanish maps to contain the name America were those in the *Atlas* of Lopez (Madrid, 1758).[3] Muñoz, in 1789, entitled his work, which was the first really critical history according to modern ideas, *Historia del Nuevo Mundo*. Among the other names suggested some may be noted. "Atlantis" was proposed by the French geographer Postel, 1561, and his example was followed among others by Sanson, 1689.[4]

Ortelius (Oertel), in 1571, desiring to do equal honor to Columbus and Vespucci, proposed to call North America "Columbana" and the southern con-

[1] Hugues, *Le Vicende del Nome "America,"* 29.

[2] *Ibid.*, 18. See Kretschmer, *Entdeckung Amerikas*, Atlas, plate 12.

[3] Hugues, *Le Vicende del Nome "America,"* 43.   [4] *Ibid.*, 23.

tinent "America." On Mercator's globe of 1541 the name America is stretched over the hemisphere, "Ame" being inscribed on the northern and "rica" on the southern continent. The names North America and South America first appear on the maps early in the seventeenth century, in Maginis's *Ptolemy* and Hondius's *Atlas*.[1]

The first indignant protest against the injustice done to Columbus in the application of another's name to the New World which he discovered was that of the celebrated Michael Servetus in that edition of *Ptolemy* whose unfortunate disagreement with the books of Moses as to the fertility of Palestine was one of the charges the stern Calvin brought against his victim.[2] Servetus declared that those were entirely mistaken who claimed that this continent should be called America, for Americus came thither much later than Columbus.[3] The case was taken up vigorously by Las Casas, who, as a friend and admirer of the admiral, felt deeply on the subject.[4] Curiously enough, there is no reference to the matter in Ferdinand Columbus's life of his father, which was written before 1539, and probably after the protest of Servetus. It would seem as if he died in ignorance of the eclipse

[1] Hugues, *Le Vicende del Nome " America,"* 39.

[2] Humboldt. *Kritische Untersuchungen*, II., 323.

[3] The passage is quoted in Winsor, *Narrative and Critical History*, II., 176, *n.*

[4] Las Casas's extensive criticism of Vespucci's narratives is given in English in Markham, *Vespucci's Letters*, 68–108.

of his father's fame by that of Vespucci in Europe outside of Spain.

The four discoverers—Columbus, John Cabot, Sebastian Cabot, and Amerigo Vespucci—have fared variously at the hands of modern historical criticism. John Cabot has been raised from almost complete obscurity to become a prominent but still shadowy figure. Sebastian Cabot has been pulled down from the lofty pedestal which he apparently erected for himself, his veracity is impugned, his scientific attainments disputed, and his lack of filial piety exposed to a glaring light. Around Vespucci the storms of controversy have raged for three centuries and a half, and he has suffered from them like Sebastian Cabot. His claims for himself have not stood the test. While he has been cleared of complicity in having his name attached to the New World, it is generally accepted that he antedated his first voyage to secure a distinction which did not belong to him, and that his narratives unduly exalt himself at the expense of others equally entitled to honor. The position of Columbus alone has not been materially affected by the modern scrutiny into his career. Opinion has differed about his character, but the record of his achievements has been unshaken and the estimate of its significance has risen rather than fallen.

CHAPTER VIII

THE SEARCH FOR A STRAIT

(1508–1514)

THE New World had proved a source of surpassing interest for Europe, but thus far of
little wealth for Spain. There was to be sure, after
nearly ten years of effort, a small importation of
gold amounting to some 400,000 pesos a year;[1] but
in the mean time Portugal had reached the Indies
and their spice markets, while in the west the ships of
Spain ran up against a mysterious barrier of land
which at every point baffled further advance. If,
as Columbus supposed—and his view was still
generally shared—this barrier was the extremity of
Asia, there must be a strait between the tropical
main-land, or Novus Mundus, of which the ancients
knew nothing, and this supposed projection of Asia.
Or if all these new lands were detached from Asia
there must be a sea beyond which led to the
spiceries. It was in search of such a passage that the

[1] Under the year 1506 Herrera estimates the annual product
at 460,000 pesos (*Historia General*, dec. I., lib. VI., chap. xviii.).
Peter Martyr, *De Rebus Oceanicis*, 118, puts the annual product
at 300,000 pesos. The peso d'oro was 450 maravedis, or about
one-sixth of an ounce, or approximately $3.

larger part of the coastal exploration of North and
South America was carried on during the sixteenth
century.

One of the earliest enterprises of Queen Isabella's
short-lived successor, Philip I. (1504–1506), was to
plan in 1506 an elaborate expedition to discover the
Spice Islands. The energetic and experienced Vicente Yañez Pinzon was selected to command it, but
two years, however, elapsed before it finally got off
(June 29, 1508).[1] Pinzon was accompanied by Juan
Diaz de Solis and Pedro de Ledesma. Starting from
Cuba, he coasted along its southern shore till he
rounded the western end, thus proving it to be an
island.[2] Before Pinzon returned, however, it was
officially circumnavigated by Sebastian de Ocampo,
1508.[3] From thence they struck across the Gulf of
Mexico to the scene of Columbus's fourth voyage,
the Bay of Honduras. From Honduras Pinzon and
Solis went carefully over the coast-line of Central
and South America as far as the fortieth degree
south latitude, the longest continuous voyage that
had then been made in American waters.[4]

---

[1] Harrisse, *Discovery of North America*, 731.
[2] Peter Martyr, *De Rebus Oceanicis*, 181 (ed. of 1574).
[3] Herrera, *Historia General*, dec. I., lib. VII., chap. i.
[4] Peter Martyr, *De Rebus Oceanicis*, 181–185; Herrera,
Historia General, dec. I., lib. VII., chap. ix.; Peschel, *Zeitalter
der Entdeckungen*, 335, 336. In Errera, *L'Epoca delle Grandi
Scoperte*, 304, 305, and Winship, *Cabot Bibliography*, xvii. and
No. 342, will be found the reasons for supposing that Sebastian
Cabot explored the northern coast of North America in 1508
in charge of an English expedition.

The next advance in knowledge of American geography was to come from the establishment of the first permanent settlements on the main-land, undertaken at their own expense by the indefatigable Hojeda and by Diego de Nicuesa, a planter who had acquired wealth and prominence in Española. Hojeda was granted the coast from Cape Vela to the Gulf of Urabá under the name of New Andalusia. Nicuesa received the Isthmus of Panama and the coast beyond to Cape Gracias á Dios, the eastern point of Honduras, and the name Castilla del Oro[1] (Golden Castile) was given to the region. Hojeda started in November, 1509, in four ships, with three hundred men and twelve horses. With him were the veteran Juan de la Cosa, and a new adventurer whose achievements were to inscribe his name high in the roll of explorers and conquerors, Francisco Pizarro.

Effecting a landing where later stood the city of Cartagena, with customary rashness Hojeda made a dash into the territory of hostile natives to get some slaves to sell to meet his expenses.[2] Their fierce resistance with poisoned arrows cost him some seventy men, including Juan de la Cosa,[3] and almost his own life. Forsaking this inhospitable region, he moved on to the west, and at the extreme

[1] This name King Ferdinand transferred in 1513 to that portion of the northern part of South America commonly called Tierra - Firme and usage subsequently followed his mandate. Navarrete, *Viages*, III., 337.

[2] Las Casas, *Historia*, III., 290.   [3] *Ibid.*, 293.

end of his territory built a fort, which he called
St. Sebastian, to enlist the saint's protection against
the death-dealing arrows that rained upon them.[1]

The appeal was vain. A few days later, for the
first time in his life, Hojeda was wounded, an arrow
piercing his thigh. By promptly cauterizing the
wound with white-hot iron plates he escaped death
this time, but his fortunes were declining. His
band of followers had wasted from three hundred
to sixty, and it was necessary for him to go to
Española for supplies. After extraordinary hardships he reached Santo Domingo only to die broken
and penniless.[2]

Nicuesa's superior resources, personal attractiveness, and the more alluring promise of the region of
Veragua brought together a large force of seven
hundred men and six horses in five ships and two
brigantines, which set sail from Santo Domingo
about ten days after Hojeda.[3]

But his fate was equally hapless. After a long
search for Veragua, during which he was wrecked,
Nicuesa resolved to transfer his settlement farther
east, and fixed upon a spot near the present
town of Aspinwall, which he called Nombre de
Dios. The climate, the lack of food, and their
arduous labors rapidly thinned the little colony
down to sixty men.

As if to rescue them from extinction, two vessels

[1] Las Casas, *Historia*, III., 298.   [2] *Ibid.*, 301–310.
[3] Peschel, *Zeitalter der Entdeckungen*, 336–338.

belonging to Nicuesa loaded with supplies appeared in November, 1510, under the command of Roderigo de Colmenares. From him Nicuesa learned of the failure of Hojeda, and that his own colonists had moved across the Gulf of Urabá from St. Sebastian to Darien, where gold had been found and a fairly prosperous settlement established. As this lay within the boundaries of Nicuesa's province he naturally expected to exercise authority over the inhabitants, but they refused submission and the unhappy governor was forced to set sail for Spain with only seventeen men in a rotten brigantine, an alternative to instant death. Nothing was ever heard of him again.[1]

The struggle for existence after Hojeda's departure had brought to the front in his colony Vasco Nuñez de Balboa, a man of great resourcefulness and courage, whose career if not so early cut off might have anticipated that of Pizarro. He had been a planter in Española, but the spirit of adventure was strong and the burden of his debts oppressive; hence, when Hojeda's lieutenant, the lawyer Enciso, was about to sail for Tierra-Firme, Balboa, not being able to evade his creditors otherwise, had himself nailed up in a barrel and put on board with the provisions.[2]   It was at his suggestion that the colonists moved over to Darien, and thenceforth he was a leader.[3]

[1] Las Casas, *Historia*, III., 329–346.
[2] *Ibid.*, III., 313.   [3] *Ibid.*, 318.

Balboa's activities embraced an energetic campaign against the natives for provisions, and an offensive and defensive alliance with one of the native rulers, including the taking of his daughter to wife. A joint expedition followed against the enemies of this chief, and then a foregathering with one of his allies at some distance to the west, who gave the Spaniards about fifty pounds of gold, worth nearly $12,000. As they were measuring it out and wrangling over it the eldest of the seven sons of this allied chief lost his patience, dashed the scales from their hands, and rebuked them for their greed, adding: "I will shewe you a region flowing with golde where you may satisfie your ravening appetites. . . . When you are passing over these mountains (poynting with his finger towarde the south mountaines) you shall see another sea where they sayle with ships as big as yours."[1]

Balboa was not able at this time to verify these assertions, but in the summer of 1513, upon receiving the news that a new governor was coming out from Spain to render judgment upon him, he resolved to forward his own cause as far as possible by a brilliant stroke. With a picked body of one hundred and ninety Spaniards and several hundred Indian porters and dogs he set out September 1

---

[1] Peter Martyr, *De Rebus Oceanicis*, 151; Eden's translation from Hakluyt, *Voyages*, V., 229, 230, Las Casas follows Peter Martyr's account, which was derived from Colmenares and Quicedo (also spelled Caicedo) upon their return from the Isthmus. *De Rebus Oceanicis*, 176; Hakluyt, *Voyages*, V., 240.

to discover the sea of which the Indians had told him. Although the isthmus is only about forty-five miles wide at the place he tried to cross, and the ridges on the average only about a thousand feet high,[1] yet so dense is the tropical forest that gloom reigns almost perpetual. Impenetrable thickets, tangled swamps, slippery cliffs, enormous trees, and interlacing vines block the way at every turn.[2] After a most arduous progress of eighteen days, a wonderful achievement as modern explorers have found out, at about ten o'clock in the morning of September 25, 1513, Balboa reached the ridge from the summits of which " he might see the other sea so long looked for, and never seene before of any man comming out of our worlde." [3] This dramatic moment may best be described in the words of Peter Martyr, whose account is based on Balboa's letters.[4]

"Approching therefore to the tops of the mountaines, he commanded his armie to stay, and went himselfe alone to the toppe, as it were to take possession thereof, where, falling prostrate upon the grounde, and raysing himselfe againe upon his knees, lyfting up his eyes and handes toward heaven he hales the South and powred forth his

[1] Peschel, *Zeitalter der Entdeckungen*, 370, 371.

[2] Prevost in 1853 found the forest so dense that for eleven days they did not see the clear sky. *Ibid.*, 371.

[3] Peter Martyr, *De Rebus Oceanicis*, 210; Hakluyt, *Voyages*, V., 255.

[4] Peter Martyr, *De Rebus Oceanicis*, 205.

boundless gratitude to God and all the Heavenly Host who had reserved the prize of so great a thing unto him being a man but of small wit and knowledge, of little experience, and lowly parentage. When he had thus made his prayers after his warlike manner, hee beckoned with his hande to his companions to come to him, showing them the great maine sea heretofore unknowne to the inhabitants of Europe, Aphrike, and Asia.''[1]   Four days later, upon the shore of the bay which he named San Miguel, he waited the rising tide.   When the billows came rolling in over the flats he rushed in, flourished his sword, and took possession of the sea with a ringing proclamation.

Eight years passed after Columbus unlocked the bars of the Ocean Sea before he was sent to Spain in irons.   The star of Balboa sank more rapidly.   In four years he was relentlessly put to death by a jealous and suspicious governor, Pedrarias Davila.[2] Columbus's work was really done; the career of Balboa was in its beginning.   He had made the most important discovery since the third voyage of the admiral, and he had displayed qualities as a leader thus far unequalled by any of the conquistadores.   He was not only a considerate and inspiring commander of Spaniards, but, in addition, he showed extraordinary ability in dealing with the

---

[1] Eden's translation in Hakluyt, *Voyages*, V., 255, here slightly changed to a closer conformity to the original.

[2] The name is sometimes written Pedro Arias de Avila.

natives. By a judicious mingling of severity with tact he won the friendship of the chieftains and the attachment of the tribesmen. Had he lived they would have been spared countless horrors, and he might have anticipated either Pizarro or Cortés.[1] Could his discovery have been reported a little sooner, Pedrarias Davila, whose jealousy brought him to ruin, would hardly have been appointed, and the history of the main-land of South America might have been very different.

The news of Balboa's discovery of the great sea beyond the main-land reached Spain soon after the departure of Pedrarias in April, 1514, and immediately aroused the greatest interest. A despatch was promptly forwarded to the new governor of Castilla del Oro to establish a settlement on the shores of the Gulf of San Miguel and to build three or four caravels for making a thorough exploration of the coast of the South Sea. King Ferdinand next turned to the veteran navigator Solis, the ablest sailor in Spain[2] now that Pinzon had retired, and familiar with the South American coast from his great voyage six years before; and on November 12, 1514, gave him a commission to take three ships, one of seventy tons and two of thirty tons, with seventy men and provisions for two years and a half, to go to explore the waters beyond Golden Castile (the isthmus) to the distance of seventeen

[1] Cf. Markham, *Narrative of Pascual de Andagoya*, ii., iii.
[2] Herrera, *Historia General*, dec. II., lib. I., chap. vii.

hundred leagues, or more if possible, yet without intruding upon any of the lands of the king of Portugal.[1] This voyage, if brought to a successful issue, must find the long-sought strait, the much-desired western route to the Spice Islands, and settle the vexed problem whether or no the New World was adjacent to the eastern verge of Asia.

The voyage proceeded with hopeful prospects until the discovery of the broad estuary of the later Rio de la Plata, which they called the "Mar Dulce" (Fresh Sea). The shores were inhabited, and Solis, expecting to find the natives friendly, landed with seven companions. No sooner had they landed than "sodenly a great multitude of the inhabitantes burst forth upon them, and slue every man with clubbes even in the sight of their fellowes. . . . They cut the slayne men in peeces," preparing to eat them. "Their companions being stricken with feare through this example, durst not come foorth of their shippes or devise how to revenge the death of their Captayne and companions. They departed therefore from these unfortunate coastes, and by the way lading their shyppes with Brasell, returned home agayne with losse, and heavie cheare."[2]

The goal at which Solis had aimed was already in the hands of the Portuguese. They reached Malacca,

<hr>

[1] Navarrete, *Viages*, III., 134.
[2] Peter Martyr, *De Rebus Oceanicis*, 316–318; Hakluyt, *Voyages*, V., 307. Based on the accounts of the survivors.

the great emporium of all eastern Asiatic commerce, in 1509. Two years later the city fell before the Portuguese viceroy Alfonso d'Albuquerque. This splendid conquest was announced by the king of Portugal to Pope Leo X. in glowing language almost exactly twenty years after the news of Columbus's first voyage. The long race had been run and the glittering prize of such unparalleled efforts was at last in the hands of King Emmanuel: "The Golden Chersonese, called Malacha by the inhabitants, situated between the Gangetic and the Great Gulf, a city of wonderful size with upwards of twenty-five thousand households, the land most fertile and most productive of merchandise in India by means of that most famous market where not only abound the different spices and all kinds of perfumes, but also gold and silver, pearls and precious stones."[1] To seal this conquest, Albuquerque despatched a fleet under Antonio d'Abreu in December, 1511, to the Spice Islands themselves, which lay farther to the east. Early in 1512 Abreu visited in turn Amboina and Banda, and, loading with cloves, returned to Malacca.

[1] Translated from the Latin text in Roscoe, *Leo X.*, I., 521, 522 (London, 1846).

CHAPTER IX

MAGELLAN AND THE FIRST VOYAGE AROUND THE WORLD

(1519–1522)

THE revelation that the islands where spices grew lay some fifty degrees of longitude to the east of Calicut could not fail to revive the old Columbian project to reach them by sailing west. That it was now again first proposed to the king of Portugal, rejected by him, laid before the king of Spain, and under his patronage at last brought to a successful issue by a Portuguese sailor, is one of those "artistries in circumstance"[1] which give its infinite variety to history and baffle all efforts to reduce its course to the regulated bounds of discernible natural law.

Fernão de Magalhães was born in the interior of Portugal of a family of the lesser nobility, about the year 1480. Early transplanted to the capital, he became a page of Queen Leonora, but at the accession of King Emmanuel in 1495 he passed into his service. In the impressionable years of his early manhood he saw the return of Da Gama from India.

[1] Hardy, *The Dynasts*, 1.

Then came the equipment of great fleets for the Indies, the discovery of Brazil and its exploration. No wonder that the youth sought service in the far East and joined the great expedition of Almeida in 1505. In this service Magellan, to adopt for convenience this anglicized form of the name, remained for seven years, during which he visited Malacca and took part in its conquest in 1511. His return to Portugal soon followed, and next came a campaign or two in Morocco.[1]

Africa was a "pent-up Utica" compared with the Indies, and the letters which Magellan received from his intimate friend Francisco de Sarrão, who penetrated still farther East, and was living in the Molucca islands and writing of "another new world larger and richer than that found by Vasco da Gama,"[2] hardened to a fixed purpose the project to seek the Spice Islands by the west. The decisive moment came when King Emmanuel denied Magellan's request for promotion and a slight increase in his stipend, and rejected his proposal for the western voyage.[3] Magellan was not the man to sit quiet with a great idea in his head. If the door was closed against him in Portugal he would find an opening elsewhere.

Hence he went to Seville in 1517, and, taking out naturalization papers, became a subject of Charles I.,

[1] Guillemard, *Life of Magellan*, 17 ff.   [2] *Ibid.*, 71.
[3] That Magellan made such a proposal is an inference. *Ibid.*, 81, 82.

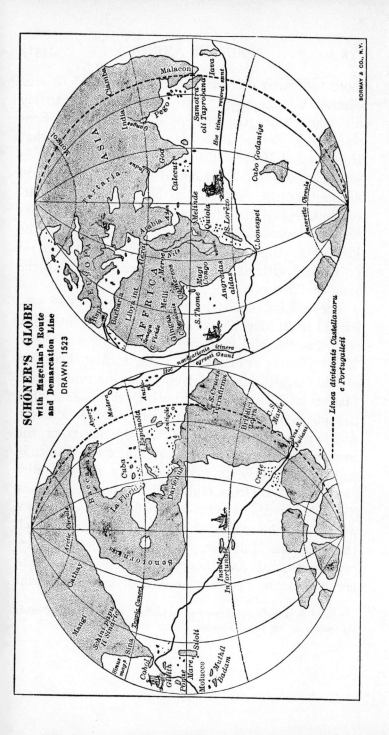

SCHÖNER'S GLOBE
with Magellan's Route
and Demarcation Line
DRAWN 1523

-------- Linea divisionis Castellanoru e Portugalleii

BORMAY & CO., N.Y.

more familiarly known under his imperial title as
Charles V. He soon found an opportunity to lay
his plan before the officials of the Casa de Contractacion, or India House. He told them that
Malacca and Maluco (the Moluccas), "the islands in
which cloves grow, belonged to the emperor on
account of the demarcation line."[1] They assent-
ed, but replied that it was impossible to go thither
without trespassing within the demarcation of the
king of Portugal. Magellan asserted that he could
go thither without touching the seas or land of the
king of Portugal.

The officials shelved the matter, but after prolonged effort Magellan was able to have an interview
with the youthful king and his immediate advisers.
Maximilianus Transylvanus, the earliest historian
of the expedition, describes the interview with
Charles as follows: "They both showed Cæsar that
though it was not yet quite sure whether Malacca
was within the confines of the Spaniards or the
Portuguese, because as yet nothing of the longitude
had been clearly proved, yet that it was quite
plain that the Great Gulf and the people of Sinae
[China] lay within the Spanish boundary. This, too,
was held to be most certain, that the islands which
they call the Moluccas, in which all the spices are
produced, and are thence exported to Malacca,,
lay within the Spanish western division, and that

[1] Lord Stanley's version of the extracts from Correa, *Lendas
da India*, in his *First Voyage Round the World*, 245.

it was possible to sail there; and that spices could
be brought thence to Spain more easily, and at less
expense and cheaper, as they came direct from their
native place." [1]

The historian Las Casas was present in Valladolid
when Magellan came thither to present his plan to
the king, and he records a conversation with him.
"Magellan had," he writes, "a well-painted globe
in which the whole world was depicted, and on it
he indicated the route he proposed to take, saving
that the strait was left purposely blank so that
no one should anticipate him. And on that day
and at that hour I was in the office of the high
chancellor when the bishop [Fonseca] brought it
[*i.e.*, the globe] and showed the high chancellor the
voyage which was proposed, and speaking with
Magellan I asked him what way he planned to take,
and he answered that he intended to go by Cape
Saint Mary, which we call the Rio de la Plata,
and from thence to follow the coast up until he hit
upon the strait. 'But suppose you do not find any
strait by which you can go into the other sea?'
He replied that if he didn't find any strait that he
would go the way the Portuguese took. . . . This
Hernando de Magallanes must have been a man
of courage and valiant in his thoughts and for
undertaking great things, although he was not
of imposing presence because he was small in

[1] Lord Stanley, *First Voyage Round the World*, 187; Blair and
Robertson, *The Philippine Islands*, I., 309.

stature and did not appear in himself to be much." [1]

The appeal to the sovereign was successful, and in a few days (March 22, 1518) Magellan received a patent under which the king was to equip five ships with provisions for two years for the expedition, upon the condition that it was to be within "the limits which belong to us in the ocean within the bounds of our demarcation." [2] No sooner had the preliminary arrangements been completed than the most strenuous efforts were made by the Portuguese minister in behalf of his sovereign to prevent the expedition; but Charles was firm and Magellan refused to give way to appeals or threats.

The fleet prepared for this momentous enterprise consisted of the *San Antonio*, of one hundred and fifty tons burden; the *Trinidad*, of one hundred and ten tons; the *Concepcion*, ninety tons; the *Victoria*, eighty-five tons; and the *Santiago*, seventy-five tons. It was far from easy to get together the crews, and when the list was finally made up it was singularly cosmopolitan. In this great world - voyage nearly all the seafaring peoples were represented: besides Spaniards and Portuguese, there were Basques, "Genoese, Sicilians, French, Flemings, Germans, Greeks, Neapolitans, Corfiotes, Negroes, and Malays;" one Englishman, Master Andrew, of Bristol; [3]

---

[1] Las Casas, *Historia*, IV., 376, 377.
[2] Navarrete, *Viages*, IV., 116–121.
[3] Guillemard, *Magellan*, 137.

natives of the Azores, Madeira, and Canary Islands; and at least two of American birth and partly of American blood.[1] The total equipment numbered about two hundred and seventy men. On board were several young men who went to see the world, among whom, fortunately for posterity, was the Italian Antonio Pigafetta, whose journal of his experiences and observations is our best history of the expedition.

Finally, on Tuesday, September 20, 1519, the little fleet weighed anchor and set sail from the harbor of San Lucar de Barrameda. The earlier part of the voyage was without startling incident save for an ominous clash with some of the captains, who questioned the wisdom of Magellan's course, and were obviously restive under the authority of a Portuguese.[2] Reaching the coast of Brazil near Pernambuco, they followed it south till they found (January 11) the mouth of the great river where Magellan's forerunner Solis had met his death. This was carefully examined, and from thence to the south not an inlet was overlooked. It was a slow process, and the name "Bahia de los Trabajos" (Bay of Labors) attached to one of the indentations on that bleak shore records its tedium and difficulties.

Cold weather was now approaching, and Magellan decided, March 31, 1520, to spend the winter in Port

---

[1] Guillemard, *Magellan*, 154, *n.*
[2] Peschel, *Zeitalter der Entdeckungen*, 492.

St. Julian, in latitude forty-nine degrees south. The
region was almost uninhabited, and the climate as
well as the latitude corresponded to that of southern
Newfoundland. It was the first attempt in history
on the part of an exploring expedition to winter
in a high latitude,[1] and the prospect to Magellan's
associates was forbidding. They urged a return to
Spain, satisfied with having carried the exploration
of the coast beyond previous navigators. This
was a natural attitude for ordinary men, especially
as they were now fifteen degrees farther south than
the Cape of Good Hope; but Magellan was not an
ordinary man. He was bound to accomplish his
purpose at any cost. He assured his commanders
that although winter was upon them it could be
weathered, and that it would be easy to succeed in
the summer of that region, where, if they continued
their course beyond the south, "the whole of its
summer would be one perpetual day."[2] He further
reminded them that the greater the difficulties the
greater the reward.

Far from being reassured, the commanders con-
spired. On the night of April 1 Captain Quesada,
of the *Concepcion*, with a body of armed men boarded the *San Antonio*, at that time commanded by
Mesquita, a cousin of Magellan, overpowered him
and put him in irons. Captain Mendoza, of the

[1] Günther, *Zeitalter der Entdeckungen*, 77.

[2] Maximilianus Transylvanus, in Lord Stanley, *First Voyage
Round the World*, 193.

Victoria, sided with the mutineers, whose plan was to take control of the fleet and return to Spain. Magellan woke to find three ships in their control. Open force would be hopeless; to give in would be humiliation and failure; to go on with the little *Santiago* was out of the question. With instant resolution Magellan risked all in a single stroke. Having retained the boat of the *San Antonio*, which brought the terms that the rebellious captains offered, he used it to despatch Gonzalo Gomez, the alguacil, with a written order to Mendoza to come on board Magellan's ship. Gomez and his five companions bore concealed weapons. When Mendoza refused to obey the order he was instantly stabbed by Gomez in the neck and struck down dead by one of his companions. At almost the same moment the vessel was boarded and carried with a rush by Magellan's brother-in-law Barbosa and fifteen picked men, the crew making little resistance; and the day was won!

With the recovery of the *Victoria* the odds now were three to two against the mutineers, with Magellan blocking their exit from the harbor. During the night the *San Antonio*, dragging her anchors, bore down upon Magellan's ships. The *Trinidad* opened fire and grappled her, and she was boarded from both the *Trinidad* and the *Victoria*. Without loss of life the *San Antonio* was recovered. There was now no hope for Juan de Cartagena, on the *Concepcion*, and he surrendered. The next day the body of Mendoza was quartered, and then the living mutineers were tried and forty found guilty and condemned to death. Magellan pardoned all but three of the ringleaders. Quesada was beheaded, and when the fleet left the bay in the August following Juan de Cartagena and the priest Sanchez were put ashore. After this grim crisis Magellan's authority was unquestioned.[1]

After four months and a half of waiting a new start was made August 24, 1520. During this period the sprightly Pigafetta had not failed to make many interesting observations of the wandering bands of natives whose immense footprints suggested to Magellan the name "Patagones" ("big feet"). Their unusual stature led the Italian to call them giants; and the quaint name of their devil god, to whom they cried in anger or terror, which he records, gave Shakespeare his Setebos, to whom Caliban appeals in "The Tempest."[2] The season, however, was not advanced enough for pushing farther south, and another tarry of two months followed in the mouth of the Santa Cruz. By October 18 the weather invited a renewal of the search, and on the 21st the entrance to the looked-for westward strait was discovered.

Threading its windings and exploring its branches took thirty-eight days, but they were days of excitement and expectation, as hitherto unknown

[1] Guillemard, *Magellan*, 163-174.
[2] Pigafetta, in Lord Stanley, *First Voyage Round the World*, 53.

wonders of nature were revealed from hour to
hour. Magellan found himself in a great cut some
three hundred and twenty - five miles long and
from two to five miles wide. For the first half of
the distance it runs southwesterly through a region
of pampas; then it turns to the northwest and cuts
through the ridge of the lower Andes. Lofty
precipices rising several thousand feet, snow-topped,
forest-clad mountains, vast glaciers, tempestuous
winds rushing down the mountain-sides like ava-
lanches, fathomless depths of black water beneath,
long antarctic days, new and strange forms of life,
the great issues at stake—all combined to make the
first passage of the Straits of Magellan one of the
most thrilling of human experiences. That the strain
told even on Magellan's "heart of triple bronze"[1]
is clear from Pigafetta's record of the announcement brought back by a reconnoitring party "that
they had found the cape and the sea great and
wide. At the joy which the captain-general had
at this he began to cry, and he gave the name
of Cape of Desire to this cape, as a thing which
had been much desired for a long time."[2]

Yet anxiety was mixed with joy, for Estevan
Gomez, with the *San Antonio*, during the passage of
the strait, had slipped away to return to Spain, and
no trace of him could be found. As they entered
the ocean again they were so favored with quiet

[1] John Fiske, *Discovery of America*, II., 204.
[2] Pigafetta, in Lord Stanley, *First Voyage Round the World*, 60.

waters and fair winds that the name "Mare Pacificum" ("Peaceful Sea") was bestowed upon it. Fortunate, indeed, was it that this vast expanse of waters deserved this name, otherwise these first venturers upon its bosom must have perished. Columbus found land approximately where he expected to; Magellan pursued his way for weeks over a pathless sea about whose width nothing was known and all conjectures were hopelessly wrong. That he faced an ocean more than twice as wide as the Atlantic or Indian oceans he could have no intimation, for no one suspected the existence of such a mass of water on the globe.

As the weeks rolled by the provisions gave out, and nothing was left but wormy crumbs. The water was thick and yellow. In their want, the weatherworn ox-hides with which the main-yard was covered to prevent chafing were soaked in the sea for days and then broiled; and rats were sold for half a ducat apiece.[1] Twice their hopes were raised by sight of land, but it was only small coral islands which were uninhabited save by birds.

March 6, 1521, they discovered a group of islands which they called the "Ladrones" (Robbers), because the natives were so thievish. Securing some provisions, they proceeded, and on March 16 sighted the island of Samar of the now familiar Philippines. That they had reached the outlying

[1] Pigafetta, in Lord Stanley, *First Voyage Round the World*, 65; Guillemard, *Magellan*, 221.

portions of the Asiatic world was evident a few days later when Magellan's Malay slave Enrique, of Malacca, was able to make himself understood. But Magellan's triumph was to be short-lived: in a little over a month he fell in a battle with the natives on the island of Matan. He was denied the proud and happy moments enjoyed by Columbus upon his return, but he was also spared the agony of declining fortunes.

Columbus and Magellan are the great figures of this heroic age in American history, but though their lives overlapped a quarter of a century, they really belong to different ages. There was none of the prophetic mysticism of Columbus in the make-up of the great Portuguese. Magellan was distinctly a man of action, instant, resolute, enduring. The first voyage across the Atlantic broke down the barriers of the ages and was a sublime act of faith; but the first navigation of the Straits of Magellan was a far more difficult problem of seamanship than crossing the Atlantic. More than half of the English and Dutch navigators who later attempted it towards the end of the sixteenth century gave it up and turned back.[1] Columbus's voyage was over in thirty-five days; but Magellan's expedition had been gone a year and weathered a subarctic winter before its real task began — the voyage over a trackless waste of waters exactly three times as long as the first crossing of the Atlantic. For

[1] Ruge, *Zeitalter der Entdeckungen*, 474.

these and other similar reasons it seems to be the mature judgment of the historians of the discoveries that Magellan is to be ranked as the first navigator of ancient or modern times, and his voyage the greatest single human achievement on the sea.[1]

The rest of the voyage lay for the most part over a region already traversed by the Portuguese. A few days after Magellan's death his two successors in command, Barbosa, his brother-in-law, and his faithful friend João Serrão, with several companions, were treacherously killed by the natives. The numbers were now reduced to about one hundred and fifteen men, and they decided to leave the unseaworthy *Concepcion* and to proceed with the *Victoria* and the *Trinidad*. After leaving the Philippines they touched on the west coast of Borneo, then turned back and went down to the Moluccas. Here they loaded with spices, refitted, and started on the long return, the *Victoria* across the Indian Ocean and up the coast of Africa, the *Trinidad* for Panama across the Pacific, an attempt which had to be given up because little headway could be made against the trade winds. Of the fifty-four who set sail with her only nineteen survived when the voyage[2] was finally given up; and

---

[1] Peschel, *Zeitalter der Entdeckungen*, 526; Guillemard, *Magellan*, 258; Günther, *Zeitalter der Entdeckungen*, 76; Lord Stanley, *First Voyage Round the World*, p. xlvi.

[2] Guillemard, *Magellan*, 302.

only four of these ever saw Spain again, and that
after years of captivity.[1]

On the *Victoria* there was much suffering from
cold and later from lack of food; and under absolute
necessity a stop was made at the Cape Verd Islands.
There it leaked out that the weather-worn navigators were returning from India with spices, and
the Portuguese held a boat-load of the sailors as
captives. The *Victoria* herself barely escaped with
the scanty number of eighteen Europeans and four
natives. At last, after an absence of three years
lacking thirteen days, on September 7, 1522, they
arrived at San Lucar and two days later at Seville.
In response to the urgent request of the emperor the
men detained at the Cape Verd Islands were sent
home by the Portuguese, and then the emperor
received at court the thirty-one who had been round
the world. Sebastian del Cano, the commander,
was given five hundred ducats, and granted a coat
of arms surmounted by a globe bearing the sublime
legend " Primus circumdedisti Me " (" First thou didst
encompass me "). Of the two hundred and thirty-
nine men who started probably about eighty returned from the Straits with the *San Antonio;*[2] of the
remainder, perhaps one hundred and sixty in number,
only thirty-six ever saw home again.[3] Yet the
financial results were such as to tempt other voyages,
for the cargo of spices brought by the little *Victoria*,

---

[1] Guillemard, *Magellan.*, 306.
[2] *Ibid.*, 267.   [3] *Ibid.*, 336–339.

consisting principally of twenty-six tons of cloves, exceeded in value the total net cost of the expedition.[1]

Among the novel experiences of going round the world is the gain or loss of a day. As the *Victoria* went round to the west, those on board saw the sun rise once less than those who stayed at home. This was first noticed upon their arrival at the Cape Verd Islands on Wednesday, July 9, as they supposed, but really on Thursday, July 10, as they were assured by the Portuguese. The discovery was alarming, for none could tell how many fasts had been violated or saints' days neglected. Absolution was sought and obtained, but the explanation of the problem apparently was beyond the historian Peter Martyr, who tried to convince the men they had miscounted or forgotten that 1520 was a leap year, and so lost the 29th of February; but, no, they insisted that no mistake had been made. Finally, Gaspar Contarini, the Venetian ambassador, gave the true solution,[2] which curiously enough was perfectly familiar to the Arabian geographer Abulfeda two centuries earlier.[3]

The approach to the Spice Islands from the east and the assertion that they lay within the Spanish field of discovery by the demarcation line precipitated a controversy which lasted several years. After some preliminary negotiations it was agreed

[1] Guillemard, *Magellan*, 310.
[2] Peter Martyr, *De Rebus Oceanicis*, dec. V., lib. VII.
[3] Peschel, *Zeitalter der Entdeckungen*, 530.

to hold a scientific congress made up on each side of three astronomers and three pilots as scientific experts, and of three lawyers as judges of documentary proofs. This body, known as the Badajos Junta, held its opening session April 11, 1524, on the bridge over the Caya River, the boundary between Spain and Portugal, meeting thereafter alternately in Badajos and Yelves until May 31. But nothing came of the congress, for the lawyers could not agree as to the priority of possession, nor the scientific experts as to the longitude of the Moluccas or the proper location of the demarcation line.[1]

King Charles then sent out an expedition to the islands under Loaysa, which met with many disasters. The difficulty of navigating the straits was such that it took Loaysa four months to make the passage. It was not discovered until 1616 that Cape Horn could be rounded. When the survivors reached their goal they could neither go on nor return. The stubbornness with which the king of Portugal maintained his claims to the islands, the impossibility of a scientific and exact determination of the demarcation line in the absence of accurate means for measuring longitude, and the pressure of financial needs led Charles V. in 1529 to relinquish all claims to or rights to trade with the Moluccas

[1] Bourne, *Essays in Historical Criticism*, 209–211; the opinions are extracted in Blair and Robertson, *The Philippine Islands*, I., 165–221.

for three hundred and fifty thousand ducats; and to accept a new demarcation line in the antipodes drawn north and south seventeen degrees on the equator east of the Moluccas. This agreement in reality renounced all claim to the Philippines, but this feature of the treaty was subsequently violated or ignored by Spain.[1]

The scientific results of Magellan's voyage were far more important than the political advantages derived from it. Once for all it gave a practical demonstration of the sphericity of the earth that convinced the ordinary mind unreached by the scientific proofs. It revolutionized all ideas as to the relative proportions of the land and water of the globe, and dissipated the traditional error on which Columbus's voyages and his whole geographical system were based, that the area of the land far exceeded that of the water. The vast width of the Pacific revealed that America was a new world in a more comprehensive sense than had been suspected. That America was entirely detached from Asia was not definitely proved until the voyage of Vitus Bering, in 1728, through the strait named for him.

[1] Bourne, "Historical Introduction" to Blair and Robertson, *The Philippine Islands*, I., 29, 30. For the important articles of the treaty, see *ibid.*, 223–239.

CHAPTER X

EXPLORATION OF THE GULF AND ATLANTIC COASTS

(1512-1541)

AFTER the complete subjection of the Indians and the first excitements of gold - hunting in Española, sugar-planting and stock-raising were too tame to satisfy the more adventurous of the settlers, and so with the restlessness of the true pioneer they sought more excitement and quicker profits in slave-hunting raids to the Bahamas, in the colonization of other islands, or in the exploration of waters not yet visited. These ventures form the prologue to the conquest of Mexico and the exploration of North America.

Juan Ponce de Leon, the discoverer of Florida, one of the most picturesque of the adventurers who sought their fortune in America, came over with the first colonists in 1493. In 1504 he proved himself a valiant and efficient officer in the Indian war in Higuey, at the eastern end of Española, and was appointed provincial governor by Ovando. Hearing from Indians that there was gold in the fair island on the eastern horizon, · Boriquen, or

San Juan de Puerto Rico, he secured permission from Ovando to explore it and to open up trade with the Indians.[1] Later, in 1509, at Ovando's request he was appointed governor of the island.

After his removal from that office in February, 1512, he secured a patent from the king authorizing him to discover and colonize the island of "Beniny" (Bimine), vague rumors of which had come to Spanish ears during slave raids in the Bahamas.[2] An incidental object in this enterprise, which has been usually considered the primary purpose, was to verify the Indian tradition of a spring or river whose waters would restore youth to the aged. Of this there is no hint in the patent, nor, apparently, in the narrative of the voyage which Herrera seems to have had before him;[3] yet to the prevalence of the legend the testimony is abundant,[4] and the story probably directed Ponce de Leon to Bimine in particular rather than to the lands north of Darien.

Winding through the Bahamas and touching at San Salvador, Ponce de Leon, on April 2, 1512, approached a coast in latitude 30° 8', which he followed till nightfall, seeking a port. He supposed it to be an island, and since it was "Pascua Florida," the Easter season, and the low-lying

---

[1] Herrera, *Historia General*, dec. I., lib. VII., chap. iv.

[2] The patent is reprinted in Lowery, *Spanish Settlements*, 437 ff., from *Docs. Ined. de Indias*, XXII., 26.

[3] Cf. Peschel, *Zeitalter der Entdeckungen*, 411, *n*.

[4] Peter Martyr, *De Rebus Oceanicis*, dec. VII., lib. VII.; Hakluyt, *Voyages*, V., 422.

shores presented a fair sight with the mass of green foliage, Ponce gave it the name of Florida.[1] He soon turned and followed the coast to the south, rounded the peninsula, and went up the west side perhaps as far as Apalache Bay. This exploration occupied from April 2 till May 23, at which date Ponce de Leon turned to retrace his course. June 14 he headed towards Porto Rico, hoping still to find Bimine. From July 25 till September 17 the search was kept up among the Bahamas, when Ponce set sail for home, leaving one ship under Juan Perez to continue the exploration for the fabled fountain of youth.

In the following December Ponce secured a patent to colonize both the "island of Beniny" and the "island of Florida,"[2] but was unable to resume his plans till 1521, when he started out anew to determine whether Florida was an island and to plant a colony there.[3] In this enterprise he expended most of his fortune, equipping two ships and two hundred men with arms, tools, and fifty horses. The history of this expedition is very obscure; but a comparison of all the evidence seems to point to

[1] Herrera, *Historia General*, dec. I., lib. IX., chap. x. The chronology is perplexing, and Peschel, *Zeitalter der Entdeckungen*, 411, *n.*, decides that the year 1513 fits the calendar of narrative better than 1512. Cf. also Harrisse, *Discovery of North America*, 142–150.

[2] Harrisse, *Discovery of North America*, 149.

[3] See his letter to Charles V., *Docs. Ined. de Indias.*, XL., 50–52, quoted in translation in Winsor, *Narr. and Crit. Hist.*, II., 234.

the west coast of Florida, not far from Tampa Bay, as the scene of Ponce de Leon's final labors.[1] In an engagement with the Indians he lost many men and was so grievously wounded that he must needs return to Cuba. There he soon died, after one of the longest and most varied careers in the New World. His epitaph reveals the contemporary appreciation of the conqueror and ruler of Porto Rico and the discoverer of Florida:

"Mole sub hac fortis Requiescunt ossa Leonis
Qui vicit factis Nomina magna suis." [2]

"Beneath this stone repose the bones
of the valiant Lion whose deeds
surpassed the greatness of his name."

The work of Ponce in exploring the gulf coast of the present United States was taken up, although not in person, by another veteran of 1493, Francisco de Garay, who had risen to be governor of Jamaica. Stirred by the reports of the discoveries made under the patronage of Velasquez, governor of Cuba, Garay equipped four vessels in 1519 to go in search of a gulf or strait dividing the main-land. This expedition was gone about eight or nine months, under the command of Alonzo de Pineda, during which they followed the gulf coast from Florida to Vera Cruz and named the region Amichel.[3] At a

[1] Harrisse, *Discovery of North America*, 162.

[2] Barcia, *Ensayo Cronologico*, 5.

[3] Navarrete, *Viages*, III., 147; Harrisse, *Discovery of North America*, 163.

point roughly in the middle of this stretch of coast they entered a large river whose banks were populated with friendly Indians. This river, named Rio del Espiritu Santo, has usually been identified with the Mississippi, although the descriptions of the stream and the numerous villages along its banks are out of accord with the experience of the survivors of De Soto's expedition. A more recent and very probable view is that this Rio del Espiritu Santo was Mobile bay and river;[1] the early maps usually depict the Rio del Espiritu Santo as emptying into a bay of the same name.[2]

The reports of the fertility of the soil and the peaceableness of the population encouraged Garay to attempt settlement, and the charter which he procured from King Charles for the purpose breathes in an exceptional degree the spirit of humanity and consideration for the natives.[3] In June, 1523, Garay's expedition was ready with an equipment far in excess of that with which Cortés had conquered Mexico; for he had eleven vessels with eight hundred and fifty Spaniards, some Indians, and one hundred and forty-four horses and an abundance of provisions and merchandise. His field of opera-

[1] Cf. Scaife, *America, Its Geographical History*, 139–176; Hamilton, *Colonial Mobile*, chap. ii. That the Mississippi was later identified by Spaniards as the Espiritu Santo and so called does not necessarily militate against this view.

[2] A tracing of Garay's map is given in Navarrete, *Viages*, III., 148.

[3] Navarrete, *Viages*, III., 147; summary in Lowery, *Spanish Settlements*, 152.

tions, however, had already been occupied by Cortés, who prepared to resist any rival. Pending the settlement of the question Garay's men yielded to the solicitations of Cortés's agents and deserted; and finally Garay himself was compelled to throw in his lot with that of the conqueror of Mexico, and concluded arrangements by which it was agreed that his son should marry a young daughter of Cortés.[1] At the following Christmas season Garay died suddenly of pneumonia.[2]

The exploration of the eastern coast of North America followed quickly upon that of the Gulf of Mexico, and in response to two different motives: the establishment of new colonies and the search for a passage into the Pacific. The first of these motives prompted Lucas Vasquez de Ayllon, a justice of the supreme court of Santo Domingo, to despatch a caravel in the year 1521 under the command of Francisco Gordillo to explore the coast of the main-land beyond the Bahamas.[3] While among these islands Gordillo ran across a caravel fitted out by Justice Matienzo of the same court for the capture of Indians. The two parties joined forces and proceeded together towards the northwest until they reached the main-land in latitude 33° 30', near the mouth of a large river, which they named St. John

---

[1] Herrera, *Historia General*, dec. III., lib. V., chap. vii.

[2] *Ibid.* Bernal Diaz, *Historia Verdadera*, chap. clxii. On the cause of his death, see Jourdanet, *Bernal Diaz*, 898.

[3] Shea, in Winsor, *Narr. and Crit. Hist.*, II., 238, on the basis of unprinted materials.

the Baptist — a site identified by Harrisse with Georgetown Entrance, South Carolina.[1] Here Gordillo yielded to the opportunity, and, contrary to his instructions, joined his colleague in loading up with Indians.

Ayllon condemned Gordillo's course, and the court at Santo Domingo liberated the Indians. In 1523, while in Spain, Ayllon secured a charter somewhat similar to the later English proprietary charters, which authorized him to explore eight hundred leagues of the coast, and to follow up a strait if he found one; to establish a colony, of which he was to be governor, sole proprietor of the fisheries, distributer of the lands, etc.; supplies were to be exempt from taxation; the Indians must not be reduced to forced labor of any kind.[2] On the strength of this patent Ayllon sent out an exploring expedition in 1525 which followed up the coast for some two hundred and fifty leagues.[3] The preparations for the colony were completed in 1526, and in June of that year Ayllon set out with three vessels, some five or six hundred people, including some negro slaves and three Dominican friars, and eighty-nine horses.

They landed at the mouth of a river, in latitude 33° 40', to which a pilot gave the name of Jordan. The site, however, was not satisfactory, and another

[1] Harrisse, *Discovery of North America*, 209.
[2] Navarrete, *Viages*, III., 153.
[3] Shea, in Winsor, *Narr. and Crit. Hist.*, II., 240.

was selected about one hundred and fifteen miles to the southwest near a large river, which was perhaps the Cape Fear. Here they established the settlement of San Miguel de Gualdape.[1] But the company was unruly, the Indians hostile, and Ayllon inexperienced in command. The ground, too, was swampy and unhealthy. The climax was reached by the approach unusually early of very cold weather. Ayllon died of fever October 18, and anarchy soon followed. Return to Santo Domingo finally was resolved upon, but only one hundred and fifty survived to reach the island.

On the map of Ribeiro in 1529 that part of North America now New York and New England is inscribed: " Land of Stephen Gomez, who discovered it by his majesty's command in 1525. Trees and fruits like those of Spain abound, and turbot, salmon, and pike. They found no gold." Gomez, it will be remembered, forsook Magellan in the passage of the straits and returned with the *San Antonio* to Spain. A Portuguese like his leader, he had proposed a similar expedition to the Orient; but Magellan's plan had been accepted and Gomez assigned to accompany him as one of the pilots. After Gomez returned to Spain he was imprisoned until the return

[1] The location of San Miguel cannot be determined with certainty. Shea, in Winsor, *Narr. and Crit. Hist.*, II., 241, believed it to be near where Jamestown, Virginia, was later settled. Harrisse, *Discovery of North America*, 213, favors the lower Cape Fear River between Wilmington and Smithville. Lowery, *Spanish Settlements*, 166, suggests the Pedee.

of the *Victoria*. In 1524 he was one of the experts
to take part in the Badajos conference on the demarcation line. In all these years he never re-
linquished his plan, which was apparently to seek
the Spice Islands by a northern route, for in 1523
he proposed to the king to make a voyage of discovery to Cathay and even to the Moluccas by a
strait to be sought for between Florida and Bac-
calaos (Labrador).[1]

The king provided Gomez with a caravel of fifty
tons burden, and he set forth from Coruña either
late in 1524 or early in 1525,[2] heading towards the
northwest. He made land somewhere between
Maine and Newfoundland, and followed the coast
very carefully down to the fortieth parallel, or approximately to the region covered by Ayllon's explorers. The severity of the northern winter convinced him that if a strait were discovered in the
high latitudes it would be of little service. Not to
return empty - handed, he loaded his caravel with
Indians as slaves.[3]

Spanish explorers had now minutely examined
the coast of North America, from Mexico to Labrador, with results of great importance for the history

---

[1] *Docs. Ined. de Indias*, XX., 74–78; Peter Martyr, *De Rebus
Oceanicis*, dec. VI., lib. X.; in Hakluyt, *Voyages*, V., 403;
Harrisse, *Discovery of North America*, 230.

[2] On the date, see Harrisse, *Discovery of North America*, 230–
232.

[3] Santa Cruz, in Harrisse, *Discovery of North America*, 235;
Peter Martyr, *De Rebus Oceanicis*, dec. VIII., lib. X.; Hakluyt,
Voyages, V., 475.

of geography, but of little significance in the building of their colonial empire.　That they should have
neglected the region where the English were to lay
the foundations of a great nation and to embody on
a grander scale their most valuable contributions to
the political life of mankind, may seem strange, yet
it was wholly natural.　Empire not plantation appealed to Spain; for she had little surplus population, and too many political irons in the fire to do
everything for which opportunity offered.

That in those days of small ships and an almost
primitive land transportation the attractions of
Mexico and Peru infinitely outweighed anything
the Atlantic seaboard could offer, need not surprise
any one familiar with the rush to California, or the
exodus in our day from town and country to the
frozen Klondike.　Spain, to enjoy a profitable trade
with her colonies under the conditions then prevailing, must confine them to regions producing
commodities for which there was a demand in Europe, but no home supply.　As Peter Martyr, a
member of the Council of the Indies, remarked,
apropos of the voyages of Ayllon and Gomez:
"What need have we of these things which are common with all the people of Europe?　To the South,
to the South, for the riches of the Aequinoctiall they
that seek riches must go, not unto the cold and
frozen North." [1]

[1] Peter Martyr, *De Rebus Oceanicis*, dec. VIII., lib. X., in
Hakluyt, *Voyages*, V., 475.

rence, and discovered the island of Anticosti, when the lateness of the season and scarcity of supplies led to his return.[1]

In May, 1535, he again set out with three ships and took the same course. Reaching a small bay near Anticosti Island on St. Lawrence's day, he called it Bay of St. Lawrence. The great river that afterwards bore the name of the saint, Cartier knew as the river of Hochelaga. This broad estuary Cartier now explored with the same care exercised by the Spaniards in exploring its counterpart, the La Plata, in South America. By September 1 he was opposite the mouth of the Saguenay. A few days more brought them to the Indian town of Stadaconé, near the historic rock of Quebec. Cartier left his larger vessels moored near the mouth of the St. Charles River, and pushed on to Hochelaga despite the dissuasion of his Indian hosts. The current proved too swift and the channel too uncertain, and the reconnoissance was completed in their rowboats. When finally they approached the Indian village of Hochelaga, beneath the stately height which Cartier named Mount Royal, the whole population came out to greet them and later to entertain them with dancing.

Further exploration was blocked by the Lachine rapids, a name afterwards conferred in mockery of

[1] Parkman, *Pioneers of France*, 199–201; narrative of Cartier's first voyage in Goldsmid's Hakluyt, *Voyages*, XIII. 77–100.

The first detailed narrative of French exploration across the Atlantic is of an attempt to find a passage to China which was contemporaneous with that of Gomez. The hardy sailors of Normandy and Brittany had early participated in the fishing voyages to Newfoundland,[1] and in occasional trading voyages to the West Indies and to Brazil.[2] Yet the spirit of exploration in distinction from trading and fishing ventures does not emerge conspicuously among the French until after the voyage of Magellan and the conquest of Mexico; and then it is under an Italian, in the French merchant service, Giovanni da Verrazano, as leader. The obscurity veiling the facts of Verrazano's life, the absence of any patent or commission in the French archives or of contemporary notices in the French historians, and the mistaken and in reality baseless identification of Giovanni Verrazano with the French pirate Jean Florin,[3] have led to keen critical questioning whether the enterprise of Verrazano was ever carried into effect. It is, however, the generally accepted belief of the best critics to-day that the voyage did take place.

The earliest notice of Verrazano's project is in a letter to the king of Portugal from his ambassador

[1] Parkman, *Pioneers of France*, 189.
[2] Harrisse, *Discovery of North America*, 693, 697.
[3] This identification dates from Barcia, *Ensayo Cronologico para la Historia de la Florida* (1723), 8. It has been disproved by Peragallo, *Bull. of the Soc. Geog. Ital.*, 3d series, IX., 189. It never had any documentary evidence to rest on.

in France, dated April 23, 1524, informing him of an expedition which the French are expecting to arm for the discovery of Cathay under the command of João Verzano. The ambassador succeeded in averting a voyage to the East Indies by the known routes, but the ultimate purpose of the voyage was adhered to.[1]

Our knowledge of the events of the voyage, which lasted from January until July, 1524, is derived from a letter purporting to have been written by Verrazano to Francis I., the original of which is no longer extant. In its Italian form the narrative is not free from perplexities, yet it is generally interpreted to indicate that Verrazano in his progress up the coast entered New York Bay and Hudson River, Narragansett Bay, and made his way north as far as Newfoundland.

The most interesting legacy of the voyage was the conjectural placing upon the maps of North America of a second isthmus, in the region of the Carolinas, dividing the hemisphere into three continental masses instead of two. This curious configuration of the coast first appears in the Maggiolo planisphere of 1527 and in a map purporting to have been made by Gerolamo da Verrazano. Both of these maps have on the Atlantic coast Norman and French names, and the Verrazano map has an inscription stating that Giovanni da Verrazano discovered the

[1] *Alguns Documentos*, 463; Murphy, *Voyage of Verrazano*, 163, 184.

country five years before.[1] These maps and their nomenclature are an adequate proof of the reality of Verrazano's voyage, and go far to quiet the doubts aroused by the perplexities in the narrative.

This hypothetical Pacific counterpart to the Atlantic Gulf of Mexico haunted the maps for over half a century and lured many subsequent navigators with its unreal promises of a strait or a portage between the oceans.[2] Verrazano himself never followed up this voyage, but apparently directed his attention to projects relating to Brazil, for he is plausibly identified with the "Terazano" who, the Portuguese ambassador in France informs his sovereign, December 24, 1527, "is going from here with five ships which the admiral is preparing for him to a great river in Brazil,"[3] etc.

Ten years elapsed before Francis I. again turned his interest to North America under the solicitation of Admiral Chabot. In 1534 Jacques Cartier, an experienced navigator of St. Malo, in Brittany, was given command of two ships and one hundred and sixty-two men to undertake the discovery of a strait to the Pacific. Setting sail in April, he passed around Newfoundland to the north, entered the straits of Belle Isle, explored the Gulf of St. Law-

[1] Harrisse, *Discovery of North America*, 220.
[2] Winsor, *Narr. and Crit. Hist.*, IV., 32–46. It was named the Sea of Verrazano. There is no reference to it in the letter of Verrazano.
[3] *Alguns Documentos*, 490; Peragallo first brought out this evidence. See above, 143.

the elusive hopes that looked to find there a way to China.[1] Cartier dropped back to the St. Charles, where they prepared to spend the winter as did Magellan in Bay St. Julian fifteen years before, but under severer conditions. Ice-bound and snow-bound from November 1 until the middle of March, wasted by scurvy, they lost twenty-five of their best men. It was the middle of July, 1536, before Cartier reached St. Malo.[2]

Yet the inhospitable severities of the Canadian winter did not deter King Francis from an attempt to plant a colony. In 1540 Jean François de la Roque, lord of Roberval, was appointed viceroy and lieutenant-general of Canada and the surrounding regions, and Cartier was made commander of the fleet. The wintry North could not appeal to the ordinary Frenchman, and so Francis repeated the unhappy experiment of Ferdinand and Isabella and authorized Roberval to recruit his ranks from the jailbirds.[3]

Cartier sailed in 1541 with colonists and cattle, goats and hogs. He built a fort a little above Quebec, explored the rapids above Montreal, and waited in vain for Roberval.[4] When the tardy viceroy reached St. John's, Newfoundland, the following spring with some two hundred colonists, he was

[1] Parkman, *La Salle*, 21.
[2] Parkman, *Pioneers of France*, 201–215; Hakluyt, *Voyages*, XIII., 101–146.   [3] Parkman, *Pioneers of France*, 217.
[4] Hakluyt, *Voyages*, XIII., 146–163.

amazed a few days later to see Cartier sail in on his way to France, because he had not force enough to withstand the savages. Roberval ordered Cartier to stay and return with him, but he slipped away in the night, leaving Roberval to taste for himself the arctic winter. Disease swept off about fifty of his men, and the colony was broken up the following summer.[1] The foundation of New France was to be the work of a later age and of a greater man than Cartier or Roberval—Samuel de Champlain.

[1] Hakluyt, *Voyages*, XIII., 163–168; Parkman, *Pioneers of France*, 216–227.

CHAPTER XI

EXPLORATION OF THE INTERIOR OF NORTH
AMERICA

(1517–1541)

THE conquest of Cuba, from which proceeded
the exploration of the western gulf coast, the
conquest of Mexico, and the interior exploration of
North America, was undertaken by Diego Colon,
the son and heir of the discoverer who was appointed
governor of Española in 1508 in recognition of his
father's rights. For carrying out so important a
work he selected Diego Velasquez, who, after service with credit under Bartholomew Columbus and
Ovando, had become the wealthiest and most highly
esteemed of the old settlers.[1] Kind-hearted and
jovial, he had been a most popular local governor,
and when he was appointed to settle Cuba his attractive qualities and their own necessities soon
brought together some three hundred men ready
for the adventure. Among those who participated
in the conquest were men of such after-fame and
diverse fortunes as Pamfilo de Narvaez, Cortés, and
the missionary historian Las Casas. In his cam-

[1] Las Casas, *Historia*, III., 57, 462, 463.

paigns Velasquez was accompanied by Las Casas, who zealously baptized all the children he could, and did much by influence and persuasion to soften the severities of the conquest.[1]

The extent of Cuba and the resources of Velasquez soon raised him to a position of partial independence of Diego Colon, and after the island was pacified he was ready to entertain other projects. The first occasion was offered by some Spaniards who had gone to Darien with Pedrarias Davila, but with his permission came to Cuba. Velasquez received them kindly and promised them the first repartimientos that fell vacant. After vainly waiting about two years they proposed an expedition to explore the waters to the west. Velasquez consented, and with some help from him three vessels were equipped under the command of Hernandez de Cordova, which set sail in February, 1517. Their pilot was Anton Alaminos, who, as a boy, had been with Columbus on his fourth voyage, and he suggested a reconnoissance of the regions to the north of the point where Columbus made land and turned southward.[2] His counsel was approved, and after four days of careful sailing beyond the western end of Cuba they made a large island called by the Indians Cozumel.

The inhabitants were clothed, and their handiwork revealed a higher culture than the natives of the Antilles. Evidences to this effect multiplied as they coasted northward and rounded the east-

---

[1] Las Casas, *Historia*, IV., 19.   [2] *Ibid.*, IV., 350.

ward projection of a region they understood the
Indians to call Yucatan.[1] If the natives marvelled
at the ships and boats, at the heavy beards and
white faces of the Spaniards, at their clothes, swords,
cross-bows, and lances, stroking their beards and
feeling of the clothes, not less amazed were the
strangers to find stone buildings with carvings,
paved streets, temples with sculptured idols, and
altars with drops of freshly spilled blood. During
the nearly twenty-five years of discoveries and explorations that had passed since the first voyage of
Columbus, thousands of miles of coast-line had been
followed, the isthmus had been crossed, and the
Pacific Ocean discovered; and yet all without once
coming in contact with people advanced beyond the
traditional state of nature.[2]

In a battle with the Indians, the commander,
Hernandez de Cordova, was wounded, and he died
some ten days after his return home, his last hours
embittered by Velasquez's selection of Juan de
Grijalva to follow up these discoveries with a trading expedition.[3] Grijalva started out from Santiago in April, 1518, with four ships, and directed his
course to the island of Cozumel; and thence followed
the coast of Yucatan and Mexico to a point a little

[1] Las Casas, *Historia*, IV., 350–357; Bernal Diaz, *Historia
Verdadera*, chaps. ii., iii.

[2] The Indians that Columbus saw in a boat on his fourth voyage, see above, p. 79, might be regarded as a single exception.

[3] Las Casas, *Historia*, IV., 361, 362, based on Cordova's letters;
Bernal Diaz, *Historia Verdadera*, chap. iv.

beyond Vera Cruz, when the pilot Alaminos advised against proceeding farther lest adverse currents should obstruct their return. Velasquez had strictly enjoined Grijalva not to attempt to plant a colony, but to confine himself to trading; but when reports from Grijalva confirmed those of Cordova, and when later he brought evidence of the abundance of gold in the new land, Velasquez was vexed that his instructions had been followed, and promptly prepared to remedy the shortcoming by securing authority from Spain to make a settlement.[1]

For the command of this new expedition, which did not await the arrival of the king's consent, Velasquez was induced to select Hernando Cortés, then about thirty-five years of age. Cortés was born in Medellin, in the province of Estremadura, in 1485, the son of a poor country gentleman. After some study of law in the University of Salamanca,[2] like many another young Spaniard he came over to Española to seek his fortune. Taking service under Velasquez, he received a repartimiento of Indians and a notary's commission from Ovando. When Velasquez went to Cuba he took Cortés as a private secretary, but the youth was too talkative to be an ideal secretary, nor had he given any indication of the remarkable abilities that he afterwards displayed. Hardly had Cortés taken charge of the

[1] Las Casas, *Historia*, IV., 422 ff., 440, 445, information derived from Grijalva in 1523.

[2] *Ibid.*, 11.   Las Casas knew Cortés's father.

rapid preparations for the new enterprise when Velasquez began to have misgivings and made a vain attempt to displace him.

The fleet comprised eleven vessels, carrying about five hundred and fifty Spaniards including the sailors, sixteen horses, two hundred to three hundred Indians, and one negro. It finally took its departure February 10, 1519, pursuing the route followed by Cordova and Grijalva.[1] An early piece of good-fortune was the rescue of a Spaniard who had been wrecked on those shores some years before,[2] and whose knowledge of the Maya language proved of great utility. A little later, as a result of the first sharp battle with the natives of Tabasco, and Cortés' tactful treatment of two captive caciques, friendly relations were secured with this people. In the peace-offering presented to Cortés were twenty young women, among them a cacique's daughter known after her baptism as the Lady Marina. Her cleverness, fidelity to the Spaniards, and knowledge of the Maya and Nahuatl languages enabled her to render Cortés inestimable services. Through the rescued Spaniard and Doña Marina, Cortés had the immense advantage henceforward of being able to communicate freely with the Mexicans.[3]

---

[1] Las Casas, *Historia*, IV., 457; Bernal Diaz, *Historia Verdadera*, chaps. xxiii., xxiv.

[2] Bernal Diaz, *Historia Verdadera*, chaps. xxvii., xxix.

[3] *Ibid.*, chaps. xxxiv.–xxxvii.

The third stroke of fortune—a singular coincidence of striking consequence—was the widely prevalent tradition in Mexico of the return of the culture hero, the fair god Quetzalcoatl, who in an earlier age had gone off towards the east. The first rumors of the approach of the Spaniards seemed a fulfilment of this looked-for event.[1] From the moment when Cortés landed at San Juan and established the little colony of Villa Rica de la Vera Cruz, with a government of its own, of whose forces he became commander, he was favored by a rare combination of circumstances, which this extraordinary man knew how to take advantage of to the utmost.

A detailed narrative of the conquest of Mexico lies outside the scope of the present volume, which is concerned primarily with the extension of geographical knowledge, and secondarily with Spanish colonial institutions, but certain significant features of that conquest may be briefly indicated.

The Aztec power was a military despotism exercised by three confederated warlike tribes, who lived upon the plunder of their enemies and the tribute of their subjects. War for food and war for victims for the sacrifices was their chief occupation. The lack of domestic animals for suitable food had contributed to the survival of the custom, partly religious and partly utilitarian, of eating the flesh of

[1] Cf. Fiske, *Discovery of America*, II., 229–238; H. H. Bancroft, *Mexico*, I., 101–108; Payne, *History of America*, I., 588 ff.

the sacrificial victims.[1] The mass of the outlying
Indian population were oppressed by their preda-
tory rulers and not disinclined to a change when
once the new-comers showed themselves superior.

The Aztec warriors, although destitute of iron,
were expert archers and possessed a most formidable weapon in a narrow club set with a double edge
of obsidian knives. Their defensive armor was
serviceable, and they were desperate fighters. The
Spaniards, on the other hand, possessed the immense
advantage of fire-arms, steel weapons, armor, and,
not least, horses, which seemed to their opponents
strange monsters. In addition they had a leader of
matchless ability and resource. Yet these superiorities would have all been in vain but for the co-
incidences mentioned above and the paralyzing
perplexity of Montezuma at the situation, which
threw the advantages into the hands of Cortés.

The shock between these two civilizations, repre-
senting widely separated stages of culture, is one of
the most romantic and unique events in history.[2]
For the history of the conquest we are fortunate in
possessing Cortés's own account in his letters to his
king, which have been appropriately compared to
Cæsar's story of his conquest of Gaul; the fascinating
memoirs of the old soldier Bernal Diaz, who went

---

[1] Cf. Fiske's summary of Bandelier's analysis of Mexican
society, *Discovery of America*, I., 103 ff.; Payne, *History of
America*, II., 499–501.

[2] Cf. Fiske, *Discovery of America*, II., 261.

through it all; the illustrations of the Mexican artists; and the Indian traditions.[1]

The story of the conquest has been made familiar to modern readers by two of the greatest of English historical narrators, Robertson and Prescott: the scuttling of the ships to cut off retreat and enforce the unity of a common fate upon opposing factions among the Spaniards; the winning of the alliance of the Tlascalans; the exemplary punishment of treacherous Cholula;[2] the bold but quietly firm summons to Montezuma to acknowledge the sovereignty of the king of Spain; the amazing audacity and equally amazing coolness of nerve that calmly compelled Montezuma to become the unwilling prisoner-guest of the Spanish leader; the instant resolution and dare-devil courage that so completely turned the tables on Pamfilo de Narvaez, and the tact that won over his soldiers; the wealth of resource and tenacity of purpose that finally recovered the city of Mexico and completely broke the Aztec power after such a set-back as the *Noche triste*—that awful night of retreat—following the rising precipitated by Alvarado's rash attempt to imitate the incident of Cholula; the heroic labors of rebuilding the city and of founding Spanish rule in New Spain and of setting in train the transmission of European culture; and, not least, the efforts to save the population from the fate of the unhappy islanders.   In all these

[1] Collected by Sahagun, Torquemada, and others.
[2] Cf. Bandelier, *The Gilded Man*, 258 ff.

exigencies Cortés revealed such inflexibility of resolution, never-failing presence of mind, unwavering
self-control, such readiness to strike or to conciliate
as best fitted the case, such consideration for his
own men and for the conquered, such constructive
statesmanship, such downright business ability,
such scientific and practical interest in geographical
exploration that he is easily the greatest of the
conquistadores, if not the ablest man that Spain
produced in that age.[1]

Cortés landed in Mexico in the spring of 1519, and
entered the city in November; in May, 1520, Narvaez
was captured and Alvarado massacred the Aztec
nobles; on June 30 occurred the disastrous retreat of
the *Noche triste*.   A little over a year later the city
again fell into Cortés's hands, after a prolonged siege,
August 13, 1521.   Then followed the razing of the old
town and the building of a new city.   To the restoration of the country to peaceful prosperity Cortés devoted every energy.   European plants and animals
were brought in, the conversion of the natives was set
on foot, and the exploration of the land undertaken.

Mexico now in turn succeeded the islands as the
starting-point of new colonizing and exploring expeditions.   Hardly had Cortés occupied the city
of Mexico when he sent four Spaniards, two by
one route and two by another, to the South Sea;[2]

[1] On the various aspects of Cortés's abilities and character,
cf. Helps, *Spanish Conquest*, III., 4–8; H. H. Bancroft, *Mexico*,
II., 484–487; Aleman, *Disertaciones*, Nos. 5 and 6.

[2] Folsom, *Despatches of Cortés*, 338.

a little later Alvarado was despatched to conquer a sea-coast province, and no sooner was word received of his success than Cortés despatched forty Spaniards, ship-carpenters and smiths, thither to build two caravels and two brigantines to explore the South Sea.[1] Alvarado, meantime, pushed on to the south and began the conquest of Guatemala, keeping in mind the discovery of a strait.[2] The same search was one of the purposes of Cristoval de Olid, who coasted along the gulf shores to Honduras; and rumors that Olid was setting up an independent rule led Cortés into one of the most arduous undertakings of his life—the overland march to Honduras.[3] In 1527 the first expedition to the Philippines from Mexico was despatched under Alvaro de Saavedra. The voyage was safely made by only one of the three ships that started, and it was unable to return.[4] In addition may be mentioned the discovery of Lower California in 1533, Cortés's own expedition thither in 1534, and the more complete exploration of the Gulf of California by Ulloa in 1539.[5]

The subsequent development of coast and interior exploration is from this point much affected by the results of an expedition begun twelve years earlier.

[1] Folsom, *Despatches of Cortés*, 349, 351.

[2] Cf. *ibid.*, 417, on Cortés's interest in discovering a strait.

[3] Cf. his *Sixth Letter*, Gayangos, *Cartas de Cortés*, 395; H. H. Bancroft, *Central America*, I., 522–583.

[4] H. H. Bancroft, *Mexico*, II., 258.

[5] Winsor, *Narr. and Crit. Hist.*, II., 441, 442; H. H. Bancroft, *North Mexican States*, I., opening chaps.; *Mexico*, II., 421.

Pamfilo de Narvaez, after a long and, on the whole, successful career in the colonies, checkered, to be sure, by the fiasco of an attempt to arrest the progress of Cortés, secured from the king the grant of all the gulf coast from Mexico to the Cape of Florida. Narvaez set out in June, 1527, with five ships and six hundred people, including friars, negroes, and the wives of some of the company.[1] Desertions and storms in the West Indies delayed his final start for his new dominions until April, 1528. Effecting a landing just beyond Tampa Bay on Good Friday, Narvaez found only a deserted Indian village. Later, communication with the Indians by signs seemed to indicate that farther to the west was a richer country, and Narvaez landed, but directed his ships to follow the shore towards Panuco (Mexico) and to await him at a harbor the pilots professed to know of. Cabeça de Vaca, the treasurer of the expedition and its historian, opposed this step, but in vain.[2] The fleet did not find the ports where the pilots expected to await Narvaez, turned back, discovered Tampa Bay, then resumed the search for Narvaez. After a year of futile effort the ships sailed for New Spain.[3]

Meanwhile, Narvaez, with three hundred men, set out May 1 to follow the coast by land. Two months were consumed in tediously pushing their course on short rations through forests and swamps

---

[1] Lowery, *Spanish Settlements*, 172-174.
[2] B. Smith, *Cabeça de Vaca* (ed. 1851), 21.
[3] *Ibid.*, 122.

until they reached the Indian town of Apalache, not far from Tallahassee.[1] Here they tarried twenty-five days, harassed by the Indians. Their failure turned them south to the coast near St. Marks, where, under extraordinary difficulties from lack of tools and materials, they contrived to put together five boats, in which the party (now reduced to two hundred and forty-two) embarked late in September. Ignorant of navigation, with overloaded and unseaworthy craft, they had no choice but to thread their way painfully along the shore, sheltered here and there by the low-lying islands. Perhaps half the distance to Mexico had been covered when the approach of winter intensified their sufferings and multiplied their perils. One after another the frail vessels succumbed, till in November about eighty destitute and enfeebled Spaniards found themselves on one of the long, narrow islands off the coast of Texas, perhaps Matagorda Island.[2] Narvaez himself, while spending the night on his boat anchored near the shore, was blown out to sea and never seen again.[3] His crew, wandering along the shore, gradually perished from cold and hunger, and a winter of misery reduced the number of the survivors to fifteen.[4]

Cabeça de Vaca and his immediate companions were forced by the Indians to become medicine-men. Unexpected success attended their breathing

[1] Lowery, *Spanish Settlements*, 185.   [2] *Ibid.*, 191, *n.*
[3] B. Smith, *Cabeca de Vaca*, 59.   [4] *Ibid.*, 48.

upon the sick and repetition of prayers, and the strangers became too valuable to lose. Five long years were passed among these Indians as healers, traders, or slaves, according as savage whims suggested. In 1534 Cabeça de Vaca, with three others of those still surviving—Dorantes, Castillo, and a negro slave Estevanico—managed to escape to another tribe whose good-will was won by apparently miraculous cures. After eight months' sojourn with this tribe they pushed on to the west. Their reputation as medicine-men spread, and soon a most extraordinary procession, living on the plunder of villages, was wending its way slowly towards the setting sun. "Frequently we were accompanied by three or four thousand persons, and as we had to breathe upon and sanctify the food and drink for each, and give them permission to do many things they would come to ask, it may be seen how great to us were the trouble and annoyance." [1] The journey from the Texas coast to the Pacific took ten months. Their route is now thought to have been westward through Texas to the Rio Grande near where the river Pecos joins it, along the Rio Grande to a point near the mouth of the Conchos, then across Mexico in a southwesterly direction to the west coast, somewhat below the middle of the Gulf of California. [2] Finally, in July, 1536, they reached the city of Mexico.

[1] B. Smith, Cabeça de Vaca, 95.
[2] On Cabeça de Vaca's route, see Bandelier, Contributions to the History of the Southwestern Portion of the United States, 28–67; Lowery, Spanish Settlements, 206–209.

A year later Cabeça de Vaca arrived in Spain, where his expectation to secure the governorship of Florida was disappointed, for it had already been granted to De Soto. After an unfortunate experience in the river Plate region he spent the rest of his life in Spain. The credibility of his narrative has been questioned, and it certainly is not free from exaggerations, yet in substance it is accepted as trustworthy. It is less easy, however, to acquit him of the charge of utterly misleading his hearers in conversation and of rousing false hopes in the breasts of the later explorers, De Soto and Coronado, by mysterious allusions and assertions, such as "that Florida was the richest country of the world." [1]

Hernando de Soto was born in Xerez de Badajos about the year 1500, and upon reaching manhood had gone to the isthmus to seek his fortune. Starting with nothing but his sword and shield, he displayed such qualities that he was sent to Peru with Pizarro, where he greatly distinguished himself. He returned to Spain with a fortune of over one hundred thousand pesos of gold [2]—roughly equal to three hundred thousand dollars—and was rewarded by the emperor with the office of governor of Cuba and adelantado of Florida, and commissioned to conquer and settle at his own expense the whole region now included in the southern part of the

[1] "The Gentleman of Elvas," in Hakluyt, *Voyages*, XIII., 546.
[2] *Ibid.*, 544, 545; Oviedo, *Historia General*, I., 544.

United States.[1] Among those who joined De Soto were several Portuguese from Elvas. To one of these we owe the best account of the expedition that has come down to us.

A prosperous voyage across the Atlantic, an inspection of his new province of Cuba, and the replenishing of his stores occupied the months from April, 1538, to May, 1539, when De Soto left Havana with nine vessels, over six hundred and twenty men, and two hundred and twenty-three horses.[2] On May 30 a landing was effected in Tampa Bay. By a strange coincidence they soon picked up a survivor of Narvaez's force, one Juan Ortiz, who had been living among the Indians twelve years. Ortiz at one time was on the point of being put to death, when his life was saved by the cacique's daughter in a way which may have suggested to Captain John Smith the romantic incident of his rescue by Pocahontas.[3]

During the first summer various short reconnoissances were made, and the main force marched up the west coast of Florida to that same region of Apalache where Narvaez gave up his march and turned seaward. There De Soto wintered. A large number of the Indian carriers died during the

---

[1] B. Smith, *Coleccion de Documentos para la Historia de la Florida*, 140–146; Lowery, *Spanish Settlements*, 215, 216.

[2] Biedma, in Rye, *Discovery of Florida*, 173; B. Smith, *Col. de Docs.*, 47.

[3] Hakluyt's first publication of the narrative of "The Gentleman of Elvas" was in 1609.

winter from exposure and lack of food.[1] In the spring De Soto resumed the march towards the northeast across the present State of Georgia, in search of the land which the Indians told him was on another sea.[2] Reaching the Savannah River, he turned northwestward, passed through the Blue Mountains [3] nearly to the border of Tennessee, then went nearly southwest through Georgia and Alabama to a large Indian village, Mauvilla, a little above the head of Mobile Bay, where he arrived the middle of October.

We are not to think of this expedition as being always on the march. From time to time longer or shorter stops were made to recruit the strength of the men and to fatten the horses.[4] The severest battle with the Indians occurred at Mauvilla, in which a large number of Indians were killed, eighteen Spaniards lost their lives, and one hundred and fifty were wounded. A less resolute and heroic spirit would have yielded at this point, for De Soto knew that his lieutenant, Maldonado, was waiting for him at Ochuse, some six days' journey distant, but he did not reveal this opportunity of escape to his men, and "determined to send no newes of himself until hee had found some rich country." [5] That

---

[1] "The Gentleman of Elvas," in Hakluyt, *Voyages*, XIII., 572.   [2] Biedma, in Rye, *Discovery of Florida*, 177.

[3] "The Gentleman of Elvas," in Hakluyt, *Voyages*, XIII., 583. The identifications of De Soto's route are based on Lowery's text and notes.

[4] Hakluyt, *Voyages*, XIII., 585.   [5] *Ibid.*, 599.

in the year and a half that he had spent in the
southern forests he had lost only one hundred and
two men from sickness or attacks by the Indians
is a brilliant proof of De Soto's abilities as a leader
and explorer.

Turning his back again on the world outside, De
Soto marched northwest for a month until he came
to the Indian village of Chicasa, in northern Mississippi, where he set up winter quarters December
17. Here in March, 1542, the worst disaster thus
far experienced fell upon him. The Indians attacked the village suddenly about midnight and set
it on fire. In this calamity eleven Spaniards were
killed and most of the survivors lost their clothes,
substitutes for which must now be devised from
skins. Fifty horses and several hundred of the
great drove of pigs, which accompanied the expedition to serve in emergencies for provisions, were
burned.[1]

Resuming the march, De Soto proceeded in a
northwesterly direction until, on May 8, 1541, they
"saw the great river."[2] "The River was almost
halfe a league broad. If a man stood still on the
other side, it could not be discerned whether he were
a man or no. The River was of great depth, and of a
strong current; the water was alwaies muddie; there
came downe the River continually many trees and

---

[1] Hakluyt, *Voyages*, XIII., 603; Oviedo, *Historia General*,
I., 571.

[2] *Ibid.*, I., 573. Lowery, *Spanish Settlements*, 237, 238, inad-
vertently says March.

timber." [1] Such are the words of the earliest description of the Mississippi by a companion of its discoverer.

A month was spent in building barges to make a
crossing, which was finally effected some distance
south of Memphis, June 8. [2] The identification of
De Soto's route west of the Mississippi is very uncertain, but apparently his marches were within the
bounds of the present State of Arkansas. They
came upon the nomadic Indians of the plains, heard
of the buffalo, and procured buffalo-robes, but did
not see the animals, and they gathered from the
Indians that to the west they could find guides to
"the other sea." [3] A long march in that direction
was made, but in vain. They then turned back to
the southeast and went into winter quarters early
in November. [4]

Such was the indomitable spirit of De Soto that
he was still ready after an exploration of two years
and a half to send word to Cuba and to New Spain
for new supplies with which to prosecute discoveries
and conquest, for he had not yet got as far west as
Cabeça de Vaca. [5] The losses among the Spaniards
now numbered two hundred and fifty men. A
winter of great severity followed, and the deep
snow kept them housed most of the time. In the

[1] "The Gentleman of Elvas," in Hakluyt, *Voyages*, XIII., 608.

[2] Cf. Lowery, *Spanish Settlements*, 237, for a discussion of the
place.   [3] Biedma, in Rye, *Discovery of Florida*, 193.

[4] Oviedo, *Historia General*, I., 577.

[5] Hakluyt, *Voyages*, XIV., 12.

spring De Soto started towards the south to reach the gulf in pursuance of his plan, but the way was arduous and the men and horses had been weakened by the winter; De Soto became much depressed at the outlook, "his men and horses every day diminished, being without succor to sustain themselves in the country, and with that thought he fell sick." [1]

The end was near, and the great explorer knew it. In a dignified and pathetic speech he bade farewell to his followers, and named Luis de Moscoso to succeed him in command. "The next day, being the 21st of May, 1542, departed out of this life, the valorous, virtuous, and valiant Captain, Don Fernando de Soto, Governour of Cuba, and Adelantado of Florida, whom fortune advanced, as it useth to doe others, that he might have the higher fal." [2] He was first buried, and then at Moscoso's order his body was taken up, wrapped in mantles with much sand, "wherein he was carried in a canoe, and thrown into the middest of the River." [3]

The new leader and his followers were ready to return to civilization, but thought it best to go overland to Mexico, and they proceeded southwesterly into Texas, perhaps as far as the Trinity River; [4] but the scarcity of provisions and the hostility of the Indians compelled them after some months to seek the Mississippi again. Early in 1543 they be-

[1] Hakluyt, *Voyages*, XIV., 19.   [2] *Ibid.*, 23.   [3] *Ibid.*, 24.
[4] Lowery, *Spanish Settlements*, 249.

gan to construct seven brigantines, which with great difficulty were built and equipped. All the pigs and all but twenty-two of the horses were killed and their flesh dried for provisions.[1] Some five hundred Indian slaves, men and women, were liberated, and about one hundred others carried along, but these were subsequently emancipated by royal orders.[2]

The Spaniards embarked July 2, 1543, and floated down the river, with many perils from the stream and from Indians, for they no longer had fire-arms. In sixteen days they reached the sea, and then coasted along the gulf shore towards Mexico for fifty-two days, arriving at the river Panuco, September 10, 1543, four years, three months, and eleven days from the landing in Tampa Bay. Out of the six hundred and twenty people who started, three hundred and eleven survived, a favorable result, if one remember that half of the one hundred colonists at Jamestown died the first winter, and over four hundred out of five hundred died in the winter of 1609–1610.[3] Thus ended the most remarkable exploring expedition in the history of North America. Its only parallel is the contemporary enterprise of Coronado, which did for the southwest what De Soto did for the eastern and central belt.

[1] Hakluyt, *Voyages*, XIV., 39–41.
[2] Lowery, *Spanish Settlements*, 249.
[3] Eggleston, *Beginners of a Nation*, 31, 40.

If Cabeça de Vaca's reports of the riches of Florida spurred on De Soto and his followers in Spain they were not less exciting in Mexico. There the ground had been in a measure prepared by the fusing of an Indian folk tale of seven caves with the old geographical myth of the Seven Cities; and the whole was made vivid by the stories told by an Indian of a visit when a child to these seven towns, which he compared to the city of Mexico.[1]

It seemed advisable to Mendoza, the viceroy of New Spain, to explore the region, and he chose a Franciscan, Friar Marcos, of Nizza, or Nice, who had been in Peru with Pizarro, and in Mexico had had some missionary experience on the frontier,[2] to make a reconnoissance. He was now instructed to make careful observations of the country, its products and people, and to report them in detail to Mendoza.[3] The negro Stephen, who had come with De Vaca, was given to him to serve as a guide, and he was also attended by some Christianized Pima Indians. Friar Marcos left Culiacan in the western frontier of Sinaloa a few weeks before De Soto landed in Florida. Following the coast as far as the Yaqui, he then went nearly due north, veering later towards the east, until he came within sight of the Zuñi villages in western New Mexico. The negro Stephen had gone on ahead with a retinue of

---

[1] Bandelier, *Contributions*, 6–12; Winship, *Journey of Coronado*, I., 1.   [2] Bandelier, *Contributions*, 107.
[3] *Ibid.*, 109–112.

Indians, and Friar Marcos now learned that he had
been killed by the Indians of Cibola, the first of the
seven cities (which are now usually identified with
the Zuñi pueblos). From a distant point of view,
the pueblo seemed to the friar in that magnifying
atmosphere as large as the city of Mexico.[1]

The magic of the association with the legend of the
"Seven Cities" reinforced the impression made by
the narrative of the friar, some of whose exaggerated reports may have arisen from imperfectly understanding his informants; and elaborate preparations were at once made to invade the new land
of wonder, and to repeat, if possible, the history of
the conquest of Mexico. The enterprise was placed
in the charge of Francisco de Coronado, the recently
appointed governor of New Galicia, the northern
frontier province of New Spain, and a personal
friend of Mendoza.[2] The vigor and energy of Mendoza's government as well as the resources of New
Spain at that early date are strikingly displayed in
the preparations for what is perhaps the most
elaborate single enterprise of exploration in North
American history. The land force under Coronado
numbered three hundred Spaniards and eight hundred Indians, and was accompanied by a large number of extra horses and droves of sheep and pigs.
There was in addition a sea force of two ships under

---

[1] Bandelier, *Contributions*, 112–178, 264–282; Fray Marcos de
Nizza, *Relacion*, in *Docs. Ined. de Indias*, III., 329–350.

[2] Winship, *Journey of Coronado*, 10.

Hernando de Alarcon to co-operate with Coronado by following the coast of the Gulf of California and keeping in communication with the army and carrying some of its baggage.[1] Alarcon discovered the mouth of the Colorado River, and August 26, 1540, started to explore it with boats. In the second of his two separate trips he apparently got as far as the lower end of the cañon, about two hundred miles up, as he estimated it.[2]

Coronado himself set out in February, 1540, marching up the west coast of Mexico. At Culiacan he left the main force and went ahead with about fifty horsemen, some foot-soldiers, and most of the Indian allies.[3] Passing across the southwestern section of Arizona they verged to the eastward till they came to Cibola, which was captured. Here they were profoundly disappointed. However plausible Friar Marcos's comparison of the distant view of the pueblo with the city of Mexico may be made to seem in our time, there is no doubt that it completely misled the men of that day who knew Mexico.[4]

Coronado now sent back Melchior Diaz to order up the main force. Diaz did so, and then set out to explore the region at the head of the Gulf of California. He crossed the Colorado River and penetrated the country to the west.[5] Another impor-

[1] Winship, *The Coronado Expedition* (Bureau of Ethnology, *Fourteenth Annual Report*), 385.   [2] *Ibid.*, 404–406.
[3] Castañeda, in Winship, *Journey of Coronado*, 20.
[4] *Ibid.*, 23.   *Ibid.*, 26–28.

tant side expedition during this summer was that of Pedro de Tovar to the province of Tusayan, northwest of Cibola, which led to the discovery of the Grand Cañon of the Colorado by De Cardenas.[1] As they looked into its depths it seemed as "if the water was six feet across, although the Indians said it was half a league wide." They tried to get down to the stream, but in vain. "Those who stayed above had estimated that some huge rocks on the sides of the cliffs seemed to be about as tall as a man, but those who went down swore that when they reached these rocks they were bigger than the great tower of Seville."[2]

When the main army reached Cibola, Coronado moved with it to about the middle of New Mexico, where he went into winter quarters at Tiguex, on the Rio Grande. Here the burden of requisitions for supplies and individual acts of outrage against the Indians of Tiguex provoked them to an attack on the Spaniards, which was successfully repelled. The cruelty of the reprisals inflicted on the Indian prisoners exceeded anything done by De Soto, and constitutes a dark stain on the expedition.[3]

In the spring of 1541 Coronado set out to reach Quivira, a town of which an Indian prisoner had given a glowing description. It seems probable that the thirty-seven days' march took them north-

[1] The Tusayan Indians are identified as the Moquis. The cañon was twenty days' journey farther west.
[2] Castañeda, in Winship, *Journey of Coronado*, 36.   [3] *Ibid.*, 51.

easterly, but constantly verging to the right, across
the plains until they reached the borders of the
present Oklahoma Territory. A further advance
with the main force now seemed inadvisable; but to
verify, if possible, the stories about Quivira, Coronado went on early in June with thirty horsemen to
the northeast. After a ride of about six weeks the
goal was reached, and proved to be nothing more
than a village of semi-nomadic Indians in the centre
of the present state. of Kansas.[1] A few hundred
miles to the southeast De Soto at this same time
was exploring Arkansas. An Indian woman who
had run away from Coronado's army fell in with De
Soto's nine days later.[2]

Fertile as was the soil of the western prairies, the
region had nothing at that time adequate to reward settlement so far inland;[3] and Coronado in
the following spring returned to New Spain with all
his force save two missionaries and a few others.[4]
The expedition, like De Soto's, failed of its immediate object, but it revealed the character of a
large part of the southwest and of the trans - Mississippi plains; and the branch expeditions had
proved that Lower California was a peninsula and
not an island. In the summer of 1542 the Pacific
coast of California was explored by Cabrillo as far

---

[1] Coronado to the king, Winship, *Journey of Coronado*, 214–219;
Bandelier, *The Gilded Man*, 223–251.

[2] Castañeda, in Winship, *Journey of Coronado*, 77.

[3] Cf. Coronado's report, *ibid.*, 220.

[4] Jaramillo, *ibid.*, 238–240; Lowery, *Spanish Settlements*, 409.

as Cape Mendocino, named in honor of the Viceroy Mendoza.

These great expeditions of De Soto and Coronado, undertaken for the exploration of the interior of the present United States a century and a half before La Salle, and over two centuries and a half before Lewis and Clark, were the natural outflow of the marvellous experiences of Cortés and of Pizarro in Mexico and Peru, and mark the highest reach of Spanish energy in our own country; nor have they ever been surpassed as exhibitions of skilful leadership and enduring labor by any similar enterprises by the French or English in North America. Their results were keenly disappointing at the time, but in the record of the exploration of the globe they occupy a high and honorable place among the great enterprises of history.

CHAPTER XII

FRENCH AND SPANIARDS IN FLORIDA
(1558–1568)

AS a term in the political geography of Spanish America, the name "Florida" was equivalent to the eastern half of the present United States, or the country from Mexico to Newfoundland.[1] In 1558, Philip II. authorized Luis de Velasco, viceroy of New Spain, to undertake the settlement of Florida. After a preliminary reconnoissance Velasco despatched, in the summer of 1559, an expedition of fifteen hundred soldiers and settlers to make a beginning at Pensacola Bay.[2] The site selected was unfavorable, but attempts to find a better one were not successful; a winter of privation followed, and during the following summer the colony was much reduced. The second summer most of the settlers went off with Angel de Villafañe to the Atlantic coast, to Santa Elena, Port Royal Sound. When he arrived there late in May, 1561, Villafañe, disappointed at the unsuitableness of the region for a colony, continued his explorations to

[1] Lopez de Velasco, *Descripcion de las Indias*, 157.
[2] Lowery, *Spanish Settlements*, 357.

Chesapeake Bay and then returned to Española. The unhappy experiences of these colonists convinced Philip II. that the region was not likely to be occupied by the French, and hence he decided that no further attempt at colonization should be made.[1]

The very next year the unexpected happened. Jean Ribaut, of Dieppe, under the patronage of Coligny, the leader of the Huguenots in France, led a party of soldiers and young nobles to the east shore of Florida, whence they coasted as far north as Port Royal Sound. Here Ribaut left thirty men and returned to France. Want, lonesomeness, and contentions drove them to the desperate expedient of building a vessel to make their escape from the desolate continent, but only at the cost of such privations as reduced them to cannibalism before they were picked up by an English ship.[2]

In 1564 the plans for a colony in Florida of French Huguenots were matured by Coligny; and the expedition set out in June under the command of René de Laudonnière, a French officer and gentleman who had been with Ribaut in the first voyage. The site selected was at the mouth of the St. John's River, Florida. Here a fort was built and parties were despatched to explore the country. There were few if any tillers of the soil in the company, and

[1] Lowery, *Spanish Settlements*, 374–376.
[2] Laudonnière, in Hakluyt, *Voyages*, XIII., 417–441; Parkman, *Pioneers of France*, 33–47.

when the first novelty wore off, restlessness and ennui led to quarrels, insubordination, and plots.

Thirteen of the sailors seized one of the vessels and set off on a buccaneering cruise against the Spaniards. Want finally brought them up in Havana, where, to save themselves, they gave information in regard to the colony.[1] Their example was soon followed by sixty-six others, tempted by the chances of wealth in plundering Spanish ships and settlements. At first successful, they came to grief, and less than half returned to the fort, where Laudonnière overpowered them and put to death four of the ringleaders for mutiny.[2]

In August, 1565, after a summer of extreme want, the wasted garrison were preparing to leave the country, when Ribaut arrived with several hundred colonists, soldiers, and young gentlemen, with some artisans and their families.[3] Ribaut also brought orders to Laudonnière to resign his command and return to France.[4]

Contemporaneous with this effort of the French Huguenots to occupy Florida was a new project to colonize the country for Spain. Pedro Menendez de Aviles, who had served as commander of the fleet to New Spain, secured a patent in March, 1565, erecting Florida into a government and constituting him adelantado, governor, and captain - general.

[1] Laudonnière, in Hakluyt, *Voyages*, XIII., 473.
[2] *Ibid.*, 479.   [3] Parkman, *Pioneers of France*, 93.
[4] *Ibid.*, 94; Hakluyt, *Voyages*, XIII., 511.

Menendez on his part was to take five hundred men, one hundred of them farmers, to explore and conquer Florida, to transport settlers thither, some of whom were to be married, support twelve friars as missionaries, and supply domestic animals for the settlements.[1] This task Menendez undertook with great energy and zeal. The hazy ideas of the width of the continent, still prevalent even after De Soto's expedition, led him to think Florida near enough to the silver-mines of Zacatecas and St. Martin, in Mexico, to be substituted for Vera Cruz as the place of export, thus avoiding the dangers to health in that town and enabling traffic to escape the perilous and tedious navigation of the gulf by an overland journey of perhaps a hundred leagues longer than that to Vera Cruz. In reality it was over one thousand miles farther from Zacatecas to Florida than to Vera Cruz.[2]

While Menendez was making his preparations the news first reached the Spanish court of the projects of the French. The king immediately gave orders that Menendez should be granted three vessels, two hundred cavalry, and four hundred infantry in the islands to drive out the French.[3] That the Spanish government should allow a French settlement in so important a strategic point in relation

---

[1] Shea, in Winsor, *Narr. and Crit. Hist.*, II., 261.

[2] Menendez to the king, Mass. Hist. Soc., *Proceedings*, 2d series, VIII., 435, 456.

[3] Barcia, *Ensayo Cronologico*, 67; Parkman, *Pioneers of France*, 100.

to their commerce with New Spain was inconceiv-
able, and one wonders why the French promoters
of the enterprise expected that it would be regarded
as anything but a declaration of hostilities.[1] The
islands were already exposed to the ravages of the
French buccaneers. The corsair French Jacques de
Sorie had sacked and burned Havana ten years
before and killed thirty-four prisoners in cold blood.[2]
To furnish a basis for attacks of this sort, it was
naturally believed by the Spanish authorities, was
the motive of Ribaut and Laudonnière; and the
conduct of the two detachments of mutineers only
confirmed the supposition.

That the intruders were heretics intensified their
exasperation. Carefully shielding the purity of the
faith in the New World by excluding all Spaniards
whose progenitors had been tainted with heresy,
they would regard an enterprise which combined
plunder of their colonies and fleets and a corruption
of the Indians with diabolical heresy as an extraordinary provocation, excluding the guilty plotters from
any claim to mercy.

Menendez, with a company of over two thousand
six hundred persons, all maintained at his own ex-

---

[1] Ribaut's instructions contemplated hostilities. Parkman,
Pioneers of France, 115, *n*.

[2] Shea, in Winsor, *Narr. and Crit. Hist.*, 261, 275. See the
certified statement in Buckingham Smith, *Col. de Docs. de la
Florida*, 202–208. Jacques de Sorie is described as a Picard or
Norman, and, "grandisimo hereje Luterano," the churches
were burned and the images mutilated.

pense, except one ship and about three hundred soldiers paid by the king, left Cadiz, June 29, about the time Ribaut must have left Dieppe.[1] On the night of September 4, off the coast of Florida, Menendez fell in with some of Ribaut's ships, and in response to inquiries announced his instructions to hang and burn the Lutheran French to be found there.[2] The French ships escaped in the darkness, and Menendez continued on his way to his new domain. September 6, 1565, a landing was made and a fort begun which may be considered the foundation of St. Augustine, the oldest town in the United States. Two days later Menendez landed and took formal possession of the territory.[3]

His forces were not so superior to Ribaut's as to prevent his situation being one of peril. A storm, however, scattered Ribaut's ships, and Menendez decided to attack the French by land. A stealthy march, a desperate assault on a sleeping garrison just before daybreak amid a pouring rain, and soon all was over. One hundred and thirty men lay dead in and around the fort.[4] The women and children under fifteen Menendez ordered to be spared.[5]

[1] Barcia, *Ensayo Cronologico*, 69.

[2] Menendez to the king, Mass. Hist. Soc., *Proceedings*, 2d series, VIII., 420; Mendoza Grajales, the chaplain of the expedition, in French, *Hist. Coll. of Louisiana and Florida*, II., 211.

[3] Mendoza Grajales, *ibid.*, 217–219.

[4] September 20, Menendez to the king, *ibid.*, 426. The statements about the number vary somewhat. Cf. Parkman, *Pioneers of France*, 127, and Shea, in Winsor, *Narr. and Crit. Hist.*, 272.

[5] Barcia, *Ensayo Cronologico*, 1.

Of them he wrote to the king, "There were, between women, infants, and boys of fifteen years and under, some fifty persons, whom it gives me the greater pain to see in the company of my men, by reason of their wicked sect, and I have feared that our Lord would chastise me if I shall deal cruelly with them, for eight or ten children were born here." [1]

About fifty persons escaped the slaughter by swimming across the river or by taking boats to the ships. One of the ships was sunk by the guns of the fort. The other slipped down the river a few miles where there were two more. Menendez determined to capture them if possible. In his absence word was brought that some twenty Frenchmen had come in from the woods, and he gave orders to execute justice upon them. [2] A few days later, after Menendez had returned to St. Augustine, he heard of a party of Frenchmen some twenty miles distant to the south. He set out immediately with a small force against them. From their spokesman he learned that Ribaut's fleet, consisting of four galleons and eight pinnaces with four hundred picked men and two hundred sailors, which had put out in search of the Spaniards, had been struck by a hurricane, that three of the galleons had gone down

[1] Menendez to the king, Mass. Hist. Soc., *Proceedings*, 2d series, VIII., 427. He sent them to Santo Domingo as soon as possible—Barcia, *Ensayo Cronologico*, 87; in English in French, *Hist. Coll. of Louisiana and Florida*, II., 218.

[2] Mass. Hist. Soc., *Proceedings*, 2d series, VIII., 426, 427.

with over two hundred persons, and that Ribaut's flag-ship had been dismasted.

In reply to a request for safe passage to the fort Menendez told him: "We held their fort, having taken and put to death those who were in it for having erected it there without the leave of your majesty, and because they were planting their wicked Lutheran sect in these your majesty's provinces, and that I made war with fire and blood as governor and captain-general of these provinces upon all who might come to these parts to settle and to plant this evil Lutheran sect, seeing that I came by your majesty's command to bring the gospel into these parts, to enlighten the natives thereof with that which is told and believed by the holy mother church of Rome for the salvation of their souls; that therefore I should not give them passage, but, on the contrary, should pursue them by sea and by land until I had their lives." [1]

The Frenchmen, through a lieutenant of Laudonnière, then offered to surrender if their lives would be spared. "I answered," writes Menendez, "that they might give up their arms and place themselves at my mercy; that I should deal with them as our Lord should command me, and that he [*i.e.*, the envoy] had not moved me from this nor could move me, unless God our Lord should inspire in me something different." [2] According to Solis, the

[1] Mass. Hist. Soc., *Proceedings*, 2d series, VIII., 428.
[2] *Ibid.*, 429.

brother-in-law of Menendez, who was a witness, his reply was that " if they wished to surrender their arms and banners and put themselves at his mercy they might do so and he would do with them as God should give him grace, they might do as they liked; other truce or friendship they could not have." [1]

It is possible that the translation of this reply into French made it seem to give grounds for a hope that did not exist. To-day, in view of what Menendez had declared to the first envoy, he does not seem to have committed himself to any mercy. Their offer of fifty thousand ducats as a ransom he promptly declined, saying "that although he was poor he would not do that weakness; when he wanted to be liberal and merciful he would be so without self-interest." [2] After consultation the Frenchmen decided to surrender. All of them, over a hundred in number, except twelve Breton sailors who had been kidnapped and four carpenters and caulkers, were put to the knife in cold blood. Ever since the spot has borne the name Matanzas ("Slaughters ").

Next came the turn of Ribaut and those with him. October 10, Menendez received news of their approach, and went out to meet them with a body of one hundred and fifty men. The French asked for a parley, which was granted, and Menendez was then informed that it was Ribaut with some three hundred and fifty men, and that they desired safe passage to

[1] Extract in Barcia, *Ensayo Cronologico*, 86; in English in French, *Hist. Coll. of Louisiana and Florida*, II., 218.   [2] *Ibid.*

their fort. Again came the unrelenting answer that "I was his enemy and waged war against them with fire and blood, for that they were Lutherans, and because they had come to plant in these lands of your majesty their evil sect and to instruct the Indians in it." [1] Ribaut himself desired an interview, which was granted. It was hard for him to believe that his fort was captured, the garrison slain, and that the other party of refugees from the wreck had been killed, but the sight of the dead bodies on the sands convinced him. In response to his request for terms, if they should surrender, Menendez made the same answer that he had made a fortnight earlier.

Ribaut consulted his men and found them divided. He returned and explained the situation to Menendez. Some wished to throw themselves on his mercy and others not. Menendez answered it made no difference to him; they might all come or part of them or none; they might do as they liked. Ribaut then said that half of them would pay one hundred and fifty thousand ducats ransom and that the other half would pay more, as there were rich men among them. Menendez replied that it was hard to lose such a sum, as he was in need of it. This answer gave an encouragement to Ribaut for which one sees little ground, for if Menendez had intended to deceive him it would have been as easy to say "he should be glad to have it."

Grasping at the chance, whatever it was, Ribaut

[1] Mass. Hist. Soc., *Proceedings*, 2d series, VIII., 438.

and one hundred and fifty of his men gave themselves up. They were led by tens back of the sanddunes and then asked whether they were Catholics or Lutherans, "and then John Ribaut replied that he and all that were there were of the new religion, and began to repeat the psalm, 'Domine, memento mei,' and when he had finished he said that they were of the earth and to the earth must return. Twenty years more or less, it was all the same thing "[1] Then all were put to the knife save two young gentlemen about eighteen years of age and a drummer, a fifer, and a trumpeter. Menendez wrote to King Philip: "I hold it the chief good-fortune that he [Ribaut] is dead, because the king of France would do more with him with five hundred ducats than with others and five thousand, and he would do more in one year than another in ten, since he was the most expert sailor and corsair known, and very skilful in this navigation of the Indies and coast of Florida." [2]

Three weeks later Indians brought information that the rest of Ribaut's party, who refused to surrender, were building a fort and a ship. Menendez set forth against them by forced marches with three hundred men. This time, affected perhaps by adverse criticism at St. Augustine,[3] or because he saw

---

[1] Barcia, *Ensayo Cronologico*, 88, 89; in English in French, *Hist. Coll. of Louisiana and Florida*, II., 220–221.

[2] Parkman, *Pioneers of France*, 114, *n*.

[3] Cf. Solis, in Barcia, *Ensayo Cronologico*, 89; French, *Hist. Coll. of Louisiana and Florida*, II., 222.

that it would be impracticable to capture them and
felt "that it would not be proper that so wicked a
sect should remain in the land," [1] and possibly because his own heart had softened, he offered them
their lives if they would surrender. One hundred
and fifty did so and were well treated. The captain
and about twenty rejected the offer, sending word
"that he would be eaten by the Indians rather than
surrender to the Spaniards." [2]

The story of this tragedy has been told from the
Spanish side, for the accounts of Menendez and
Solis bear upon them the marks of truth so far as
these are discoverable. They do not blink the facts,
nor do they show signs of consciousness that there
was need of concealment or apology. The accounts
of the French who escaped accuse Menendez of having promised on oath to save the lives of those who
surrendered. This it is difficult to believe in view
of the whole tone of Menendez's correspondence with
the king. [3] That a man of honor and religion could
have done such a deed seems impossible to-day.
Yet if the perplexed student will read Oliver Cromwell's account of the massacre at Drogheda, and if
he will read Carlyle's comments, he may be able to
understand why the historian Barcia accorded admiration to Menendez. [4]

[1] Menendez, in Mass. Hist. Soc., *Proceedings*, 2d series, VIII., 440.

[2] Solis, in Barcia, *Ensayo Cronologico*, 90.

[3] Shea, whose account is critical and impartial, rejects the
French assertions on this point.

[4] The massacre of the English at Amboyna by the Dutch in

The French king, Charles IX., and his stronger mother, Catherine de' Medici, demanded reparation urgently and repeatedly; but Philip II. only said that he was sorry for what had happened, and insisted that Admiral Coligny was responsible for having authorized the French to occupy Spanish territory, and that he ought to be punished; redress he refused to give.[1] To Menendez, however, he expressed his approval of his conduct. In the state of politics and religion in France a breach with Spain seemed to the leaders of the Catholic party out of the question; they did not venture beyond protests.

A private adventurer, Dominic de Gourgues, so the accepted story runs, then took upon himself the responsibility of avenging his countrymen, setting out from France in the summer of 1567 with three vessels, under a commission to capture slaves in Africa. After selling his cargo in Española, when off the western end of Cuba he revealed his project to his men. They soon fell in with the plan, and De Gourgues made his way to the St. John's River to attack the Spanish fort San Mateo, which was the successor of Laudonnière's Fort Caroline. First two outposts lower down the river, then the fort itself, were taken by assault. All the Spaniards

---

1623, although the numbers were much smaller, was attended by more pitiless cruelties than was the case in Florida. Cf. Gardiner, *History of England*, V., 242.

[1] Parkman, *Pioneers of France*, 151–156.

that escaped the sword were hanged, with the inscription placed above them: "Not as Spaniards, but as traitors, robbers, and murderers." He then razed the forts, and returned to France, hoping for a recognition which only the Huguenots gave.[1]

It is a singular fact that a most careful search in the Spanish archives failed to find "the slightest allusion to any such capture of San Mateo and the two adjacent forts";[2] nor do the papers of the Menendez family appear to have contained any material on this incident, since the Spanish historian Barcia, who utilized those papers, had no sources save the French narrative. That account says nothing of the existence of St. Augustine, and, on the other hand, the existence of two forts besides San Mateo is unknown to the contemporary Spanish sources.[3] To these perplexities may be added the fact that Juan Lopez de Velasco, the cosmographer of the Council of the Indies, writing in 1571-1574, in his account of Florida, knows nothing of De Gourgues's raid in 1568, but says that Fort San Mateo was abandoned in 1570.[4]

Historians have told the tale as one of poetic

---

[1] Parkman, *Pioneers of France*, 157-177; *La Reprinse de la Floride par le Cappitaine Gourgues*, in French, *Hist. Coll. of Louisiana and Florida*, II., 267-289. The story of De Gourgues's expedition first appeared in detailed form in 1586, nineteen years after the event, in Basanier, *L'Histoire Notable de la Floride*.

[2] Shea, in his edition of Charlevoix, *New France*, I., 338.

[3] Shea, in Winsor, *Narr. and Crit. Hist.*, II., 280, 297.

[4] Juan Lopez de Velasco, *Geografia y Descripcion Universal de las Indias desde el año de 1571 al de 1574*, 162.

justice, and religious sympathies have naturally been enlisted on the side of the avenger. Yet it should not be forgotten that, merciless and cruel as was Menendez's deed—the nearest parallel to the bloody massacres of the Crusades or of the religious wars in Europe that ever happened in our country's history—he was the constituted authority in Florida, and was acting in general pursuance of instructions from his king. He looked upon the French colonists as corsairs, which, in fact, at least some of them were. That the French had a right to establish a colony in Florida can hardly be maintained; their own claim was based on a purely fictitious discovery in the fifteenth century. De Gourgues, acting as a private adventurer, had no color of law on his side.

The tragedy was the end of French colonization on the southern main-land for nearly a century and a half; and the end forever of the attempts to establish a Huguenot refuge and power on this side of the sea. Their contribution to American life was to be made as individuals, a sturdy leaven in a congenial though foreign society. On the other hand, neither Menendez nor his heirs or descendants succeeded in founding a flourishing Spanish community in Florida. Equally without permanent success were the repeated efforts of missionary bands to convert the Indians.

CHAPTER XIII

THE ACHIEVEMENT OF THREE GENERATIONS

(1492–1580)

GREAT as have been the political and religious changes of the last one hundred years, they fall short of those which took place in the three generations following the first voyage of Columbus. A man like Las Casas, who was approaching maturity in 1492, saw the discovery of a new world, the opening to European traffic of the three vast oceans, the circumnavigation of the globe, the setting forth of the Copernican theory of the solar system, the establishment of the Spanish Empire in the New World, and the Protestant revolution, events in their novelty and their far-reaching consequences surpassing anything in the history of mankind since the establishment of the Roman Empire and the advent of Christianity.

In three of these epoch-making processes Spain took the leading part; and it will be suitable in this place before taking up the special phases of her work in America to make a brief survey of what had been accomplished by Spanish enterprise in somewhat less than a century. To appreciate the total achievement, it is necessary to remind the reader that Spain was not a rich country, that her area was about equal to that of New England, New York, Pennsylvania, and Ohio combined, that her population at the end of this period was somewhat smaller than that of New York to-day, and somewhat larger than that of Pennsylvania.[1] Most of this work, however, fell to natives of the kingdom of Castile, whose population was probably half a million less than that of Pennsylvania.

Taking up first the extension of geographical knowledge, we have to record the exploration of the Atlantic coast-line from Nova Scotia to Cape Horn[2] and of the Pacific coast-line from the Straits of Magellan as far north as Oregon.[3] The Pacific had been crossed both north and south of the equator going west; and the proper eastward course, after repeated failures, was discovered in 1565 by Urdañeta.[4] The empires of Mexico and of the Incas had been conquered, and their wealth had become the support and the stimulus to the most arduous and heroic overland explorations of modern times. Pedro de Alvarado, in 1534, tempted by the desire to rival the Pizarros, diverted an expedition des-

[1] Häbler, *Die Wirthschaftliche Blüte Spaniens im 16 Jahrhundert und ihr Verfall*, 150, places the population of Spain in 1550 at about 6,800,000.

[2] Cape Horn was discovered, but not rounded, in 1526 by Francisco de Hoces. Hugues, *Cronologia*, 35.

[3] By Juan Roderiguez Cabrillo, 1542–1543, *ibid.*, 59.

[4] *Ibid.*, 71.

tined to the Spice Islands to the region north of
Peru, and forced his way through the snowy passes
of the Andes to Quito, only to find that he had been
anticipated by Sebastian de Benalcazar.[1] In 1537
Benalcazar made his way to Bogotá, which place
was also reached up the Magdalena River from the
Caribbean Sea by Gonzalo Ximenes de Quesada,
and from the basin of the Orinoco by the German
Federmann, sent out by the Welsers, of Augsburg,
under a license from the emperor Charles V.[2] In
1537 also the lawyer Vadillo organized an expedition
at an expense of one hundred thousand pesos to
march overland from Cartagena to Peru. After
a year of extraordinary exertions and hardships,
during which ninety-two of the three hundred and
fifty Spaniards died, they reached Cali, in the
southern part of the modern Colombia, where, like
Alvarado, they found themselves anticipated.[3]

Juan de Ayolas, in 1535, went up the Paraná and
the Paraguay as far as twenty degrees south latitude, and then across the plains to Peru.[4] Five
years later Martinez de Irala went up the Paraguay
to the seventeenth parallel and opened the permanent line of communication between Peru and the
river Plate region.[5] In the middle of the continent
Gonzalo Pizarro crossed the eastern Andes from

---

[1] Prescott, *Conquest of Peru*, II., 13–22.
[2] Hugues, *Cronologia*, 48.
[3] Herrera, *Historia General*, dec. VI., lib. VII., chap. iv.
[4] Hugues, *Cronologia*, 49.   [5] *Ibid.*

Quito, and his lieutenant Orellana, embarking on the Napo, floated down that stream into the Marañon and the Amazon, and reached the Atlantic after a navigation of seven months and three thousand miles.[1] In the western Cordilleran region Almagro penetrated Chili from Peru and returned by the coastal lowlands, 1535-1537, with difficulties and sufferings as great in the sandy deserts as in the mountain wilderness.[2]

In the present United States the story of the interior exploration is more familiar. Beginning with the wanderings of Cabeça de Vaca from eastern Texas to the Gulf of California, it was followed up in the southwest by Friar Marcos, of Nice, introducing the vaster enterprise of Coronado, who covered the region from Mexico to Kansas; and in the east by the expedition of De Soto, which, while failing of its immediate objects, enriched geographical knowledge with the earliest descriptions of our southern inland region from Florida to Arkansas, and recorded the first undoubted discovery of the Mississippi.

During this period the explorations of the French were limited to the voyages of Verrazano, Cartier, and Roberval; while the English, after the first ventures of John Cabot, did nothing to add to the knowledge of geography, with the possible exception of the Cabot voyage of 1508-1509. Even the great

[1] Prescott, *Conquest of Peru*, II., 153-170.
[2] *Ibid.*, II., 83-90.

achievements of Champlain, La Salle, and other French explorers of the seventeenth century pale before the exploits of the Spaniards in the previous age.

If we turn to colonization and conquest we find the same disparity; for the results of the first eighty years of English and French colonization, compared with the work done by the Spaniards, were small, notwithstanding their great significance for the future. In the first three generations that followed the settlement at Jamestown, communities of Englishmen had been planted on the Atlantic coast and along the course of streams from Maine to South Carolina. New England had a white population of perhaps eighty thousand in 1700;[1] in New York, in 1698, there were perhaps eighteen thousand of European extraction;[2] Virginia was the home of about forty thousand in 1671,[3] and in Maryland there were perhaps twenty thousand in 1676. In the Carolinas and the Jerseys by 1690 there were perhaps twenty-five thousand more, making a total of certainly less than two hundred thousand whites in the English colonies about the year 1690. Chalmers estimated the white population of the English settlements in 1715 at about three hundred and seventy-five thousand.[4] Of Christianized Indians there were few outside of New England, and there

---

[1] Doyle, *English in America*, II., 497, 498.
[2] Lodge, *Short Hist. of the Eng. Cols.*, 312.
[3] Governor Berkeley's report, in Hart, *Contemporaries*, I., 239.
[4] Fiske, *Old Virginia*, II., 169.

the number was much less than before King Philip's
War. In 1674 Gookin estimated the total for Massachusetts and Plymouth at eighteen hundred.[1]

In the English colonies institutions for the education of the Indians were projected in the seventeenth
century, but not realized except in so far as the
foundation of Harvard College was designed to effect that end.[2] Roger Williams had written on
their language and customs, and Eliot had translated the Bible into the Natick dialect. For the
higher education of the whites Harvard was the sole
foundation until 1693; and only two other colleges
were established during the next fifty years. There
were in the colonies during their first century little
accumulated wealth, but hardly any poverty, few
fine buildings, and scant traces of artistic feeling.
On the other hand, the English in America were
building up self-governing communities which in
some cases were almost independent states. They
were the scenes of experiments of democracy and
religious toleration of epoch-making significance.
The foundations of a great people had been laid.

If we now compare what the Spaniards accomplished in the sixteenth century with the work of
the English in the seventeenth we shall appreciate
that, although it was different in character and less

[1] Doyle, *English in America*, II., 202.

[2] In Virginia in 1619, Bruce, *Economic History of Virginia*, I.,
228; in Massachusetts, Doyle, II., 78; *Cal. of State Pap., Col.*,
1650; charter of Harvard College, 1650, *Harvard University
Catalogue*.

in accord with our predilections or prejudices, it was, nevertheless, one of the great achievements of human history. They undertook the magnificent if impossible task of lifting a whole race numbering millions into the sphere of European thought, life, and religion. Yet this thought and life and religion were so different in many respects from the ideals which now appeal to the descendants of the seventeenth-century English Protestant that we instinctively appraise the attempt of the Spaniards both by modern standards and by the measure of their failure, rather than by the degree of their success.

An outline of what they had accomplished may be drawn from what is substantially a census of Spanish America in 1574. In 1576 Juan Lopez de Velasco, in his capacity as cosmographer and historian to the Council of the Indies, prepared a "Description of the Indies" which far surpasses in detail and completeness any official report on the English colonies till the time of Chalmers.[1] In 1574 Velasco enumerates in the New World some two hundred Spanish cities and towns with some mining settlements. These towns, together with the stock-farms and plantations, contained about one hundred and sixty thousand Spaniards, of whom about four thousand were encomenderos—*i.e.*, lords of Indian serfs—and the rest settlers, miners, traders, and soldiers. Of Indians there were approximately

[1] Juan Lopez de Velasco, *Geografia y Descripcion Universal de las Indias* (Justo Zaragoza's ed.).

eight or nine thousand villages, inclusive of tribes or parts of tribes not yet civilized, containing one million five hundred thousand Indian men of tribute-paying age (fifteen to sixty), or an aproximate Indian population of about five million, not counting the considerable number who escaped taxation either because not yet reduced to village life or because they hid away. The Indians were divided into three thousand seven hundred repartimientos belonging to the king or to private persons. In addition there were about forty thousand negro slaves and a large number of mestizos and mulattoes. The great mass of the Indians were nominally Christians and were living as civilized men and their numbers increasing.[1]

In following Velasco's account of the various colonies we see how the superior attractiveness of Mexico, Central America, and Peru, and the restrictions on commerce, had largely depleted the population of the islands. In Española there remained only ten Spanish villages with a population of about one thousand Spaniards, engaged principally in sugar-growing and stock-raising, with the labor of some twelve thousand negro slaves. The city of Santo Domingo a few years before had a Spanish population of one thousand seven hundred, but in 1574 only one thousand and two. Of Indians there were left only two villages. In Cuba there were seven towns (villas) and one city, but their total Spanish

---

[1] Velasco, 1, 2.

population was only two hundred and forty. There were nine Indian hamlets and about two hundred and seventy married Indians. Santiago, which had once contained a thousand Spaniards, now was the home of only thirty. The Spanish population of Havana was only seventy. Porto Rico and Jamaica were in the same plight, slowly stifling for lack of a market.[1] Venezuela was somewhat better off, but here, too, the tale is of poverty.

It is only when we follow the islanders and go to New Spain that we find progress and prosperity. In the city of Mexico in 1574 there were about fifteen thousand Spaniards — encomenderos, merchants, miners, mechanics — and about one hundred and fifty thousand Indians. Besides the public buildings, the churches, and the monasteries, there were a university, a boys' and girls' high-school, four hospitals, of which one was for Indians; in the Spanish quarter well-built houses of wood, stone, and mason work.[2] To the north of Mexico lay a typical Indian province, that of Teotlalpa, of some six hundred square miles, with no Spanish towns save two mining settlements with perhaps one hundred and thirty Spaniards. There were twenty-six Indian villages with one hundred and fourteen thousand Indians paying tribute, fifteen monasteries averaging three or four friars each.[3]

In the bishopric of Tlaxcala to the east there were only two Spanish towns, Los Angeles and Vera

[1] Velasco, 94–134.   [2] Ibid., 188–190.   [3] Ibid., 194–196.

Cruz. The two hundred Indian villages contained two hundred and fifteen thousand tributaries, divided into one hundred and twenty-seven repartimientos, worth one hundred and twelve thousand pesos a year. Sixty-one belonged to the crown, yielding thirty-eight thousand pesos, and sixty-six yielding seventy-four thousand pesos to private encomenderos. In the town of Vera Cruz lived some two hundred Spanish families, all merchants and shopkeepers, but no Indians. The heavy work was performed by some six hundred negro slaves as porters and stevedores. The sickly climate accounts for the three hospitals in so small a place.[1]

In Yucatan, not counting Tabasco, there were four Spanish towns, with some three hundred householders, one hundred and thirty of them encomenderos, the rest planters living on their plantations, traders, and officials.[2] In South America, Velasco reckoned one hundred Spanish settlements with a total of thirteen thousand five hundred households. Some two thousand of the Spaniards were encomenderos, the rest farmers and traders. The Indians were not reduced to village life as generally as in the north, but the number of tributaries is put at eight hundred and eighty thousand. The Indians on the plains were diminishing in number, while those in the uplands were increasing.[3] The aspects of Spanish life were not dissimilar to those in the

[1] Velasco, 207–213.   [2] *Ibid.*, 247.   [3] *Ibid.*, 401.

north: stock-raising, growing cereals, sugar-cane, wool, etc., were the principal occupations.[1] The city of Quito contained some four hundred Spanish families, three monasteries, and a hospital. In the Franciscan monastery there was an Indian school.[2]

In Lima, the "City of the Kings," the capital of the viceroyalty of Peru, there were some two thousand Spanish families, thirty of them encomenderos, the rest traders and officials. The Indian population of the district was twenty-five or twenty-six thousand, divided into one hundred and thirty-six repartimientos, of which six belonged to the crown. The wealth of Peru redounded to the prosperity of the church, for Lima contained five monasteries and two convents, a convent for mestizo girls and a house of sisters of charity, two large and rich hospitals, one for Spaniards and one for Indians.[3] In institutions of learning Lima was in 1570, as always, far behind Mexico.

The foregoing presents the results of Spanish colonization from the stand-point of the historian and geographer of the Council of the Indies. If now we review the same events with the eyes of the old campaigner of the conquest, Bernal Diaz, as he looks back forty-seven years, we see that first there come to his mind the wonderful changes in the life and condition of the Indians, changes in range and character perhaps not equalled before in the history of the race in so short a time. Instead of the fearful

---

[1] Velasco, 337.   [2] Ibid., 432.   [3] Ibid., 463–466.

temples of Huitzilopochtli and Tezcatlipoca, smok-
ing with human sacrifice and dripping with blood of
victims, there are Christian churches; while upon the
Indians themselves have been bestowed the hardly
won prizes of ages of slow progress, the developed
arts, the various domestic animals, the grains, vegetables, and fruits, the use of letters and the printing-
press, and the forms of government.[1] As the child
physically and mentally passes rapidly through the
earlier stages of the development of the race, so the
natives of New Spain in a generation and a half were
lifted through whole stages of human evolution.   If
these gifts came through war and conquest, so Roman culture came to Gaul and Britain.

[1] Bernal Diaz, *Historia Verdadera*, chaps. ccviii., ccix.

CHAPTER XIV

THE BEGINNINGS OF SPANISH COLONIAL POLICY

(1493-1518)

THE Spanish colonial empire lasted three centuries, a period nearly as long as that of the sway of imperial Rome over western Europe. During these ten generations the language, the religion, the culture, and the political institutions of Castile were transplanted over an area twenty times as large as that of the parent state. What Rome did for Spain, Spain in turn did for Spanish America. In surveying, therefore, the work of Spain in the New World, we must realize from the start that we are studying one of the great historical examples of the transmission of culture by the establishment of imperial domain, and not, as in the case of English America, by the growth of little settlements of immigrants acting on their own impulse.

The colonial systems of Spain and of England have often been compared, to the great disparagement of the work of Spain; but the comparison of unlike and even contrasted social processes is more misleading than instructive. If we seek in English history a counterpart to the Spanish colonial empire, we shall find it rather in India than in Massachusetts or Virginia. Even here qualifications are necessary, for America never sustained such enormous masses of people as are found in India; and, small on the whole as was Spanish migration to the New World, it was relatively much larger than the English migration to India. Nor as yet have the people of Hindustan absorbed so much of the culture of the ruling nation in its various aspects as did the Indians in the American possessions of Spain.

It will be nearer the truth if we conceive of Spanish America as an intermediate and complex product, approximating on the political side to British India, on the social side in some respects to Roman Africa, and in the West Indies to the English plantation colonies in Virginia and South Carolina. British India is a more extreme example of imperial rule than is presented by New Spain and Peru; there was a far less ethnic divergence between the Roman and the Gaul or Briton than between the Spaniard and the red men, and the absorption of Roman culture was more complete in the ancient than in the modern instance.

In the West Indies and southern colonies of the English the same conditions confronted both England and Spain, and here a comparison of their respective systems is instructive; but for a fair counterpart to the English colonies of the north Atlantic seaboard we look in vain in the Spanish world, for

Spain, in the commercial interest of Peru, steadily neglected the opportunity to develop the La Plata River country, where, alone of all her empire, there has sprung up since the era of independence and the rise of steam transportation a community rivalling the Mississippi Valley, in its wealth from agriculture and grazing, in its attractiveness to European emigration, and in the rapidity of its growth.

Of the three general divisions of their empire—the imperial dependencies of Peru and Mexico, the plantation colonies of the islands, and the unutilized areas of La Plata—the Spaniards always regarded the first as the most important; and it was only when these slipped from their grasp that the resources of the West Indies were adequately developed. Hence in a survey of Spanish colonial institutions our study will be mainly directed, after a brief examination of the beginnings of the West Indies, to Mexico, Central America, and Peru.

The earliest outline of a distinctive colonial policy for the new discoveries was drawn up by Columbus shortly before his second voyage. In this paper he proposed that emigration should be allowed at first up to the number of two thousand households to Española; that three or four towns should be founded, with municipal governments similar to those in Castile; that gold hunting should be restricted to actual settlers in the towns; that there should be churches with parish priests or friars to conduct divine worship and convert the Indians; that no

do set sail with thirty-two ships and two
d five hundred colonists and adventurers,
est number in any one expedition in early
n history. Among them was Las Casas, the
n and advocate of the Indians. The ex-
s of these colonists bring out into strong light
lexing problem of the situation. The num-
paniards in the colony before the arrival of
e was about three hundred.[1] Many of these
rvivors of the criminals taken over by Co-
on his third voyage. Bobadilla, in pursuance
eak policy of conciliation, had allowed them
d the system of compulsory labor by the
; and the indignant Las Casas records that
ht see rabble who had been scourged or
of their ears in Castile lording it over the
hiefs.[2] Most of the Spaniards had Indian
es, and other Indians as household servants
aughted laborers.[3] The Spaniards who had
on mining were in poverty; the farmers were
osperous, and directed their efforts to breed-
e and cultivating cassava and yams and
tatoes.[4]

was the community now overrun with
kers and new settlers. The prospectors
off to the mines, but found there unex-
bor, "as gold did not grow on the trees."
climate, the failing supply of food quickly

colonist should go off prospecting without a license
or without having given his oath to return to his
town and render a faithful account of his findings;
that all gold brought in should be smelted at once
and stamped with the town mark; that one per cent.
be set apart for the support of the church; that the
privilege of gold hunting be limited to certain seasons so that planting and other business would not
be neglected; that there should be free opportunity
to all to go on voyages of discovery; that one or two
ports in Española be made the exclusive ports of
entry, and that all ships from the island should report at Cadiz.[1]

In the following January, Columbus, further instructed by experience as to the actual difficulties
of establishing a colony in a distant tropical island,
supplemented these proposals with the recommen-
dations which were summarized above.[2] The most
notable addition is the suggestion to ship to Spain
captives taken from the cannibals so as to pay for
the importations of cattle and provisions. Of all
the productions of this new world the only ones immediately marketable in Spain were the precious
metals and the inhabitants. These two documents
reveal Columbus's ideas as to a colonial policy for
Spain. They forecast several features of the system as subsequently developed, and establish his
right to be regarded as the pioneer law-giver of the

Las Casas, *Historia*, III., 33.
[2] *Ibid.*, 3.   [3] *Ibid.*, 5.   [4] *Ibid.*, 35.

[1] Thacher, *Columbus*, III., 94–113, also translated in Amer.
Hist. Assoc., *Report*, 1894, pp. 452 ff.   [2] See above, p. 37.

New World, a distinction which has been eclipsed by his failure or misfortunes as viceroy.

In the narrative of the second voyage of Columbus the beginnings of the history of the colony in Española were touched upon.[1] It was there noted that after the suppression of the revolt of the natives in 1495 a system of tribute was imposed upon them. In commutation of this tribute, perhaps in pursuance of the suggestion of the cacique Guarionex,[2] the labor of the Indians on the farms of the Spaniards was accepted, this being the manner in which they rendered services to their own caciques.[3]

Two years later, one of the conditions exacted by the followers of the Spanish insurgent Roldan, when they came to terms with the admiral, was to be granted citizenship and lands. In fulfilling this last stipulation Columbus allotted to each of them the cultivated lands of the Indians, apportioning to one ten thousand cassava plants or hillocks and to another twenty thousand. These allotments, repartimientos, or encomiendas, as they were subsequently called, carried with them the enforced labor of the Indians,[4] and were the beginning of a system almost universally applied in Spanish America to make the colonies self-supporting.

[1] See above, chap. iv.
[2] Las Casas, *Historia*, II., 103.
[3] Herrera, *Historia General*, dec. I., lib. III., chap. xiii.
[4] Las Casas, *Historia*, I., 373. Las Casas draws no other distinction between " repartimiento " and " encomienda " than that noted in the text, that " encomienda " was the later term.

The next advance in the d institutions was made under Ovando, who came out in 15 Bobadilla and upon whom fe lishing ordered life there. scrupulous integrity and unb the Spaniards, but relentless and terrible blows if convin tended Indian revolt. Las of some instances of these blackened Ovando's name, a ing his many admirable qua which Oviedo dwells with e

An examination of Ovand reveals the ideas entertaine nand and Isabella. Their fi vide for the kindly treatme maintenance of peaceful rel the settlers. The Indians were to help in the colle wages for their labor. stricted to natives of Sp arms to the natives, nor w converts from Mohammed thither. Negro slaves bor be taken to Española, bu should be exercised not against Christianity.[1]

[1] Herrera, *Historia General*, d *Spanish Conquest*, I., 127-130.

exhausted them, and they straggled back to the town stricken with fever. Here, without shelter, they died faster than the clergy could conduct funerals.[1] More than a thousand perished thus and five hundred were disabled by sickness. The fate that impended over the American soldiers in Cuba in 1898 fell upon these new settlers without mitigation.

Ovando had been ordered to treat the Indians as free men and subjects of the king and queen, but he soon had to report that if left to themselves they would not work even for wages and withdrew from all association with the Spaniards, so that it was impossible to teach or convert them. To meet the first of these difficulties, the sovereigns instructed him, March, 1503, to establish the Indians in villages, to give them lands which they could not alienate, to place them under a protector, to provide a school-house in each village that the children might be taught reading, writing, and Christian doctrine, to prevent oppression by their chiefs, to suppress their native ceremonies, to make efforts to have the Indians marry their wives in due religious form, and to encourage the intermarriage of some Christians with the Indians, both men and women.[2]

To meet the difficulty of getting the Indians to work, a royal order was issued in December, 1503,

---

[1] Las Casas, *Historia*, III., 36.
[2] Fabié, *Ensayo Historico*, 52; Herrera, *Historia General*, dec. I., lib. V., chap. xii.

that the Indians should be compelled to work on
buildings, in collecting gold, and farming for such
wages as the governor should determine. For such
purposes the chiefs must furnish specified numbers of men, "as free men, however, and not servants." [1] These two edicts fairly represent the
colonial policy of the crown and its intentions to
civilize the Indians. As time went on these two
lines of effort were more and more evenly carried
out; but at first attention was principally directed
to making use of the labor of the Indians, and only
incidentally to their systematic civilization. [2]

In pursuance of the royal order, Ovando allotted
to one Spaniard fifty and to another one hundred
Indians under their chiefs; other allotments, or repartimientos, were assigned to cultivate lands for
the king. These assignments were accompanied
with a patent reading, "To you, so-and-so, are given
in trust ("se os encomiendan") under chief so-and-
so, fifty or one hundred Indians, with the chief, for
you to make use of them in your farms and mines,
and you are to teach them the things of our holy
Catholic faith." [3]   At first the term of service in the
mines lasted six months and later eight months. As
the mines were from thirty to two hundred and fifty
miles distant this involved prolonged separations of

---

[1] Las Casas, *Historia*, III., 65; Fabié, *Ensayo Historico*, 57;
text in *Docs. Ined. de Indias*, XXXI., 209.

[2] Las Casas, *Historia*, III., 70. See Van Middeldyk, *History
of Puerto Rico*, 29, 45, for tables illustrating Indian allotments
in that island.   [3] Las Casas, *Historia*, III., 71.

husbands and wives, and upon the wives fell the entire burden of supporting the families. According to Las Casas this separation, the consequent overwork of both husbands and wives, and the general despair led to high infant mortality and a very great diminution of births. If the same conditions existed throughout the world the human race, he writes, would soon die out.[1]

The rapid melting away of the population of the West Indies during the first quarter of a century of the Spanish rule was the first appearance in modern times of a phenomenon of familiar occurrence in the later history of the contact of nature peoples with a ruling race.[2] Through the impassioned descriptions of Las Casas, which were translated into the principal languages of Europe, it is the most familiar instance of the kind; and, as a consequence, it is generally believed that the Spaniards were cruel and destructive above all other colonists, in spite of the fact that in their main-land settlements the native stock still constitutes numerically a very numerous element in the population. That the wars of subjugation were very destructive of life is only too clear; that famine followed war to prolong its ravages is equally certain; that the average

[1] Las Casas, *Historia*, III., 72.
[2] Waitz, *Introduction to Anthropology* (London, 1863), 144–167, amasses a great variety of evidence illustrating this decay of population. Cf. also Peschel, *Races of Man*, 152–155; and G. Stanley Hall, *Adolescence*, II., 648–748, on "Treatment of Adolescent Races."

Spaniard recklessly and cruelly overworked the
Indians there is no doubt.

Nevertheless, there were other and more subtle
causes in operation. Diseases were imported by the
whites, which were mitigated for them by some degree of acquired immunity, but which raged irresistibly through a population without that defence.
Of these new diseases small - pox was one of the
most destructive.[1] In the epidemic of small - pox
in 1518 the natives, Peter Martyr reports,[2] died
like sheep with the distemper. Small - pox appeared in Mexico at the beginning of the conquest.
When Pamfilo de Narvaez was despatched to recall
Cortés, a negro on one of his ships was stricken
with the disease, which was soon communicated
to the Indians and raged irresistibly, sweeping off
in some provinces half the population.[3] Mortality
was greatly increased because in their ignorance
they plunged into cold water when attacked. The
disease seems to have been particularly fatal to
women. Eleven years later came an epidemic of a
disease called "sarampion," which carried off great
numbers.[4] At more or less long intervals the Indian
populations were swept by a pestilence from which

[1] On the small-pox, see Waitz, *Introduction to Anthropology*,
145.
[2] Peter Martyr, *De Rebus Oceanicis*, dec. III., lib. VIII.;
Hakluyt, *Voyages*, V., 296.
[3] Motolinia, *Historia de los Indios de la Nueva España*, in *Col.
de Docs. para la Hist. de Mexico*, I., 15; Herrera, *Historia
General*, dec. II., lib. X., chap. xviii.
[4] Motolinia, *Historia*, 15.

the whites were exempt. It was known in Mexico as the "matlazahuatl," and in 1545 and 1576 it caused an enormous mortality.[1] Humboldt conjectured that possibly this might be the same as the pestilence which visited Massachusetts in 1618, sweeping off the vast majority of the Indian population.[2] Jourdanet finds evidence of endemic typhus and pleuropneumonia in Mexico at the time of the conquest, but that yellow fever did not appear until the next century. Besides the famines consequent upon the conquest, those incident to a failure of the crops were a wide-reaching cause of depopulation from which Mexico on occasion suffered comparably to India in the nineteenth century.[3]

Just what the population of Española was when Columbus discovered the island there is no means of knowing, but there can be no doubt that the estimates of Las Casas that there were over three million people in the island is a wild exaggeration.[4] Oscar Peschel, an experienced ethnologist and a critical historian, after weighing all the evidence, places the population of Española in 1492 at less than three

---

[1] See Jourdanet, "Considérations Médicales sur la Campagne de Fernand Cortés," in his ed. of Bernal Diaz, 895.

[2] Cf. extract from Johnson, "Wonder-working Providence," in Hart, *American History Told by Contemporaries*, I., 368; H. H. Bancroft, *Mexico*, III., 756.

[3] Cf. Humboldt, *New Spain*, I., 121.

[4] Las Casas, *Historia*, III., 101. The prevalent Spanish estimate was one million one hundred thousand, *ibid.*; Oviedo, *Historia General*, I., 71; Peter Martyr, *De Rebus Oceanicis*, III., dec. III., lib. VIII.; Hakluyt, *Voyages*, V., 296.

hundred thousand and at over two hundred thousand. In 1508 the number of the natives was sixty thousand; in 1510, forty-six thousand; in 1512, twenty thousand; and in 1514, fourteen thousand.[1]

In 1548 Oviedo doubted whether five hundred natives of pure stock remained, and in 1570 only two villages of Indians were left. A similar fate befell all the islands. Accelerated as this extermination was by the cruelty and greed of the early Spanish colonists, the history of the native stock in the Sandwich Islands, which has been exempt from conquest and forced labor, indicates that it was perhaps inevitable, without the adjunct of ruthless exploitation. The same phenomenon appeared among the less numerous aborigines of our eastern states where there was little enslavement of the Indians. But here there was no Las Casas, and the disappearance of the natives was regarded as providential.

Daniel Denton in 1670, in recording the rapid decrease of the Indian population of Long Island, quaintly observes: "It hath been generally observed that where the English come to settle, a divine hand makes way for them by removing or cutting off the Indians either by wars one with the other or by some raging mortal disease."[2]

The melancholy fate of these nature folk and the romantic incidents of the Spanish conquest have

---

[1] Peschel, *Zeitalter der Entdeckungen*, 430; Oviedo, *Historia General*, I., 71; Lopez de Velasco, *Geografia y Descripcion*, 97.

[2] Denton, *New York* (ed. 1902), 45.

naturally obscured the more humdrum phases of their earlier colonial history, and have given rise to such erroneous assertions as the following: "Not the slightest thought or recognition was given during the first half-century of the invasion to any such enterprise as is suggested by the terms colonization, the occupancy of soil for husbandry and domestication."[1] How far from true such a sweeping statement is, appears from the equipment of Columbus's second voyage, from the offer of supplies for a year to all settlers in 1498,[2] and from the provisions made by the sovereigns to promote colonization in connection with his third voyage, which have been summarized in an earlier chapter.

In addition to the arrangements there quoted, in order to promote colonization the king and queen exempted from the payment of duties necessary articles taken to the Indies; and granted a similar exemption upon articles of every sort imported from the Indies.[3] Further, they ordered that there should be prepared a sort of public farm open to cultivation by Spaniards in the island, who should receive as a loan to start with fifty bushels of wheat and corn and as many couple of cows and mares and other beasts of burden.[4] This loan was to be paid back at harvest with a tenth part of the crop; the rest the cultivators could retain for themselves or

[1] G. E. Ellis, in Winsor, *Narr. and Crit. Hist.*, II., 301.
[2] *Memorials of Columbus*, 91; Navarrete, *Viages*, II., 167.
[3] Fabié, *Ensayo Historico*, 32.
[4] *Memorials of Columbus*, 74; Navarrete, *Viages*, II., 183.

sell. In July of the same year, 1497, in response to petitions from actual and proposed settlers in Española for lands for cultivating grain, fruits, and sugar-cane, and for erecting sugar and grist mills, the king and queen authorized Columbus to allot lands free of charge to actual settlers, subject to the condition that they live there four years and that all the precious metals be reserved for the crown.[1]

Five years later Luis de Arriaga, a gentleman of Seville, proposed to take out to the island two hundred Biscayans, or more, with their wives, to be settled in four villages; and the sovereigns on their part offered free passage for these colonists, free land for cultivation, and exemption from taxes excepting tithes and first-fruits for five years. Large reservations of the sources of monopoly profits, such as mines, salt-pits, Indian trade, harbors, etc., were made for the crown; but the terms for farming were certainly liberal. Arriaga was unable to get together more than forty married people, and they soon petitioned for a reduction of the royalties payable on gold mined and for other concessions. These were granted, but the colony did not preserve its identity and soon merged in the mass.[2]

In 1501 the crown, to promote trade with the Indies, and especially exports from Castile, relieved

---

[1] *Memorials of Columbus*, 127–129; Navarrete, *Viages*, II., 215.

[2] *Docs. Ined. de Indias*, XXX., 526; Las Casas, *Historia*, III., 36–38; Southey, *History of the West Indies*, 77.

this commerce entirely from the payment of duties.[1] Still further, as early as 1503, Ovando was instructed to promote the cultivation of mulberry-trees that the silk culture might be developed.[2]

One of the most remarkable efforts of the Spanish government to promote the colonization of the New World by actual workers was that made in 1518 in response to Las Casas' representations of the evils of the compulsory labor of the Indians. Those that would go to Terra-Firma were offered free passage and their living on board ship, promised the attendance of physicians, and upon arrival at their destination lands and live-stock; for twenty years they were to be relieved of the alcabala, or tax on exchanges, and all taxes on their produce except the church tithes. Further premiums were offered of $200 for the first one who produced twelve pounds of silk; of $150 for the one who first gathered ten pounds of cloves, ginger, cinnamon, or other spices; of $100 for the first fifteen hundredweight of woad, and $65 for the first hundredweight of rice.[3]

A formal expression of contemporary opinion in Española as to the needs of the colony towards the end of Ovando's administration affords us an interesting picture of its general condition and of the

---

[1] *Docs. Ined. de Indias*, XXXI., 62 ff.; Fabié, *Ensayo Historico*, 40.

[2] Herrera, *Historia General*, dec. I., lib. V., chap. xii.; Southey, *History of the West Indies*, 91.

[3] *Col. de Docs. Ined. de Ultramar*, IX. (*Docs. Leg.*, II.), 77–83; Fabié, *Ensayo Historico*, 163–164.

spirit of the inhabitants, and of the defects in the government trade policy. Two proctors or representatives of the people presented a petition to King Ferdinand in 1508 in which they ask for assistance in building stone churches and additional endowments for their hospitals; for permission to engage in the local coasting trade; that all the natives of Spain be allowed to engage in trade with Española; that their imports of wine be not limited to that grown near Seville; that they may bring in Indians from the neighboring islands, which are of little use and not likely to be settled; that by this means the Indians could be more easily converted; for the devotion of the product of salt-mines to the building of public works; for the establishment of a higher court of appeals; for more live-stock; that no descendants of Jews, Moors, or of heretics, burned or reconciled, down to the fourth generation, be allowed to come to the island; that hogs be considered common property as they have multiplied so greatly and run wild; that the towns be ennobled and granted arms, likewise the island; that the artisans who come to the island may be compelled to stick to their trades and not be allowed, as they desire, to desert them and to secure an allotment of Indians; for the choice of sheriffs and notaries by election of the regidores, etc.[1]

That the Spanish authorities were not indifferent to the establishment of agricultural colonies in the West Indies is abundantly evident. That their suc-

[1] *Col. de Docs. Ined. de Ultramar*, V. (*Docs. Leg.*, I.), 125–142.

cess was not more striking was quite as much the result of the superior attractiveness of Mexico and Peru as of any defects in their policy. The early history of Española compares not unfavorably with the early years of Virginia. Had a California of 1849 been as accessible to the Virginia of 1620 as Mexico was to Española in 1520, Virginia might have suffered a similar eclipse.

CHAPTER XV

SPANISH COLONIAL GOVERNMENT AND ADMIN-
ISTRATION

(1493-1821)

THE legal relation between Spain and her American dominions was strikingly like that which
the promoters of the American Revolution maintained to be the proper relation between England
and her colonies.   James Madison, in 1800, wrote,
"The fundamental principle of the Revolution was
that the colonies were co-ordinate members with
each other and with Great Britain of an empire
united by a common executive sovereign":[1] so far
the description exactly applies to the relation between Castile and New Spain and Peru.   "The
legislative power," Madison goes on to say, "was
maintained to be as complete in each American
parliament as in the British Parliament."   Similarly,
legislative detachment and co-ordination existed in
the Spanish Empire; but since neither Spain nor the
Spanish colonies enjoyed self-government, there was
no question of parliamentary supremacy.   The laws
of Castile were made by the king with the advice

[1] Madison, *Writings*, IV., 533.

of his councils; and the laws of Spanish America were made by the king through the Council of the Indies. In fine, Spanish America did not belong to Spain, but was a part of the hereditary domains of the sovereigns of Castile as heirs of Queen Isabella, with which the cortes of Castile had little more to do than with the kingdom of Naples or the Netherlands.

That English political institutions were transplanted to America by the colonists is one of the most familiar as well as one of the most fundamental facts in our history. That contemporary Spanish institutions and the general machinery of government were likewise transplanted and adapted to Spanish-American conditions is less familiar but not less important.

The first step in framing an administrative system for the government of their new possessions was taken by the sovereigns in May, 1493, when they appointed a member of their council, Juan de Fonseca, archdeacon of Seville, to act with the admiral in making preparations for a second voyage.[1] For the next ten years, until the establishment of the Casa de Contractacion, and, in fact, during the entire reign of Ferdinand and Isabella, Fonseca was practically the colonial minister and zealously guarded the interests of the crown. His character has been blackened by the partial biographers of Columbus, who have followed the lead of Ferdinand

[1] Navarrete, *Viages*, II., 48.

Columbus and of Las Casas; but though some of his appointments were bad, and he was opposed to some of the plans of Columbus and to the policy of Cortés, he retained the confidence of his sovereigns, who steadily promoted him. Bernaldez, the curate of Los Palacios, the friend and host of Columbus, tells us that Fonseca deserved his promotions and that he sustained all his dignities worthily.[1]

The second decade of Spain's colonial administration opens with the establishment at Seville, the mercantile capital of Castile, of the Casa de Contractacion, "at once a board of trade, a commercial court, and a clearing-house for the American traffic."[2] In its earliest form this body consisted of a treasurer, an auditor, and a factor or manager. The casa, or house, was to contain ample stores of the commodities to be shipped to the Indies, and its officials were to exercise close supervision over all commerce with the Indies, Barbary, and the Canaries, to select proper captains for the ships, and to keep themselves informed regarding conditions in the Indies and ways of extending trade.

In a measure, this ordinance formally established what had been gradually growing up under Fonseca and his assistants.[3] As subsequently developed, the

[1] Bernaldez, *Historia de los Reyes Catolicos*, chap. cxx., in Mass. Hist. Soc., *Collections*, 3d series, VIII., 36.

[2] Armstrong, *The Emperor Charles V.*, II., 47.

[3] Ordinance of January 20 and June 5, 1503, Navarrete, *Viages*, II., 285; H. H. Bancroft, *Central America*, I., 282, *n.*; Prescott, *Ferdinand and Isabella*, II., 491.

Casa de Contractacion consisted of the president, the treasurer, the auditor, and the manager—the four bearing the title of "judges *ex officio*"—three assistant judges, and the attorney-general, and a steadily growing body of subordinate officials, among whom may be noted a high-sheriff, inspector-general, pilot-major (to examine and license pilots), the post-master-general ("correo mayor"),[1] etc.

In 1552 a professorship of cosmography and navigation was established under the control of the casa, and all candidates for the office of pilot were obliged to take the courses of study provided in these subjects.[2] A regulation of great importance to science, established by Philip II., was the requirement that all pilots and ship-masters should keep an accurate daily record of their course, of the weather, and of the ocean currents, as well as a precise description of all shores coasted, etc., which were to be deposited with the pilot-major in Seville.[3] The efficiency of this institution became widely known, and it was imperfectly imitated by Henry VIII. of England in the incorporation of the association called the Trinity House, at Deptford, in 1512,[4] which is still in existence, although its most important functions were taken over in 1853 by the Board of Trade.[5]

[1] Cf. H. H. Bancroft, *Central America*, I., 282, for further details.

[2] *Recopilacion de Leyes de las Indias*, lib. IX., tit. XXIII., leyes 5 and 25. [3] *Ibid.*, ley 37.

[4] Anderson, *History of Commerce*, year 1512.

[5] *Encyclopædia Britannica* (9th ed.), art., "Trinity House."

The variety of the political questions presented by the organization of the Spanish possessions in the New World led gradually to the formation of a new royal council, which took its place beside the Council of Castile, the Council of State, and the other royal councils. At first these matters had been considered by the sovereigns in consultation with Bishop Fonseca. In 1507 Governor Ovando and the officials of the Casa de Contractacion were ordered to confer with Fonseca and Lope de Conchillos, the king's secretary in Indian affairs.[1] These two men continued in charge for several years, consulting in cases of some difficulty informally with other members of the king's council.[2] It would appear that as early as 1509 their decisions were recorded as those of the Council of the Indies.[3]

With the accession of King Charles I. (Emperor Charles V.) a nucleus of the more extensive council later established was formed in 1517 with seven members, among whom were Fonseca, Francis de los Cobos, one of Charles's ablest ministers, and Peter Martyr, the first historian of America. In this group Fonesca's influence was paramount.[4] The formal organization of this body as a permanent in-

[1] Herrera, *Historia General*, dec. I., lib. VII., chap. i.; Las Casas, *Historia*, III., 269.

[2] Herrera, *Historia General*, dec. I., lib. X., chap. vi.

[3] Saco, *Historia de la Esclavitud en el Nuevo Mundo*, 138, cites a manuscript volume in the library of the Academy of History, Madrid, entitled, *Extracto del Indice General de los Registros del Consejo de Indias desde 1509 á 1608.*

[4] Herrera, *Historia General*, dec. II., lib. II., chap. xx.

dependent council in distinction from a varying group of advisers on Indian affairs dates from August 4, 1524. At its head was placed Garcia de Loaysa, the general of the Dominican order and the king's confessor. In October, when the king was ill with the quartan fever, he authorized the council to despatch all matters relating to justice without waiting to consult him.[1]

In 1542 and later the composition of the council was specified in detail. The high chancellor of the Indies was to be president; the number of ordinary councillors who were lawyers might be enlarged as business grew, but should be eight for the present; an attorney and two secretaries, and a deputy of the high chancellor came next in order. All these were to be of noble birth, pure lineage, and God-fearing. In addition there were to be three reporters and a clerk, four expert accountants, a treasurer, two treasury solicitors or attorneys, an historian,[2] and a cosmographer and mathematician, a judge to appraise damages, an advocate, a proctor of the poor, a chaplain, four ushers, and a sheriff.[3]

To this body was intrusted the supreme legislative and judicial control, under the king, of Spanish America. It was to meet twice daily except on church holidays, three hours in the morning and two in the afternoon; and the different branches of

---

[1] Herrera, *Historia General*, dec. III., lib. VI., chap. xiv.
[2] The historian Herrera held this position.
[3] *Recopilacion de Leyes*, lib. II., tit. II., ley 1.

business had each its allotted week-day. Business might be divided among "halls" or committees, but legislation of general importance must be acted on in full council and required a two-thirds vote for passage. The council was to use all available means to accumulate information about the Indies so that action would be based on knowledge.[1] It was also felt to be desirable, although not enforced by law, that some of the members of the council should have seen official service in the Indies so as to be able to give advice based on experience. Besides making the laws for the New World and serving as the final court of appeal, the council served as an advisory or nominating board in regard to all civil and ecclesiastical offices in the Indies.[2] The literary monument of nearly two centuries of its activity is the great *Recopilacion de Leyes de los Reinos de las Indias*, a body of law which, in spite of shortcomings as to finance and variances with modern ideas, is, in its broad humanity and consideration of the general welfare of the king's American subjects, far superior to anything that can be shown for the English or French colonies.[3]

In the history of English colonial policy in the

---

[1] *Recopilacion de Leyes*, leyes 5 and 6; cf. also Herrera's account of its duties and methods; *Descripcion de las Indias Occidentales*, chaps. xxx., xxxi.; H. H. Bancroft, *Central America*, I., 280.

[2] Solorzano, *Politica Indiana* (ed. 1703), lib. V., chap. xv., 463.

[3] On the history of this code, see H. H. Bancroft, *Central America*, I., 285–288; on other collections of the colonial laws, see H. H. Bancroft, *Mexico*, III., 550.

eighteenth century the Board of Trade and Plantations, in its advisory and judicial functions, suggests some comparison with the Spanish Council of the Indies, but it was a much weaker and less effective body. In name the English India Council of our own day challenges a comparison with its Spanish prototype, but its similarities are on the whole superficial: it is mainly advisory in character, has no power of initiation, and only a very limited power of veto. The making of laws, which was so important a part of the work of the Spanish council, under the English system for India falls to the lot of the governor-general and his council, as specially expanded for the purpose.[1]

Turning now to the Spanish organization in America, we observe a general disposition to adjust the existing machinery of Spanish administration to the problem of governing the colonies, just as it was the policy of the crown to assimilate the laws of the Indies as far as possible to those of Spain.[2] In 1507 the towns in Española sent two delegates to Spain to petition the king for the privileges possessed by municipalities in Spain.[3] The request was granted, and in addition coats of arms were bestowed upon fourteen towns. A court independent of the governor was established in 1510 to hear appeals from the decisions of the governor's justices.

[1] Ilbert, *The Government of India*, 113, 118.
[2] *Recopilacion de Leyes*, lib. II., tit. II., ley 13.
[3] Herrera, *Historia General*, dec. I., lib. VII., chap. ii.

This may be taken as the beginning of the Audiencia, or supreme court, of Española, a body which also became the mouth-piece of colonial needs by presenting memorials to the Council of the Indies.[1]

It is particularly interesting to find conventions of the proctors or delegates of the towns, meeting to take common action for pressing their needs. For example, in 1518 the proctors of the towns met and petitioned for freer commerce with Spain.[2] By 1540 such meetings were annual in Cuba.[3] In 1542 this inchoate cortes petitioned the king that each householder might import four negroes free of duty.[4] In 1530 Charles V. accorded the city of Mexico the first place in New Spain and the first vote in the congresses "that meet by our command. Without our command it is not our intention or will that the cities and towns of the Indies meet in convention."[5] The whole drift of Spanish political life in the sixteenth century, however, was towards the strengthening of the power of the crown and the loss by the cortes of its legislative function; and traces of an opposite tendency in America were sporadic and temporary. The government of Spanish America was pre-eminently monarchical, and a consideration of its political machinery may well begin with the

[1] Cf. H. H. Bancroft, *Central America*, I., 269.
[2] Saco, *Historia de la Esclavitud en el Nuevo Mundo*, 86.
[3] *Ibid.*, 179; Alaman, *Historia de Mejico*, I., 39.
[4] Saco, *Historia de la Esclavitud*, 184.
[5] "Se juntar," *Recopilacion de Leyes*, lib. IV., tit. VIII., ley 2; Alaman, *Historia de Mejico*, I., 39.

representative and counterpart of the king, the viceroy.

In the year 1574 the Spanish-American world was officially described as consisting of two kingdoms: New Spain, comprising the main-land and islands north of the isthmus, and also that part of South America which is now Venezuela; and Peru, comprising the isthmus and all the territory from New Spain to Patagonia except Brazil. The kingdom of New Spain was subdivided into four audiencias, or supreme court districts, and seventeen or eighteen "governments." The court districts were Mexico, Española, including the other islands and Venezuela, New Galicia, and Guatemala. The viceroyalty of Peru contained five audiencias—Lima, Los Charcas, Quito, New Granada, and Panama—and ten governments.[1]

The viceroy was the personal representative of the king, and was to govern and labor for the welfare of the king's subjects and vassals as he would do if present in person.[2] Over seventy laws in the *Recopilacion* are devoted to specifying his duties, and a conscientious ruler found it a position of arduous labor and trying responsibility.[3] The fourth viceroy, Don Martin de Enriquez, informed his successor that he was expected to be the father

---

[1] Lopez de Velasco, *Geografia y Descripcion*, 40, 41.

[2] *Recopilacion de Leyes*, lib. III., tit. III., ley 1.

[3] On the daily routine of the viceroy of Peru, see Ulloa, *Voyage*, II., 41, 42.

of the people, the patron of monasteries and hospitals, the protector of the poor, and particularly of the widows and orphans of the conquerors, and the old servants of the king, all of whom would suffer were it not for the relief afforded them by the viceroy.[1] It was the duty of the outgoing viceroy to draw up a general report embodying information and counsel for his successors. These reports constitute to-day one of our most complete and trustworthy sources of knowledge.[2]

The normal term of office was three years, lengthened in the eighteenth century to five, but it could be extended or shortened by the king.[3] The first two viceroys reigned fifteen and fourteen years respectively. From 1535 down to 1821' sixty-two viceroys held the office. In the seventeenth century the salary of the viceroy of New Spain was twenty thousand ducats and that of the viceroy of Peru thirty thousand ducats.[4] In the middle of the eighteenth century the salary of the viceroy of Mexico was fixed at sixty thousand pesos, twelve thousand of which he was expected to devote to his captain-general.[5] The increase was more nominal

[1] H. H. Bancroft, *Mexico*, II., 661.

[2] For those of viceroys of Peru that have been published, see Winsor, *Narr. and Crit. Hist.*, VIII., 342; for Mexico, cf. H. H. Bancroft, *Mexico*, III., 551.

[3] *Recopilacion de Leyes*, lib. III., tit. III., ley 71; Alaman, *Historia de Mejico*, I., 44.

[4] *Recopilacion de Leyes*, lib. III., tit. III., ley 72. The ducat equals approximately $2.25.

[5] Alaman, *Historia de Mejico*, I., 44.

than actual, owing to the gradual fall in the value of money. As appears from the difference in the salary, the viceroyalty of Peru ranked as a higher dignity than that of New Spain, and successful vice-roys of New Spain were often promoted to Peru.[1]

As the Spanish rule extended in America, the great distances required additions to the number of independent governments; of these, two were viceroyalties, New Granada (created in 1717) and Buenos Ayres (1778); the other and lesser divisions, styled captaincies-general, were Guatemala (1527), Venezuela (1773), Cuba (1777), Chili (1778). The powers and duties of the captain-general were similar to those of the viceroy; he was the king of a smaller kingdom. In Venezuela his term of office was usually seven years and his salary nine thousand pesos.[2]

At the expiration of their term of service all administrative officers had to undergo a "residencia," an inquest into their conduct in office. One or more commissioners appointed for the purpose opened a court, at which all persons with grievances or injustice to complain of against the outgoing official could present their charges. The residencia for a viceroy was limited to six months. The commissioner then prepared his report of the hearing, and the

---

[1] Ulloa describes the arrival of a new viceroy, *Voyage*, II., 46–52. He thought the ceremonials excessive and demoralizing, *Noticias Secretas*, 452.

[2] Depons, *Voyage to the Eastern Part of Terra-Firma*, II., 17.

papers were forwarded to the Council of the Indies for the final decision. This method of enforcing responsibility was of varying efficacy. Depons, who lived several years in Caracas, said, "I resign all criticism on its operation to those who know the seductive influence of Plutus over the feeble and pliant Themis." [1] A viceroy of Peru compared the residencia "to the whirlwinds which we are wont to see in the squares and streets, that serve only to raise the dust, chaff, and other refuse and set it on our heads." [2] Sometimes favor at court exempted a viceroy from a residencia. [3]

The only other check on the arbitrary powers of the viceroy was that exercised by the appropriate audiencia, which combined the functions performed in Spain by the chanceries of the different kingdoms and by the Council of the Indies. The audiencia was, therefore, at the same time, the viceroy's or governor's council and the highest colonial court of appeal. The number of these bodies gradually increased until Philip IV., in the seventeenth century, divided his dominions beyond the sea into twelve audiencias—Santo Domingo, Mexico, Panama, Lima, Guatemala, Guadalajara, Bogotá, La Plata, Quito, Manila, Chili, Buenos Ayres. The executive in these lesser subdivisions was the governor and captain-

[1] Depons, *Voyage to the Eastern Part of Terra-Firma*, II., 25.

[2] Helps, *Spanish Conquest in America* (new ed.), III., 102–109, traces the history of the institution. Presumably the residencia was more effective with subordinate officials.

[3] Alaman, *Historia de Mejico*, I., 43.

general, who was *ex officio* president of the audience. The number of members of the audience depended upon its position and importance. The royal audience of Mexico, for example, consisted of eight auditors (oidores), or civil judges, four alcaldes de crimen (criminal judges), and two prosecuting attorneys, one for civil, the other for criminal cases, a sheriff, etc.[1] In the subordinate audiences the number of auditors was less and they served as criminal judges as well.[2]

As a council the audience deliberated with its president, or, in Mexico and Peru, with the viceroy, on appointed days, in regard to the more weighty or perplexing questions of government. Such a session was called an "acuerdo."[3] The executive, however, had no vote in matters of justice, but he could determine whether a question was really one of justice or political in character.[4] Persons who felt themselves wronged by any act or decision of the viceroy could appeal to the audience.[5] The subordinate audiences could communicate independently of their president to the viceroy, and the principal or royal audiences equally independently to the king. If a vacancy occurred in the viceroyalty or government the audience assumed the adminis-

---

[1] *Recopilacion de Leyes*, lib. II., tit XV., ley 3.

[2] *Ibid.*, ley 4; Solorzano, *Politica Indiana* (ed. 1703), 394.

[3] *Recopilacion de Leyes*, lib. III., tit. III., ley 45; Depons, *Voyage*, II., 31.

[4] *Recopilacion de Leyes*, lib. II., tit. XV., ley 38.

[5] *Ibid.*, ley 35.

tration. In questions involving sums under six thousand pesos the decision of the audience was final ; in matters of greater import an appeal could be carried to the Council of the Indies.

Every three years one of the auditors was to be delegated by the viceroy or president to make a tour of inspection throughout the entire district, to inform himself as to the economic condition of the people, as to the number of churches and monasteries necessary to provide for their good, as to whether the Indians were lapsing into idolatry, as to the conduct of the corregidors, whether the slaves in the mines were instructed, whether the Indians were enslaved or employed as freight - carriers, whether the drugs in the apothecary shops were pure, etc.[1] Extraordinary precautions were taken to detach the auditors from social connections or business relations which would impair their impartiality.[2]

The administrative subdivisions of the audiences were the "gobiernos," or governments, the "corregimientos," and the "alcaldias mayores."[3] The executives for these local governments were ap-

---

[1] *Recopilacion de Leyes*, lib. II., tit. XXXI., ley 1.

[2] Cf. Depons, *Voyage*, II., 29, 30.

[3] *Recopilacion de Leyes*, lib. V., tit. II., ley 1. As the encomienda system was abolished the Indians were placed under a corregidor, who was a sort of Indian superintendent, *ibid.*, ley 3; H. H. Bancroft, *Mexico*, II., 329. The alcalde mayor was a district or county magistrate, sometimes a local governor, *ibid.*, 520.

pointed by the crown, but *ad interim* appointments could be made by the viceroy.[1]

It was only in the colonial towns, both Spanish and Indian, that there existed some degree of self-government. The conquerors often established municipal governments of their own initiative in a way that reminds one that self-government might have grown up spontaneously in Spanish America if the arm of the home government had not been so long. Thus in Darien the colonists established a municipality and elected Balboa alcalde in 1510.[2] Again, when the followers of Cortés founded Vera Cruz they elected the alcaldes and regidores making up the town council, a chief of police (alguacil mayor), treasurer, etc.[3]

In 1523 it was enacted that in founding new towns the citizens might elect the regidores unless the right to nominate them had been accorded to the commander of the colony; and this privilege was confirmed by Philip II.[4] But since in Spain the town councils had been changed from a body elected by the citizens to be a close corporation, permanent membership in which was inherited or purchased,[5]

[1] *Recopilacion de Leyes*, lib. V., tit. II., ley 4. In 1786 the local government was reorganized and the viceroyalties and captaincies-general were subdivided into intendencias. The corregidors and alcaldes mayores were then displaced by the subdelegados of the intendants, H. H. Bancroft, *Mexico*, III., 520.

[2] Irving, *Columbus*, III., 155; H. H. Bancroft, *Central America*, I., 330.   [3] Bernal Diaz, *Historia Verdadera*, chap. xlii.

[4] *Recopilacion de Leyes*, lib. IV., tit. X., ley 3.

[5] Armstrong, in Hume, *Spain*, 19.

the cabildos, or municipal councils, of Spanish America took the same course. Those in ordinary places had normally six regidores, or aldermen, and two alcaldes, or justices, elected by regidores each year.

In the larger cities the number of regidores was greater, and they were divided into different classes. For example, in Santiago, Chili, in the first half of the eighteenth century, the cabildo consisted of six regidores, part of whom inherited and part had purchased the dignity, two alcaldes, one alferez real (royal ensign), one alguacil mayor (sheriff), and a depositary or trustee of trust funds.[1] In Caracas, in Depons' time, the cabildo consisted of the governor *ex officio*, two alcaldes, twelve regidores whose positions could be bought or sold, four other regidores nominated by the king from among the Spaniards resident in the town,[2] and four other officers, the alferez real, alcalde mayor, alguacil mayor, and fiel executor (sealer of weights). These last offices were purchasable.[3] At the close of the colonial period the cabildo of the city of Mexico consisted of fifteen permanent regidores, whose dignity was entailed, who elected each year two alcaldes and every two years six honorary regidores, including a syndic, from prominent business-men or property owners.[4] It was in the cabildos only of all the

---

[1] Frézier, *Voyage*, I., 179.
[2] These honorary regidores were of recent origin.
[3] Depons, *Voyage*, II., 45.
[4] Alaman, *Historia de Mejico*, I., 57.

machinery of government that the Spanish creoles had a prominent or controlling share.

The functions of the cabildo embraced the ordinary duties of the town council—local legislation, sanitary and humane regulations, etc.[1]   In Castile the cortes had come to consist mainly of the procuradores (proctors), or delegates of the cities.   The initial steps in the development of what might have become colonial cortes have already been noticed, as well as the opposition of Charles V. to any such tendency.   The institution of proctors of the towns, however, continued to exist with narrowly defined functions.   In the sixteenth century the towns in the New World were authorized to elect proctors to represent their interests before the Council of the Indies.   In the seventeenth they were to empower resident agents in Spain to look after such matters.   These elections or commissions proceeded from the regidores of the towns.[2]   In general, these proctors of the towns may be compared with the agents maintained in London by the English colonies and even by the town of Boston.

One feature of the administrative system which now seems strange and unsuitable was the purchase and sale of offices.   One of the regular branches of the royal revenue was the income derived from the increase in public offices as the king's domains in the New World expanded, which from 1557 on was a

---

[1] Cf. Saco, *Historia de la Esclavitud*, 201, 221, 251.
[2] *Recopilacion de Leyes*, lib. IV., tit. XI.

regular part of the governmental system. The principal offices that were offered for sale and for which bids were received were those of sheriffs, city and court clerks and notaries, proctors, depositaries, ensigns, regidores, treasurers, sealers of weights and measures, assayers.[1] In 1620 it was enacted that the office of regidor should be no longer filled by election or lot, but that bids should be called for by the officials of the royal treasury during a period of thirty days, and that the persons to whom the award was made should possess the requisite qualifications for the office, giving the preference to the conquerors, the first settlers, and their descendants.[2]

This system offered opportunity for a successful business-man to become a member of the official class, thereby improving his social station and securing a permanent position for his family. The office conferred distinction, and the income from it would be a secure form of investment. The system is, of course, repugnant to present-day ideas, but it was not so in the seventeenth and eighteenth centuries. In fact, it secured the positive approval of the most eminent writer on comparative politics who knew it at first hand.[3] It is the opinion of Bancroft that the policy of salable offices "does not appear to have been attended with so many evils as might have been expected."[4] Indeed, the system

[1] *Recopilacion de Leyes*, lib. VIII., tit. XX., ley 1.
[2] *Ibid.*, ley 7.
[3] Montesquieu, *L'Esprit des Lois*, liv. V., chap. **xix**.
[4] H. H. Bancroft, *Mexico*, III., 530.

had many advantages over the practice of paying a heavy assessment to a party machine for a nomination and the chance of being elected. To most Americans to-day the letting out of public work by private contracts to the lowest bidder seems natural and a sound business policy. Perhaps in a century or so it may seem as strange to let out the paving of a street to a contractor as to call for bids for a county clerkship.

That the Spanish colonies were oppressed and exploited by the mother-country is a widely spread opinion. The well-known fact that the king derived a large net revenue from his American dominions is in itself no evidence of oppression or exploitation. Not to do so would have been a proof of extraordinarily bad finance, for the source of the net revenue was the king's royalty of one-fifth on the yield of the gold and silver mines. That the state should receive a part of the pure rent of such natural monopolies rather than it should be entirely appropriated by the lucky prospector commends itself to-day to an increasing number of people. It was calculated in the latter half of the eighteenth century that the fifth of the annual product of the mines was about $7,425,000, and that the king's net revenue from America was about $6,750,000.[1]

The main sources of government revenue in the New World besides the mining royalties were: the tribute, or poll-tax, paid by the male Indians of work-

[1] See Robertson, *History of America*, notes 196 and 197.

ing age, roughly equal in the later period to about
$2.25 per capita annually; the alcabala, or excise,
levied on goods sold, varying from two to six per
cent.; the almojarifazgo, or export and import duties,
averaging perhaps fifteen per cent.; the averia, or con-
voy tax, equalling about two per cent. on the value
of the cargoes; the receipts from the sale of offices;
the receipts from the sale of the bulls of the crusade
—*i.e.*, indulgences; monopolies of gunpowder, salt,
tobacco, and quicksilver, and a portion of the church
income. The taxes were, as a whole, much the same
as those in Spain.[1] In 1746 the total revenue of
New Spain was estimated at 3,552,680 pesos.[2] A
little less than half a century later, 1796, it had risen
to $19,400,000,[3] of which probably $3,500,000 [4]
represents the king's mining royalties, leaving about
$16,000,000 from taxation from a population of
about five million — certainly not an oppressive
amount, especially when we consider the great
wealth among the Spaniards, who constituted about
one-fifth of the population.

The burden bore unequally heavy on the Indians,
who as a class were poor and could not escape the
tribute or the indulgences. Financial corruption

[1] Cf. Bancroft, *Mexico*, III., 655–668; Robertson, *History of
America*, note 196.

[2] By Villa Segnor, in his *Teatro Americano;* Robertson, *History of America*, note 196.

[3] Bancroft, *Mexico*, III., 676.

[4] Estimated at between a fifth and a sixth on the basis of
Bancroft, *Mexico*, III., 399.

no doubt absorbed a large amount which was collected but which did not appear in the returns; yet, all in all, it does not seem that the Spanish government can be charged with exploiting the colonial population by oppressive taxes. The real burden which lay upon them was not that of intentional oppression, but that of unintelligent commercial legislation, which sacrificed the colonial opportunities to the protection of the manufactures and trade of Spain. A vastly larger sum could easily have been borne if the unproductive restrictions of the trade legislation had been relaxed earlier and more completely.

Another indication that the colonies suffered from lack of opportunities rather than from extortion is afforded by the fact that fertile regions of great natural advantages never produced revenue enough to pay the expenses of government. The Philippines, Cuba, and the other islands, Venezuela before the establishment of the Guipuzcoa commercial company, Florida, and Louisiana after 1765, were all subsidized from the treasury of New Spain to an amount of between three and four million dollars a year.[1] Peru, in her turn, contributed one hundred thousand pesos to Chili and seventy thousand to Valdivia.[2] If it had not been for the mines it is probable that Spain could neither have formed nor maintained her American empire under any such

[1] Bancroft, *Mexico*, III., 676, *n*.
[2] Roscher, *The Spanish Colonial System*, 40.

commercial policy as she pursued. Her trans-
atlantic establishments would have been feeble and
of slow growth, and very likely South and Central
America would have waited as long as North America for effective occupation, which then might have
been accomplished by Spain's later and more powerful rivals.

Without a prolonged and detailed discussion it
would be difficult to reach a general conclusion
on the government and administration of Spanish
America. Severe judgments have been passed upon
it. Justice was slow and uncertain; the evidence of
financial corruption, especially of bribery of judges
and custom-house officials, is abundant; but, after
all, the general impression derived from the narratives of English residents in New Spain and other
early travellers is that they observed no particular
contrast between governmental conditions in Europe and America. It is the opinion of the writer
that, all things considered, Spanish America was
quite as well governed as was Spain, and was, on the
whole, more prosperous; that the condition of Peru
and the rest of South America was below that of New
Spain in many respects; and that at no time in the
history of Mexico, up to within the last quarter of a
century, has the government been so good as her
people enjoyed under the abler viceroys such as
Mendoza or Velasco in the beginning, or the younger
Revillagigedo at the end of Spanish rule.

CHAPTER XVI

SPANISH EMIGRATION TO AMERICA

(1500–1600)

THE beginnings of Spanish emigration to the New World have already been outlined, and the efforts of the government and of the colonists to restrict the privilege to Spaniards of the old Christian families have been noted.[1] Yet the enforcement of these regulations was delayed, and in 1511 the Casa de Contractacion was instructed to allow any Spaniards to go to the Indies without formalities beyond registration of their names and residence.[2] In 1518, however, the earlier prohibitions were formally re-enacted and extended to include the grandsons of heretics.[3]

An interesting illustration of the thoroughness with which this rigorous sifting of emigration was later carried out, and of the completeness with which New Spain was sheltered from the invasion of heresy,

---

[1] *Docs. Ined. de Ultramar*, V., 134.   Cf. above, pp. 209, 220.

[2] Veitia Linage, *Norte de la Contractacion*, 219.

[3] *Recopilacion de Leyes*, lib. IX., tit. XXVI., ley 16.   The Jeronimite fathers wrote the king in January, 1517, from Española, that it was reported that there were many heretics in the island who had come to escape the Inquisition, *Docs. Ined. de Indias.*, I., 274.

is afforded by the case of the English merchant Tomson, whose trial for heresy in 1556 is perhaps the earliest recorded instance in Mexico of such a prosecution.[1] The strangeness of the event aroused great curiosity, and "there were that came one hundredth mile off, to see the said Auto (as they call it), for that there were never none before, that had done the like in the said country, nor could not tell what Lutheranes were, nor what it meant; for that they never heard of any such thing before."[2] This was almost forty years after the posting of Luther's theses. Perhaps an even more striking demonstration is that in an activity extending over two hundred and seventy-seven years the Inquisition put to death in Mexico only forty-one unreconciled heretics, a number surpassed in some single days in Spain in Philip II.'s time.[3]

These restrictions unquestionably conformed to prevalent public opinion in Spain and the colonies, yet here and there a protest was uttered. In 1518 the lawyer Zuazo, who was then in America as the agent of the crown, urged that the Indies be thrown open freely to emigration from all parts of the world, excluding only Moors, Jews, heretics, and their descendants.[4] The restriction of the right of emi-

---

[1] Cf. Icazbalceta, "Autos de Fe celebrados en Mexico," *Obras*, I., 279.   [2] Hakluyt, *Voyages*, XIV., 146.

[3] Icazbalceta, *Obras*, I., 316. For autos in Spain in 1559, cf. Motley, *Dutch Republic*, I., 221, 222.

[4] *Docs. Ined. de Indias*, I., 328. The Jeronimite fathers urged the same, *ibid.*, I., 287.

gration to the people of Spain was contrary to the instincts and preferences of Charles V., and in 1526 he issued an ordinance giving full liberty to all his subjects of all his kingdoms and lordships, including the empire and Genoa and all the rest, to go to, to traffic in, and to live in the Indies, "since it was reasonable after such vast territories had been discovered that they should be peopled with Christians." [1] How extensively this privilege was used it would be difficult to say. Charles granted Venezuela to the Augsburg banking-house of the Welsers [2] and the coast of Chili to the Fuggers, [3] but no German settlements resulted in either case.

That foreigners did secure licenses to go to and to trade in the Indies is indicated by the laws of 1569 requiring the Casa de Contractacion to keep an exact record of such instances, and the law of 1557 requiring such foreigners to stay in the ports and not to go into the interior. [4] The Italian Benzoni seems to have had no difficulty in going to the Indies in 1541. [5] In 1555 the English merchant Field, who had lived in Seville eighteen or twenty years, purchased a license to go to the Indies with his family, and took with him Robert Tomson, who had been in Seville only a year. [6]

[1] MS. ordinance quoted by Saco, *Historia de la Esclavitud*, 85; Herrera, *Historia General*, dec. III., lib. X., chap. xi.

[2] See Häbler, *Die Uberseeischen Unternehmungen der Welser* (1903). [3] Armstrong, *Charles V.*, II., 47.

[4] *Recopilacion de Leyes*, lib. IX., tit. XXVII., leyes 2 and 4.

[5] Benzoni, *History of the New World*, 1.

[6] Hakluyt, *Voyages*, XIV., 138, 139.

With the accession of Philip II., however, the lines were more strictly drawn; and the regulations in regard to passengers to the Indies and to foreigners reveal an elaborately developed policy to preserve, so far as European intermixture was concerned, the purity of the Spanish stock in the New World, and to prevent, so far as possible, the diffusion of knowledge in foreign countries of the wealth and resources of the king's American possessions. In regard to Spaniards the policy adopted was one of restriction and rigid supervision. No one, either native or foreigner, was allowed to go to the Indies without a permit from the crown (or in some cases from the Casa de Contractacion) under penalty of forfeiting his property. Officers of the fleets or vessels were held strictly responsible for infractions of this rule. In the code the details of these restrictions are amplified in seventy-three laws. The reason for such strict regulations covering emigration was to protect the Indies from being overrun with idle and turbulent adventurers anxious only "to get rich quickly, and not content with food and clothing, which every moderately industrious man was assured of." [1]

In 1592 all unnaturalized foreigners were prohibited from going to the Indies;[2] yet a complete exe-

[1] Velasco, *Descripcion de las Indias*, 36. Cf. the Venetian ambassador Soriano's characterization of most of the emigrants as "broken and desperate men or fugitives from justice." **Albéri**, *Relazioni Venete*, 1st series, III., 343.

[2] *Recopilacion de Leyes*, lib. IX., tit. XXVII., ley 1.

cution of the law seems not to have been attained, for the law of 1602 recognizes increasing inconveniences from foreigners going to the New World, and directs their deportation because "the ports are not safe in the things of our holy Catholic faith, and great care should be taken that no error creep in among the Indians."[1] In 1621, however, exception is made of such as are engaged in the useful mechanical arts, but the law is to be enforced against the traders in the towns.[2] Foreigners were defined to be those not born in Spain or Majorca or Minorca. This policy of exclusion was maintained to the downfall of Spain's rule on the main-land. In five years' travel in Spanish America Humboldt happened upon only one German resident.[3] The inhabitants of the remote provinces, he tells us, had difficulty in conceiving that there could be Europeans who did not speak Spanish.[4]

These strict regulations stand out in sharp contrast to the later English indifference as to what sort of people went to the colonies. The purely secular policy of Cromwell, who shipped Irish papists and rebels wholesale to the West Indies,[5] would have been impossible for the scrupulous Philip II.; but by the middle of the seventeenth century commercial and secular motives and ideals in state policy had

[1] *Recopilacion de Leyes*, lib. IX., tit. XXVII., ley 9.
[2] *Ibid.*, ley 10.   [3] Humboldt, *Travels*, VII., 441.
[4] Humboldt, *New Spain*, I., 210.
[5] Cf. *Cal. of State Pap., Col.*, I., 421, 427, 428.

nearly displaced the religious. Then again the existence in New Spain and in Peru of a large population of Christianized natives whom the crown wished to protect so far as possible from exploitation, made the question of unrestricted immigration essentially different in the Spanish colonies from what it was in the settlements of the English.

That the difference between the policies of the two home governments was not a difference between the two nations so much as between two periods and their respective ruling ideas is shown by the earlier English projects to enforce religious uniformity in the colonies.[1] Our own exclusion of laborers under contract, of speculative anarchists, and of the Chinese should not be overlooked in passing judgment on the Spanish restrictive policy.

Concurrently with this sifting of emigration the government continued to encourage the settlement of farmers and artisans in the islands. In 1519 colonists were offered exemption from taxation for twenty years. But soon Mexico, and later Peru, with their wealth of gold and silver and more salubrious climate, proved so attractive that the island colonies were threatened with depopulation.[2]

To counteract this peril, the king in 1525 offered free transportation of families to Española,[3] and in

---

[1] Cf. Eggleston, *Beginners of a Nation*, 231, 235; *Cal. of State Pap., Col.*, I., 177, 310; Hart, *American History told by Contemporaries*, I., 183. [2] See above, p. 199.
[3] Saco, *Historia de la Esclavitud*, 141.

1526 the extreme measure was adopted of prohibiting under penalty of death and confiscation migration from the islands to the continent. The founders of main-land settlements, however, were allowed to draw from the islands if they would contract to replace their recruits by an equal number of Spaniards. So severe a law was naturally a dead letter.[1]

In 1529 a new plan was tried—that of establishing feudal lordships. If any one would take over to Española fifty married couples, twenty-five free whites and twenty-five negro slaves, build a church and fort and support the clergyman, pay the freight and supply provisions for the emigrants, build their houses, give each couple two cows, two bulls, fifty sheep, one mare, ten pigs, and six chickens, and make the settlement within a year, completing twenty-five stone houses within five years and fifty within ten—he was to receive an area of about sixty square miles, with its mines (subject to the king's royalty of one-fifth), its fisheries, one-fifth of the royal income from the territory, the right of patronage for the church, etc.; and finally his family should be raised to the nobility and granted a coat of arms.[2] It is possible that the sixty laborers with their wives and a clergyman, brought to Santo Domingo in 1533 by one Bolaños under contract with the crown, came

---

[1] Saco, *Historia de la Esclavitud*, 142; Herrera, *Historia General*, dec. III., lib. X., chap. ii.

[2] Saco, *History de la Esclavitud*, 147–149.

in response to this effort,[1] but in general the allure-
ments of Mexico could not be withstood or counter-
acted.   In one period of five months (1535) there
arrived in Panama on their way to Peru six hundred white men and four hundred negro slaves.[2]   In
1551 the crown agreed to advance to Cuban planters
the capital required for building sugar-mills.   The
islands, however, never really prospered until the
relaxation of the restrictions on their trade in the
eighteenth century.

To estimate the amount of emigration from Spain
to America is very difficult, but it probably did not
average much over one thousand or one thousand
five hundred a year during the sixteenth century.
Robert Tomson tells us that in the fleet of 1556 there
were eight ships, and that on one of them, the *Carion*,
of five hundred tons burden, there were one hundred
and thirty - nine persons — men, women, and children.[3]   He estimated the Spanish population of
Mexico city at about one thousand five hundred
households.   Velasco's estimate, twenty years later,
was three thousand households.   Counting a household at five persons this would give about seven
thousand five hundred as the growth in twenty
years of the Spanish population in the city.   Velasco,
in 1574, estimated the total Spanish population of
the New World at thirty thousand five hundred

---

[1] Herrera, *Historia General*, dec. V., lib. V., chap. v.
[2] Saco, *Historia de la Esclavitud*, 164.
[3] Hakluyt, *Voyages*, XIV., 142.

households, or one hundred and fifty-two thousand five hundred people. If this population, like that of Mexico city, had doubled in twenty years we should have an average annual increase of about three thousand eight hundred from excess of births over deaths, and from immigration. It is clear, then, after making reasonable allowance for high mortality, that the annual immigration could not have furnished more than three thousand of this number, and that in all probability it was much less. The estimate, therefore, of one thousand to one thousand five hundred a year seems a reasonable one.

Nevertheless, the movement impressed contemporary observers as considerable. The Venetian ambassador Priuli, in 1576, refers to the emigration to the Indies as "the great numbers of people who have gone and go continually to those parts." [1] In 1617 the Casa de Contractacion wrote the king of the serious embarrassment occasioned by the multitude of passengers desiring to go to the Indies who came before it with incomplete or unsatisfactory credentials.[2] At a later date, in the early eighteenth century, Campillo, a minister of King Philip V., estimated the annual emigration to America at fourteen thousand,[3] but this figure is supported by no actual records. Adam Seybert placed the annual emigration to the United States from 1790 to 1810

[1] Albéri, *Relazioni Venete*, 1st series, V., 233.
[2] Veitia Linage, *Norte de la Contractacion*, 225.
[3] Colmeiro, *Hist. de la Econ. Polit.*, II., 48.

at not more than six thousand a year.[1]   It is difficult,
moreover, to see where and how any such number
as Campillo suggests could have got transportation,
for the fleet system was on the steady decline after
the treaty of Utrecht (1713).

In the previous centuries, notwithstanding the
first excitement of the conquests of Mexico and
Peru, there were no agencies of colonial companies
nor any system of indentured servants such as supplied the English colonies.   A record of the expense
of crossing the Atlantic in the sixteenth century was
made by the Englishman Miles Philips, who in
1581 paid sixty pesos for a passage from Honduras
to Spain, and provided his own chickens and bread.[2]
The peso in Mexico at this time is usually the gold
peso, which was equivalent to about three dollars.
The legal fare for such as secured passage on the
war galleons was twenty silver ducats.[3]

[1] Seybert, *Statist. Annals*, 29.
[2] Hakluyt, *Voyages*, XIV., 223.
[3] Veitia Linage, *Norte de la Contractacion*, 228.

CHAPTER XVII

RACE ELEMENTS AND SOCIAL CONDITIONS IN SPANISH AMERICA

(1500–1821)

THE preservation and civilization of a large proportion of the native stock on the continent is a feature of the Spanish colonial system remarkable in itself and inadequately appreciated by the average American, whose familiarity with the Spanish Indian policy rarely goes beyond the days of the conquest and of the extinction of the natives of the islands. To the prolonged efforts of the crown in behalf of its Indian vassals many a popular history gives less space than to the terrible stories of cruelties which Las Casas heaped up.

In Spanish America the natives from the start were regarded as the subjects of the crown of Spain, whereas in English America they were generally treated as independent nations, friends, or enemies, as the case might be; and the relations of the English crown and colonial governments to them were diplomatic rather than those of ruler and governed. The consequence was that the English did not exert over the Indians a strong protective power, but that they were left in the main to take their chances in a sort of struggle for existence. A contributing factor in shaping the different policy pursued by Spain in its final form was the conquest by Cortés and Pizarro of states of a developed civilization, themselves in turn resting on the conquest and combination of smaller political aggregates. The peoples under the sway of Montezuma and Atahualpa accepted a change of rulers with no great resistance, and became the subjects of the king of Spain, whose captains displaced their earlier conquerors. Only in the case of the wilder tribes, the "unreduced" Indians, do we have a situation more like that in English America.[1]

The inhabitants of the newly discovered tropical Africa knew Europeans only as slave-buyers and kidnappers; that a similar fate did not befall the natives of America may be attributed to the long-continued efforts of the Spanish kings and missionaries, seconded by public opinion in Spain.[2] These new subjects must be converted, must be reduced to civilized life and to regular industry. It was a compulsory process, and it bore down at times in the remoter fields of execution with terrible severity, especially on such as were not inured to work. That the Indians, excepting prisoners of war and the wild Caribs resisting conquest, should not, either in theory

[1] Cf. Farrand, *Basis of American History*, chap. xii.
[2] See Armstrong, *Charles V.*, II., 100, for petitions of the communes and the cortes for the freedom of the Indians.

or in fact, be enslaved, was from the start the policy of the crown. The encomienda system, the genesis of which has been described in an earlier chapter, tended to degenerate into a serfdom approaching slavery and capable of great abuses; but the crown tried to prevent these evils so far as possible. In the code for the Indies prepared in 1542, commonly called the "New Laws," the future enslavement of the Indians was absolutely prohibited, and all slaves whose masters could not prove a just title were to be liberated; encomiendas belonging to officials, churchmen, and charitable institutions were to be given up; encomenderos who had abused their Indians were to forfeit their holdings; no new encomiendas were to be granted, and existing ones were to lapse on the death of the holder.[1]

In securing this legislation Las Casas, "the apostle of the Indians," had been pre-eminently influential, but the practical difficulties of its execution proved insuperable.[2] The problem was not an easy one. A realm had been wrested from its earlier conquerors by the heroism and sacrifices of private adventurers: how were they to be rewarded and their families supported? That they should have great estates with a numerous body of serfs and live like the nobles in Europe seemed a practical

---

[1] Icazbalceta, *Obras*, V., 287; Bancroft, *Mexico*, II., 516. The text of the "New Laws" is given in Icazbalceta, *Documentos para la Historia de Mexico*, II., 204–227.

[2] Charles V. repealed the prohibition of encomiendas in 1545, *Recopilacion de Leyes*, lib. VI., tit. VIII., ley 4.

solution of the difficulty. That "the American conqueror with his encomienda of Indians differed little from the Andalusian or Valencian noble with his Moorish vassal peasantry"[1] was no slight confirmation of this view. On the other hand, Cortés and the Spanish crown keenly felt the unwisdom and the wrong of any such wasting of the population as had taken place in the islands. Hence, after prolonged discussion and several experiments, it was decided that the encomienda system was to go on through four generations, after which the encomiendas would lapse to the crown. Subsequent further extensions took place, and the lapse of the system was not accomplished until the eighteenth century.[2] The Indian legislation of the Spanish kings is an impressive monument of benevolent intentions which need not fear comparison with the contemporary legislation of any European country affecting the status of the working-classes.

The details of the history of the Spanish Indian policy are too voluminous for presentation in this survey of the population of Spanish America; yet they form an important and instructive chapter in the history of the contact of the "higher" and "lower" races, of which unfortunately only the tragic prologue has been made generally familiar through the wide diffusion of Las Casas' tracts on

[1] Armstrong, *Charles V.*, II., 99.

[2] *Recopilacion de Leyes*, lib. VI., tit. XI., leyes 14, 15; Humboldt, *New Spain*, I., 183. On the whole question, see Icazbalceta, *Obras*, V., chap. xv.

the Indian question. His *Breuissima Relacion de la Destruycion de las Indias*, a voluminous plea prepared to present to Charles V. in 1540, was first published twelve years later. Translations into all the principal languages of Europe followed, and its pictures of terrible inhumanity, its impassioned denunciations of the conquerors, and its indictment of the colonial officials became the stock material of generations of historical writers.

It is forgotten that his book was the product of a fierce agitation, or that it was written before the Spaniards had been fifty years in the New World, where their empire lasted three hundred years. Two centuries of philanthropic legislation has been thrown into the background by the flaming words which first gave it impulse. Las Casas was the Lloyd Garrison of Indian rights; but it is as one-sided to depict the Spanish Indian policy primarily from his pages as it would be to write a history of the American negro question exclusively from the files of the *Liberator;* or, after a century of American rule in the Philippines, to judge it solely from the anti-imperialistic tracts of the last few years. That the benevolent legislation of the distant mother-country was not, and probably could not be, wholly enforced will not seem strange to those familiar with our experience with federal legislation on the negro question; but that a lofty ideal was raised and maintained is as true of the Indian laws of Spain as of the Fifteenth Amendment.

All that can be attempted here is an outline sketch of the typical features of Indian society as reorganized by the conquest. The distinctive features of the Spanish Indian policy were the reduction of the Indians to village life, their conversion to the Christian religion, the suppression of their vices and heathen practices, and a training to industry and sobriety so that they should support themselves and contribute to meet the expenses of the colonial establishment. A portion of their labor was to belong either to their encomenderos or to the crown. On the other hand, they were to be protected from the struggle for existence in competition with the heterogeneous elements of a colonial population.

In pursuance of these aims the Indians were to live in villages under their own magistrates. Each village, according to its size, had one or two alcaldes and from one to four regidores, who were annually elected by the residents in the presence of the cura, or pastor.[1] These offices were not purchasable, as was the case in the Spanish towns.[2] Each village must contain a church with a mission priest, the expense to be borne by the encomendero out of his tributes.[3] No Indian could live outside his village, nor could any Spaniard, negro, mestizo, or mulatto live in an Indian village; Spaniards could

---

[1] *Recopilacion de Leyes*, lib. VI., tit. III., ley 15.
[2] *Ibid.*, ley 29; Depons, *Voyage*, I., 229.
[3] *Recopilacion de Leyes*, lib. VI., tit. III., leyes 4, 5.

not tarry over one night, except merchants, who might stay two nights.[1]

In these villages the Indian social life, their marriages, and the like were to be regulated in accordance with Christian principles;[2] schools for teaching Spanish were to be opened;[3] no wine could be sold there, and precautions were to be exercised that the native pulque should not be adulterated or fortified with spirits.[4] Indians could not purchase or bear arms nor ride on horseback.[5] In their religious relations they were exempt from the jurisdiction of the Inquisition.[6] The caciques who had been the chiefs of the Indians before their conversion or reduction might retain that office, and it was recognized as hereditary. They exercised minor jurisdiction, but could not try capital offences. In case they were reported to be oppressive the Spanish officials were to look into their conduct.[7]

The question of Indian tribute and labor was carefully regulated. All male Indians between eighteen and fifty were liable for an annual payment, which was payable in kind either to the crown or to the encomendero, as the case might be; but sometimes it could be commuted into money. The tribute was assessed by officials for the purpose, and protectors of the Indians were appointed to

---

[1] *Recopilacion de Leyes*, lib. VI., tit. III., leyes 19, 21, 23, 24.
[2] *Ibid.*, lib. VI., tit. I., passim.   [3] *Ibid.*, ley 18.
[4] *Ibid.*, leyes 36, 37.   [5] *Ibid.*, leyes 31, 33.
[6] *Ibid.*, ley 35.   [7] *Ibid.*, lib. VI., tit. VII., passim.

look after their interests. The amount of the
tribute in money value was in the later period two
or three pesos.[1]

Slavery was absolutely prohibited;[2] the caciques
could not hold Indian slaves. In granting encomiendas the descendants of the conquerors, discoverers, and first settlers were to be preferred.
Encomenderos could not be absentee landlords.
They must provide for the religious instruction of
the Indians and protect their rights. If negligent
they were liable to forfeit their tributes. In the case
of the larger encomiendas the tributes in excess of
two thousand pesos were to be available for pensions
of deserving persons. Encomenderos must not live
in their Indians' villages, nor build houses there,
nor allow their slaves to go thither, nor maintain
stock-farms in the neighborhood of a village. They
must marry within three years after receiving a
holding, and could not leave their province without
a license, or go to Spain except for some extraordinary emergency.[3]

Many regulations safeguarding the good treatment of the Indians illustrate evils which needed
correction. For example, no Spaniard of whatever
station could be carried in a litter by Indians.[4] The
older form of draughting Indians for labor had been

---

[1] *Recopilacion de Leyes*, lib. VI., tit. V., passim.
[2] *Ibid.*, lib. VI., tit. II., ley 1, end ley 3.
[3] *Ibid.*, lib. VI., tits. VIII., IX., passim.
[4] *Ibid.*, tit. X., ley 17.

prolific in abuses and was later abolished. Indians could be assigned by the proper officials to work for wages, and the same was done with idle Spaniards, mestizos, and negroes; but it was forbidden that the Indians should be carried off against their will or kept overtime. If they demanded excessive wages the rate was to be settled by the officials. The absence of beasts of burden in New Spain, before they were introduced by the Spaniards, had necessitated all freight being carried by Indian porters; but the Indians were no longer to be compelled to carry burdens. Nor were Indian laborers to be apportioned to work in vineyards or olive groves, factories or sugar-mills. If, however, boys wished to work in a factory to learn the art of weaving it was permitted.[1]

The required service of Indians in the mines was called the "mita." In Peru not more than one-seventh part of the Indians could be assigned on the "mita" at once; nor could an Indian be draughted again until all his fellow-villagers had completed their turn. In New Spain the "mita" drew only four from each hundred. For this as for all other services they received wages. They were not to be sent to poor mines, or employed in draining them of water.[2]

One of the fullest pictures that we have of the conditions of Indian life in the middle of the colonial

---

[1] *Recopilacion de Leyes*, tit. XII., passim.
[2] *Ibid.*, tit. XV., passim.

era is that of the English friar Thomas Gage, who
was for several years stationed in Indian towns in
Guatemala, and also served as a teacher of Latin in
Chiapa and as lecturer on divinity in the University
of Guatemala.   After his return he became a Protestant, and his subsequent views in some respects colored his narrative.   His incidental notices of Indian conditions impress the reader as indicating on
the whole a status superior in its economic possibilities to that of the European peasantry of that
day.   His chapter devoted to a particular description of Indian life [1] is darkly colored, but not more
so than the average conventional picture of peasant
life in France on the eve of the Revolution.   Gage
tells us that the apportionment of Indians as laborers was the occasion of much oppression, and that
the wages were inadequate, being only about ten
cents a day.   Yet it does not appear that the system in Mexico was more oppressive than the French
corvée.

After describing the government of the Indian
towns, he writes: "They live as in other Civil and
Politick and Well governed Commonwealths; for in
most of their Townes, there are some that professe
such trades as are practised among Spaniards.
There are amongst them Smiths, Taylors, Carpenters, Masons, Shoomakers and the like." Some of
the Indians were excellent architects. "For paint-
ing they are much inclined to it, and most of the

[1] Gage, *New Survey of the West Indies*, chap. xix. (London, 1648).

pictures and altars of the country towns are their workmanship. In most of their townes they have a schoole, where they are taught to read, to sing, and some to write." [1]   Humboldt at the beginning of the nineteenth century estimated that one-third of the Indians lived nearly in the manner of the lower people of Spain;[2] the other two-thirds were poorer. He quotes an interesting memorial of a bishop of Michoacan to the king which takes the ground that the laws shielded the Indians too much from the world, and so hindered their development that the regulation should now be relaxed and the Indian given free opportunity to make the most of himself.[3] Depons was led by his observations in Caracas to a somewhat similar view.[4]

In South America, particularly in Peru, the condition of the Indians was much worse than in Mexico. Ulloa charges the corregidors—the royal officials for collecting the tribute—with ruthlessly exploiting the Indians by collecting tributes from ages and classes exempt from it, and particularly by means of the repartimiento system of supplying them with mules and European goods. The corregidor arbitrarily allotted the mules or the cloths to the Indians, which they were compelled to buy at

[1] Gage, *New Survey of the West Indies*, 146.
[2] Humboldt, *New Spain*, I., 198. Cf. Bancroft, *Mexico*, III., 750, who thinks "their material condition much better than that of the lowest classes in Europe."
[3] Humboldt, *New Spain*, I., 89.
[4] Depons, *Voyage*, I., 226–248.

exorbitant prices.[1] In the application of the "mita"
system, which in Peru and Quito was extended to the
stock-farms and woollen factories, they were practically reduced to slavery, overworked, underpaid,
underfed, and scourged for falling short in their
tasks.[2] Ulloa goes so far as to say that whatever
may have been the tyranny of the encomenderos
of the conquest he does not believe it was as bad as
that of the corregidors and the bosses in the factories or the overseers on the plantations and stock-
farms.[3]

In a later work Ulloa says that the severity of the
"mita" in the mines had been much exaggerated;
that more Indians were killed in a year by the im-
moderate use of brandy than by the mines, including all accidents, in fifty years. The inhumanity
and destructiveness of the labor in the factories
he still condemns without qualification.[4] The prohibition of factory assignments would seem to have
been a dead letter in Peru.

The Spanish authorities on the whole encouraged
marriage between Spaniards and Indian women.
When Ovando arrived he found most of the three
hundred Spaniards in Española living with Indian
women, often the daughters or sisters of chiefs,

[1] Juan and Ulloa, *Noticias Secretas*, 234, 235.

[2] *Ibid.*, 268–279. Cf. Frézier, *Voyage*, II., 464–472, and Tschudi,
Peru, 330. The hopelessness of securing reforms led to the
Indian revolt under Tupac Amaru in 1780.

[3] Juan and Ulloa, *Noticias Secretas*, 279.

[4] Ulloa, *Noticias Americanas*, 281.

as concubines. The Franciscan fathers protested against this practice, and Ovando ordered the Spaniards to marry the women or to separate from them.[1] As a temporary expedient King Ferdinand in 1512 urged the sending of Christian white slaves to the Indies, and especially to Porto Rico, to become wives. This policy Diego Columbus, the governor, opposed, so far as Española was concerned, because there were Castilian women in the island, converts,[2] and the settlers would pass them by in favor of the white slaves, who were presumably "old Christians."[3] In 1514 King Ferdinand, apparently recognizing the inevitable, issued an ordinance approving of the marriage of Spaniards with Indian women.[4] The interest of the wives left at home by adventurers enlisted the concern of Ovando, and in 1505 the king approved of his plan to send such husbands back to Spain to fetch their wives.[5] Later, married men, even officials of the highest rank, were not allowed to go to the Indies without their wives.[6]

In striking contrast to the subsequent policy of Louis XIV. in Canada and Louisiana and of the English generally, the emigration of single women to the colonies was not favored in the later legislation, and the king reserved to himself the power to

[1] Herrera, *Historia General*, dec. I., lib. VI., chap. xviii.
[2] *I.e.*, from Mohammedanism, or "New Christians."
[3] Saco, *Historia de la Esclavitud*, 81.
[4] *Docs. Ined. de Ultramar*, IX., 22.
[5] Fabié, *Ensayo Historico*, 64.
[6] *Recopilacion de Leyes*, lib. IX., tit. XXVI., ley 28.

grant the necessary license if exception was to be made.[1]   It was therefore inevitable that there should be an excess of white men in the colonies and that marriage with Indian women should be common. It was Humboldt's estimate in 1803 that not one-tenth of the European-born Spaniards in Mexico were women.[2]

This mixture of races produced a variety of types in the population of Spanish America. The whites were divided into the peninsular Spaniards, who were called in Mexico gachupines (those who wear spurs[3]), and chapetones; and in South America,[4] usually chapetones, and the American-born Spaniards or creoles. The word creole, contrary to a prevalent idea, indicates nothing as to blood, but only connotes the place of birth:[5] there were creole whites and creole negroes, the latter being thus distinguished from the bozals or African-born negroes.

Below the whites came the castas, the mixed breeds or blends. Of these the commonest were the mestizos, those born of Spaniards and Indian women; in addition, there were the mulattoes, of white and negro parentage; the zambos, of negro and Indian parentage. Then there were the Indians, and lastly

---

[1] *Recopilacion de Leyes.* lib. IX., tit. XXVI., ley 24.

[2] Bancroft, *Mexico*, III., 752.

[3] Alaman, *Mejico*, I., 7; Gage, *New Survey of the West Indies*, 56.

[4] Ulloa, *Voyage*, I., 29.

[5] Saco, *Historia de la Esclavitud*, 124; Tschudi, *Travels in Peru*, 80.

the negroes. Subdivisions of the mulattoes were the quadroons and octoroons (quinteroons in Spanish). An alternative name for the zambos in use in Mexico and Lima was chino, and the name zambo came to be applied to the offspring of a negro and mulatto or chino. A black zambo was the offspring of a negro and a zambo woman. The extremes of the mixtures between whites and negroes were, therefore, octoroons (seven-eighths white), and black zambos (seven-eighths black).[1]

The European Spaniards were most active in commerce and filled the governmental offices in church and state. If the Spanish emigrant rose in fortune he would marry into a wealthy creole family; if he fell he would marry into one of the blends. Many of the Spaniards came over only to make their fortunes and return, but those that stayed constantly replenished the creole stock with new blood and energy, to yield again in the next generation to idleness and ease.[2]

Manual labor was disdained by the white; and even if he had been inclined to engage in it he could not compete with the Indian with his simple tastes and low standard of living. Miles Philips reports that "in that country (Mexico) no Spaniard will serve one another."[3] Similarly Henry Hawkes,

[1] Humboldt, *New Spain*, I., 243–247. The English translator mistakenly renders chino, Chinese woman. Tschudi, *Peru*, 80, 81, gives the technical names of some twenty varieties of blends.
[2] Alaman, *Mejico*, I., 10; Bancroft, *Mexico*, III., 744.
[3] Hakluyt, *Voyages*, XIV., 208.

a merchant who lived in Mexico five years, told Hakluyt in 1572 that the Indians were expert artisans and would "do worke so cheape that poore young men that go out of Spain to get their living are not set on worke; which is the occasion there are many idle people in the country. For the Indian will live all the weeke with lesse than one groat; which the Spanyard cannot do, nor any man els." [1] In Lima most of the mechanics were colored, although some were Europeans. [2] In Quito, however, the whites avoided any mechanical labor, and all the handicrafts were left to mulattoes and Indians. [3] There was a spirit of jealousy prevalent among the different classes of the population and a pride proportionate to the degree of whiteness of the complexion. Between the office - holding, enterprising Spaniard and the easy-going creole there was little sympathy of race and much antagonism. The Indians, of a morose disposition by nature, smothered their resentment against the ruling race. The home government welcomed rather than tried to allay these antipathies regarding them as an element of security. [4]

[1] Hakluyt, *Voyages*, XIV., 178.
[2] Ulloa, *Voyage*, II., 55.   [3] *Ibid.*, I., 263.
[4] Cf. Humboldt, *New Spain*, I., 261, 262; Bancroft, *Mexico*, III., 740–745; Roscher, *Spanish Colonial System*, 8.

CHAPTER XVIII

NEGRO SLAVES

(1502–1821)

THE introduction of negro slavery into the New World dates from the year 1502, and its history in the Spanish dominions illustrates more than one phase of their colonial policy. The instructions to Ovando in 1501, which prohibited the passage to the Indies of Jews, Moors, or recent converts, authorized him to take over negro slaves that had been born in the power of Christians.[1] This permission indicates that there were negro slaves in the peninsula that had been born there, and that at first it was thought best to allow only Christian slaves to go to the Indies. Yet even this restricted importation Ovando found unwise, and he requested the next year that no more should be sent, averring that they ran away and demoralized the Indians.[2] Isabella gave ear to Ovando's protest and withdrew the permission to import negroes.[3]

[1] *Docs. Ined. de Indias*, XXXI., 23. Ovando set sail in February, 1502.

[2] Herrera, *Historia General*, dec. I., lib. V., chap. xii.

[3] Saco, *Historia de la Esclavitud*, 62.

After her death, however, Ferdinand reverted to the plan of 1501, and in 1505 sent Ovando seventeen negro slaves to work in the copper-mines.[1] Apparently the regulation excluding any but Christianized negroes was evaded, for Ovando received orders in 1506 to deport all Berber slaves.[2]

The severity of the labor in the mines proving destructive to the Indians, Ferdinand directed the Casa de Contractacion in 1510 to send over immediately fifty slaves, and later on others, up to two hundred, to be sold to the settlers. In April of that year over a hundred were bought in the Lisbon market. This is the beginning of the African slave-trade to America. The change of climate and the hard work caused a very rapid death rate, which perplexed the king.[3] Notwithstanding their mortality the negroes were so much more efficient than the Indians that Ferdinand took measures in 1511 to develop the transportation of negroes direct from Guinea.[4]

The problem of labor in tropical colonies where nature's bounty relieves man from the necessity of hard work for food and clothing has never yet been solved in a way that has satisfied at once the demands of economic production and humane feeling. The Spanish government tried to accomplish both ends,

[1] Saco, *Historia de la Esclavitud*, 63.
[2] *Ibid.*, 63; Herrera, *Historia General*, dec. I., lib. VI., chap. xx.
[3] Saco, *Historia de la Esclavitud*, 67.
[4] Herrera, *Historia General*, dec. I., lib. IX., chap. v.

in a measure, by sparing the Indian at the expense
of the African. In 1517 this policy commended
itself to the Dominican clergy in Española,[1] to the
special commission of Jeronimite friars sent out to
take charge of Indian affairs,[2] to the lawyer Zuazo,
who accompanied the Jeronimites,[3] to the proctors
of the towns in Española, to Justice Figueroa,[4]
president of the audiencia, and to Las Casas, the
ardent champion of the Indians.[5] Las Casas,
however, still adhered to the policy of importing
negroes from Spain, while the Jeronimites and
Zuazo urged the importation of the bozal negroes,
those direct from Africa.

The government, convinced by Las Casas' arguments, which apparently antedated somewhat
those of the Jeronimite friars, decided in 1517 to
ship four thousand negroes to the islands, and thus
initiated what became the historic policy of Spain
in controlling the slave-trade—the letting it out by
contract, or asiento as it was called; which, however,
did not prevent the crown from granting limited
licenses to other courtiers and to settlers. The
first contractor, Lorenzo de Gomenot, the governor
of Bresa, agreed to introduce four thousand negroes

[1] Saco, *Historia de la Esclavitud*, 89.
[2] *Docs. Ined. de Indias*, I., 284. Cf. also Helps, *Spanish Conquest* (Oppenheim's ed.), I., 362–365.
[3] *Docs. Ined. de Indias*, I., 326.
[4] Saco, *Historia de la Esclavitud*, 92.
[5] *Historia de las Indias*, IV., 380. Saco reviews the discussion as to Las Casas' suggestions, *Historia de la Esclavitud*,
99–109.

in eight years, and he immediately sold his contract to some Genoese for twenty-five thousand ducats.[1] The development of the sugar industry and the growth of slavery were dependent upon each other, especially after the mines in the Antilles gave out. Each trapiche, or sugar-mill, run by horses or mules, required thirty or forty negroes, and each water-mill eighty at the least.[2] Had the commerce of the islands been reasonably free, plantation slavery on a large scale would have rapidly developed, and the history of Hayti and the English islands would have been anticipated a century by the Spaniards.

The number of negroes to be imported under the various contracts and the size of the bonus paid for the privilege rose steadily. The asiento made with the Germans Ciguer and Sailler in 1528 provided for a bonus to the government of twenty thousand ducats, in consideration of which the contractors were allowed to take four thousand negroes to the Indies in four years, to be sold at not more than forty-five ducats apiece. The Germans sublet the contract to some Portuguese, who supplied slaves of so poor a quality that many protests came to the Council of the Indies from the islands.[3] In consequence no new asiento was made for several years.

In 1536 contractors offered the government twenty-six thousand ducats down for a new asiento to import four thousand in four years, but they were out-

[1] Saco, *Historia de la Esclavitud*, 111.
[2] *Ibid.*, 128.   [3] *Ibid.*, 146, 147.

bid by others; neither proposal was accepted. In 1552 a contract was made with one Ferdinand Ochoa, by which he was to buy licenses to introduce twenty-three thousand negroes, paying eight ducats per license, or one hundred thousand down and twelve thousand per year for seven years. This contract was annulled before it was entirely carried out.[1]

The personal union between Spain and Portugal from 1580 to 1640 led to the practice of awarding slave-trading contracts to Portuguese, since the trading stations on the African coast belonged to Portugal. The contract of 1595 with Gomez Reynel was the most elaborate and extensive up to that date: it provided for the exclusive privilege of importing during nine years thirty-eight thousand two hundred and fifty negro slaves at the rate of four thousand two hundred and fifty per annum, of whom at least three thousand five hundred must be landed alive in America. In return, the enormous bonus of nine hundred thousand ducats was payable in annual instalments of one hundred thousand. For every negro short of the yearly quota the contractor was to forfeit ten ducats. The negroes must be fresh from Africa, with no mulattoes, mestizos, Turks, Moriscos, or any other nation mixed in.[2] Owing to Reynel's death in 1600, the contract was transferred to one Juan Rodriguez Cutiño and ex-

[1] Saco, *Historia de la Esclavitud*, 210.
[2] *Ibid.*, 240–245.

tended till 1609.[1] After that date the business was carried on in the name of the king till 1615, when Rodriguez Delvas agreed to pay one hundred and fifteen thousand ducats a year for the privilege, under which he might import up to five thousand, but never less than three thousand five hundred annually.[2]

The foregoing examples illustrate the nature of the asientos, or contracts for importing slaves, made by the Spanish government. The chief changes in the later years may be briefly indicated. In 1696 the Portuguese Royal Guinea Company secured the contract, but its business was interrupted by the European war and the company was dissolved in 1701.[3] The alliance between Spain and France and the establishment of the French Royal Guinea Company led to the asiento being granted to this company in 1701, which undertook to import three thousand to four thousand eight hundred a year for ten years.[4] The results of the War of the Spanish Succession cut short the experience of the French with the asiento, which the English obtained for the South Sea Company as one of the spoils of war by the treaty of Utrecht. The new asiento was to last thirty years and to secure the importation of one hundred and forty-four thousand negroes at the rate of four thousand eight hundred per year. For four thousand a duty of 33⅓ pesos [dollars] was to

[1] Saco, *Historia de la Esclavitud,* 247.
[2] *Ibid.,* 250.   [3] *Ibid.,* 289.   [4] *Ibid.,* 292.

be paid (the odd eight hundred being exempt from duty). The company agreed to pay the king $200,-000. This arrangement lasted, with interruptions caused by wars, until 1750.[1]

It will be seen that our data for estimating the annual importation of slaves into Spanish America are far more numerous and satisfactory than for the immigration of Spaniards. For the two hundred years, 1550 to 1750, we may estimate the importations of the asientists at an average of at least three thousand a year. Besides these were the illicit forced importations of the English and French corsairs, who, like Sir John Hawkins, would market kidnapped Africans with guns trained on reluctant customers.[2] Such illicit importations we can only guess at, but perhaps five hundred a year is not far wrong. This would give a total of seven hundred thousand for the two centuries. In 1808 Humboldt estimated the negro population of Spanish America at seven hundred and seventy-six thousand.[3] It would seem from these figures that the negro population barely held its own from generation to generation and increased solely by importation.[4] At the beginning of the nine-

----

[1] Saco, *Historia de la Esclavitud*, 295–311. In the eighteenth century the peso is the familiar Spanish dollar.

[2] Hakluyt, *Voyages*, XV., 146.

[3] Humboldt, *Travels*, VI., 835.

[4] Humboldt notes that in the eighteenth century in Cuba the number of males greatly exceeded the females.—*Travels*, VII., 142.

teenth century the annual death rate of the newly imported Africans in Cuba was seven per cent.[1] Hence, as the Spanish were on the whole easy masters, one may well doubt whether the prevalent view is correct that the negro was readily acclimated in the New World.[2] Under the earlier asientos the slave-ships were to go to America with the annual fleets, but of the size of the ships and the conditions of the voyage we have few particulars. Sandoval, in his work on the negro, reports one captain as confessing his misgivings about the business ; he had just suffered a shipwreck in which only thirty out of nine hundred on board escaped.[3]

In the earlier days of slavery in the colony it was felt to be necessary for the sake of security not to have the ratio between slaves and whites higher than three to one, though some were ready in 1532 to risk five to one. Prices varied at this time from fifty to seventy pesos on the islands, and from one hundred to one hundred and fifty on the isthmus. Twenty years later a scale of prices fixed by law

[1] Humboldt, *New Spain*, I., 236; cf. also *Travels*, VII., 153.

[2] Shaler, *The Neighbor*, 131–132. "The negro endured such a transition without any perceptible shock," etc. In Humboldt's time the English West Indies contained seven hundred thousand negroes and mulattoes, free and slave, while the custom-house registers proved that from 1680 to 1786 two million one hundred and thirty thousand negroes had been imported from Africa. *Travels*, VII., 147.

[3] Sandoval, *De Instauranda Æthiopum Salute* (Madrid, 1647), 102.

varied from one hundred ducats in the West Indies to one hundred and eighty in Chili.[1]

There is hardly any trace in the whole history of the Spanish system of anything analogous to the indented servants of the English colonies or the engagés of the French islands. The only parallels which have been noted are the following instances in the earlier period of the carrying of white slaves to the Indies; and these white slaves seem to have been chattel slaves and not temporary bond servants. In 1504 Ojeda was authorized to take five white slaves, and in 1512 Peralta received permission to take two white Christian slaves to Porto Rico. In the same year the king instructed the Casa de Contractacion to send over white Christian slaves to become wives of the colonists, as they would be preferable to the Indian women. Twenty years later, in 1532, the Council of the Indies granted twenty licenses to Spaniards to take white slaves to the Indies.[2]

We are accustomed to think of the Pennsylvania Quakers and Judge Sewall as uttering the first public protest in America against negro slavery; but the Jesuit Alphonso Sandoval, born in Seville, but educated in Peru, where his father was the king's treasurer, in his work on the history and customs of the negroes, lifts his voice clearly against slavery and the slave-trade, and brings out the point that

[1] Saco, *Historia de la Esclavitud*, 144, 159, 164, 173, 212.
[2] *Ibid.*, 62, 73, 80, 164.

the constant market for slaves on the coast is a prolific cause of wars in the interior of Africa.[1]

Slavery never became deeply rooted in Spanish America outside of the Antilles and the northern coast region of South America, for reasons in the main similar to those which limited its extent in the middle and northern English colonies. The altitude in New Spain was unfavorable to the negro, and the work was mainly done by the Indian peasants. Humboldt estimated that not more than a hundred negroes were imported annually into Mexico. In the census of 1793 only six thousand negro slaves were returned.[2] That independent Mexico abolished slavery came about as naturally as the abolition of the institution in New York.

In Peru negro slavery was most conspicuous in Lima as a phase of the luxury that characterized the lives of the Spaniards and creoles. The total number of negroes in Peru, while much greater than in New Spain, was small compared with Venezuela and Cuba. In a statement of the population drawn up towards the end of the eighteenth century the number of free colored people is placed at forty-one thousand four hundred and four and the number of

[1] Sandoval, *De Instauranda Æthiopum Salute*, part I., lib. I., chaps. xxii., xxvii.; extracts in Saco, *Historia de la Esclavitud*, 253–256. Sandoval, p. 100, quotes a letter of Padre Luis Brandaon, rector of the College of São Paulo de Loanda in 1611, estimating the annual export of slaves from São Paulo de Loanda at ten thousand to twelve thousand.

[2] Humboldt, *New Spain*, I., 236, 237. The total number of slaves was not more than ten thousand.

slaves at forty thousand three hundred and thirty-seven.[1] In the captaincy-general of Caracas, Depons estimated the number of slaves at two hundred and eighteen thousand and the descendants of freedmen at two hundred and ninety-one thousand, the two outnumbering the whites as seven to two.[2] In 1775 the number of slaves in Cuba was about forty-six thousand and the number of free colored about thirty thousand.[3]

With the relaxation of the trade laws the economic development of Cuba went forward by leaps, and the average importation of slaves for the ten years, 1790-1799, was over five thousand.[4] In spite of the great increase of the slave population Cuba never became so extreme a type of the old plantation colony as the English and French West Indies. A comparison of Cuba and Jamaica in 1823, when the number of slaves had been rapidly increasing beyond what had been the relative proportions of the population under the earlier régime, will illustrate the point.

	Total population	Whites	Free colored	Slaves
Cuba	715,000	325,000	130,000	260,000
Jamaica	402,000	25,000	35,000	342,000 [5]

In Jamaica the ratio of slaves to whites was about

[1] Markham, in Winsor, *Narr. and Crit. Hist.*, VIII., 321.
[2] Depons, *Voyage*, I., 105.
[3] Humboldt, *Travels*, VII., 111, 112.
[4] *Ibid.*, 146.   [5] *Ibid.*, 101.

thirteen and a half to one.   In Hayti, in the French part, the ratio between slaves and whites was about eleven to one.[1]

A comparative study of the status and treatment of slaves in the Spanish, French, and English colonies reveals the fact, surprising to-day, so widespread is the view that the Spanish colonial system was pre-eminently oppressive, that the Spanish slave code was far more humane than either the French or the English slave laws.   In law the Spanish slave had a right, if ill treated, to choose a master less severe if he could induce him to buy him, to marry a wife of his own choice, to buy his liberty at the lowest market rate, and to buy his wife and children.   If he were cruelly treated he could appeal to the courts and might be declared free. In fact, the Spanish laws and the administration favored emancipation at every turn.[2]   If negroes questioned the legality of their enslavement the courts were to hear their cause.[3]   Sandoval mentions such a case in which the audiencia of Mexico liberated a claimant on rather slight evidence.[4] Charles III. laid down the principle in 1789 that fugitive slaves who by just means obtained their liberty were not to be restored.[5]   In Peru the slaves

[1] Humboldt, *Travels*, VI., 824.

[2] *Ibid.*, VII., 276–278; Humboldt, *New Spain*, I., 241; Depons, *Voyage*, I., 164–166, summarizes a royal ordinance of 1789, which demanded so much for the slaves that the local authorities nullified it.   [3] *Recopilacion de Leyes*, lib. VII., tit. V., ley 8.

[4] Sandoval, *De Instauranda Æthiopum Salute*, 103.

[5] Saco, *Historia de la Esclavitud*, 361.

were permitted to work for themselves five or six hours a day.[1]

The beneficent consequences of this humane legislation appear in the large number of free colored people everywhere in the Spanish colonies. In Peru they slightly exceeded the slaves in number; in Caracas the excess was larger, the free constituting four-sevenths of the colored population; in Cuba, in 1775, the slaves stood to the free as four and six-tenths to three. In Jamaica, on the other hand, the number of free colored persons was less than one-tenth the number of slaves, and in Hayti less than one-sixteenth.[2]

On the relative humanity of the Spanish laws in regard to slavery there can be no doubt; but whether Spanish slaves were more kindly treated than French or English is a different and more difficult question. Prevalent public opinion, Depons tells us, believed they were, but he expresses his dissent in some respects. In his view the slaves suffered from neglect rather than severities. The Spanish masters were very solicitous in Caracas that the slaves should say their prayers, but unconcerned as to whether they had enough to eat and to wear. Shiftlessness and not harshness was the cause of their sufferings.[3]

[1] Tschudi, *Peru*, 76.
[2] See above, p. 281, and Humboldt, *Travels*, VI., 820, 824.
[3] Depons, *Voyage*, I., 159–164.

CHAPTER XIX

COLONIAL COMMERCE AND INDUSTRY
(1495–1821)

THE first impulse of Ferdinand and Isabella was to throw open the commerce with the newly discovered lands to all their subjects; and this was done in 1495, with the proviso that trading voyages should start from Cadiz and return thither. Columbus, however, although his right to load an eighth part of every cargo was reserved, protested; and the privilege was revoked in 1497.[1] When the Casa de Contractacion was established in 1503 the trade with the Indies was to be confined to Seville, the commercial and political capital of Castile. In 1505 King Philip I. extended the privilege of trading with the Indies to resident foreigners in Spain provided that they employed native Spaniards as their agents.[2]

The confinement of the trade to Seville was early felt to be detrimental to the colonists, and the representatives of the towns in Española vainly petitioned in 1508 that the trade might be thrown open to the other Spanish ports.[3] In 1525, in the

[1] Navarrete, *Viages*, II., 165 ff., 201; *Memorials of Columbus*, 89 ff., 96. [2] *Col. de Docs. Ined. de Ultramar*, V., 78, 79.
[3] Fabié, *Ensayo Historico*, 78.

expectation that the Spice Islands might be reached by a northern route, a casa de contractacion was established in Coruña and from that port Estevan Gomez sailed on his exploring expedition.[1]

Four years later, in 1529, Charles V. authorized ships to sail to the Indies from Coruña, Bayonne, Aviles, Laredo, Bilbao, San Sebastian, Cartagena, Cadiz, and Malaga, provided that on their return they reported at Seville.[2] This last condition was unfavorable to any considerable export trade of agricultural products from the islands, and in 1532 the audiencia of Española petitioned that the colonists be allowed to carry sugar, cassia, hides, and other products of the island, not only to Flanders, but to other European ports, asserting that it was the restriction of their trade to Seville which was most ruinous to the islands.[3] Any relaxation, however, of the monopoly of Seville was strenuously opposed by her merchants and by the other towns in Castile, and there is a doubt whether the decree of 1529 was ever actually put into operation;[4] certainly the arrangement was of short duration. Again in 1540 the authorities of Española complained that prices were depressed by restriction to Seville ships, which were inadequate to carry off their sugar, hides, and cassia.[5] In 1558 ships from

---

[1] Herrera, *Historia General*, dec. III., lib. VIII., chap. viii.
[2] Fabié, 227; *Col. de Docs. Ined. de Ultramar*, IX., 401.
[3] Saco, *Historia de la Esclavitud*, 158.
[4] *Ibid.*, 150; Armstrong, *Charles V.*, II., 47.
[5] Saco, *Historia de la Esclavitud*, 182.

Española and Porto Rico were permitted to unload their cargo, including specie and pearls, at Cadiz, provided the latter were in proper packages and legally reported to the Casa de Contractacion.[1]

In the earlier days, before the gold and silver of Mexico and Peru constituted so important a part of the return cargo, commerce was carried on in independent vessels; but the development of piracy gradually compelled the Spanish ships to and from the Indies to go in fleets.[2] When the Italian Benzoni went to America in 1541 he found ships constantly going to the Indies from the Canaries; when he returned in 1556 it was with a fleet of fourteen vessels.[3] In 1555 Robert Tomson waited in the Canaries for the Seville fleet, which that year consisted of eight vessels.[4] But apparently the Indian commerce was not yet wholly confined to these fleets, for Badoero, the Venetian ambassador, reported on his return in 1557 that perhaps a hundred ships went yearly from Seville to the Indies.[5] Tiepolo, who made his report in 1563, places the number at sixty or seventy.[6]

In 1561, however, the system of fleets was legally established and lasted nearly two hundred years.

---

[1] *Recopilacion de Leyes*, lib. IX., tit. XLII., ley 27.

[2] Cf. Häbler, *Die Wirthschaftliche Blüte Spaniens*, 54, *n.*, for the dates of earlier fleets.

[3] Benzoni, *History of the New World*, 1, 258.

[4] Hakluyt, *Voyages*, XIV., 139–141.

[5] Albéri, *Relazioni Venete*, 1st series, III., 261.

[6] *Ibid.*, I., 35.

The ordinance of that year required, for the protection of the Indian trade, that every year there should be equipped in the river by Seville and in the ports of Cadiz and San Lucar de Barrameda two fleets and a naval escort for the Indies—one for New Spain, the other for Terra Firma.[1]   In the sixteenth century on the outward voyage the fleets ordinarily put in at the Canaries, whence they sailed to the West Indies.   At the island of Dominica the vessels for the islands and for Mexico would separate.[2]   On the return voyage the two fleets and the ships from the islands, from Honduras and Yucatan would rendezvous at Havana and sail for Spain together, making a stop at the Azores to learn if the coast of Spain was free from corsairs.[3]   If, however, there were as many as six ships from Española they might secure a license to come on together without waiting for the fleet.[4]

The safe arrival of the fleets was announced and official orders transmitted to the viceroys by packet-boats of not more than sixty tons burden, which were not to carry any freight or passengers.   This despatch service consisted of two trips each year to Terra Firma and two to New Spain.[5]   During the

[1] *Recopilacion de Leyes*, lib. IX., tit. XXX., ley 1.   Terra Firma was the usual Spanish name for the northern coast region of South America.

[2] Velasco, *Descripcion de las Indias*, 64.

[3] *Ibid., Recopilacion de Leyes*, lib. IX., tit. XLII., ley 24.

[4] *Ibid.*, ley 26.

[5] *Ibid.*, tit. XXXVII., ley 5, and note after ley 22.

latter part of the sixteenth century the. regularity
of the voyages of the fleets to New Spain was disturbed by the war with the Netherlands and England, so that only eleven fleets arrived at Vera Cruz
in the last twenty years of the century.[1]

It would appear, however, that the limitation of
commerce to the fleets was evaded, although at the
risk of confiscation of vessel and cargo. Shipmasters and traders, under the pretence of having been
driven out of their course by storms, would put into
West Indian ports.[2] Ships in the Canaries, osten-
sibly loaded for France or England, would cross the
Atlantic westward. Ships, too, owned in the Canaries would load with wines, linens, or other contra-
band goods bought of foreigners and then slip over
to the West Indies.[3] Such may have been the case
with the ship in which John Chilton, an English
Seville merchant, went to Mexico in 1568, as there
is no reference to a fleet in his account.[4]

The Venetian ambassador Donato, who gives a
fuller account of the Indies in 1573 than is to be
found in the other Venetian relations, says that the
two fleets to New Spain and Peru consisted of thirty
vessels each.[5] After 1578 the naval escort normally
consisted of nine galleons and eight frigates, with

---

[1] Alaman, *Disertaciones*, III., App. No. 20; Bancroft, *Mexico*,
II., 752.

[2] *Recopilacion de Leyes*, lib. IX., tit. XXXVIII., ley 6.

[3] *Ibid.*, tit. XLII., ley 15.

[4] Hakluyt, *Voyages*, XIV., 156.

[5] Albéri, *Relazioni Venete*, VI., 453, 454.

one thousand five hundred persons, of whom nine hundred and fifty were marines, the rest officers and crews.[1] When Miles Philips returned in 1582 there were thirty-seven ships, "and in every one of them there was as good as thirty pipes of silver one with another, besides great store of gold, cochinilla, sugars, hides, and Cana Fistula with other apothecary drugs." [2]

The Indian fleet of 1625 on which Thomas Gage sailed for Vera Cruz, intending to go to the Philippines, consisted of thirty-three ships and eight galleons as escort. Gage reports the destination of the vessels as follows: "To Puerto Rico went that year two ships; to Santo Domingo three; to Jamaica two; to Margarita one; to the Havana two; to Cartagena three; to Campeche two; to Honduras and Truxillo two; and to St. John Dilua, or Vera Cruz, sixteen; all laden with Wines, Figs, Raisins, Olives, Oyle, Cloth, Carsies, Linnen, Iron, and Quicksilver for the mines." [3]   Among the passengers were a new viceroy for Mexico, a new president for Manila, with a mission of thirty Jesuits and a Dominican mission of twenty-seven friars for the Philippines, and twenty-four Mercenarian friars for Mexico— their escort was to protect them from the Turks and Hollanders.

The fleet that came in 1637 to Porto Bello con-

[1] Velasco, *Descripcion de las Indias*, 88.
[2] Hakluyt, *Voyages*, XIV., 223.
[3] Gage, *New Survey of the West Indies*, 15.

sisted of eight galleons and ten merchant ships.[1]
Alvarez Osorio, writing about the year 1686, gives
the make-up of the Porto Bello fleet as eight galleons,
one galleon for the silver, the tender from Margarita, and ten ships of different burden, with a
total capacity of fifteen thousand tons for the whole
fleet.   The fleet from New Spain was composed of
two galleons, a tender, and twenty ships, with a total
capacity for the whole fleet of twelve thousand five
hundred tons.[2]

The average length of the voyage from Spain to
Mexico was two months and a half and the estimated distance about six thousand five hundred
miles.[3]   Experience showed that the most favorable
seasons for setting out for New Spain was from
April 1 to the end of May; and for the isthmus,
August or September.   Later, however, it was or-
dained that the Terra Firma fleet should start
between March 15 and March 31.[4]   On the Pacific
the voyage from Panama to Lima, owing to head
winds and adverse currents, usually took two months,
although the distance was not over one thousand
five hundred miles.   If the voyage was continued to
Chili another two months was consumed; but the return could be accomplished in less than half the time.[5]

[1] Gage, *New Survey of the West Indies*, 196.
[2] Colmeiro, *Historia de la Economia Politica de España*, II.,
404.
[3] Velasco, *Descripcion de las Indias*, 64.
[4] *Recopilacion de Leyes*, lib. IX., tit. XXXVI., ley 13 (1619).
[5] Velasco, *Descripcion de las Indias*, 83.

A curious phase of the commercial regulations of the Spanish colonial system grew out of the trade with the Philippine Islands, where the foundations of Spanish rule were laid by Legaspi (1564–1565) in an expedition equipped in Mexico. The Portuguese monopoly of the Eastern seas and the difficulty and danger of navigating the Straits of Magellan made these islands, lying on the outmost verge of the Spanish Empire, a dependency of New Spain. In the early years of the conquest of the islands their commerce was unrestricted; but soon the fear of the competition of Chinese silks with those of Spain in the Lima market led to a series of protective measures which seem highly unwise to-day. First came the prohibition of the importation of Chinese fabrics into Peru; then a prohibition of all direct trade between South America and the Philippines or China; and then a law limiting the shipments from the Philippines to Mexico to two hundred and fifty thousand pesos annually, and from Mexico to the Philippines to five hundred thousand. The trade between China and the islands was restricted to the Chinese.[1]

Notwithstanding these restrictions Chinese goods were smuggled into Lima, and in consequence all trade between New Spain and Peru was interdicted in 1636.[2] So complete an embargo could not be enforced, and Ulloa reports that it was systemat-

[1] Tit. XLV. of lib. IX. of the *Recopilacion de Leyes* is devoted to the trade with the Philippines.   [2] *Ibid.*, ley 78.

ically evaded at Guayaquil with the collusion of the officials.[1] In the cargo of the annual ship from Manila to Acapulco every Spaniard in the Philippines could share in proportion to his means or standing, and these chances were bought and sold.[2] The passenger service was, of course, limited mainly to officials and missionaries. The fare from Manila to Acapulco at the end of the eighteenth century was $1000, and $500 for the return.[3] When the Italian traveller Gemelli went from Manila to Acapulco he was two hundred and four days on the sea. He described it as a voyage "which is enough to destroy a man or make him unfit for anything as long as he lives." Ordinarily the voyage to Manila required ninety days.[4]

Another strange example of the vagaries of Spanish protective policy is presented by the severe restrictions on trade between Spain and Buenos Ayres, now the commercial metropolis of Spanish America. From 1535 to 1579 direct trade between Buenos Ayres and Spain was prohibited. Thereafter the policy vacillated between absolute prohibition and the permission of a few vessels especially licensed. In 1580 Buenos Ayres was refounded, but its interests were wholly subordinated to those of Peru. The effective reasons for not opening that

[1] Juan and Ulloa, *Noticias Secretas*, 201, 202.

[2] For details, see E. G. Bourne, "Historical Introduction" to *The Philippine Islands*, ed. by Blair and Robertson, I., 62–70.

[3] Zuñiga, *Estadismo de las Islas Filipinas*, I., 268.

[4] Churchill, *Voyages*, IV., 491, 499.

port to direct trade with Spain were: that the region did not produce gold and silver; that its trade would attract capital from Peru; that merchandise would enter Buenos Ayres for Peru and Chili cheaper than via Panama, which would be detrimental to the fleet, and would bring upon the Porto Bello fair losses which would more than counterbalance the gains to Buenos Ayres; and lastly, that the La Plata region was a healthy country and could be self-sufficient.[1]

Total prohibitions and stifling restrictions on trade alike proved incapable of complete execution. The authorization of the slave-trade to the extent of importing six hundred negroes a year (1595–1596) opened the door for smuggling.[2]   In 1623 the evil was so great as to call for heavy penalties by an ordinance which recorded the fact that many passengers enter the port of Buenos Ayres for Peru, and that ships load in Portugal with all kinds of goods and then go to Buenos Ayres.[3]

The fleet system has been compared to the mediæval caravan system of transportation, and, like its prototype, it involved the fair as the agency of exchange and distribution. The Peru fleet in the eighteenth century first made the port of Cartagena the distributing centre for what is now Colombia and Ecuador.   At one time the overland trade from Quito was extended to Peru, to the detriment

---

[1] Mitré, *Historia de Belgrano*, I., 29.   [2] *Ibid.*, 30.
[3] *Recopilacion de Leyes*, lib. VIII., tit. XIV., ley 13.

of the Lima merchants who attended the Porto
Bello fair; and consequently, in response to their protest, all trade in European commodities between
Quito and Lima was prohibited after the arrival of
the fleet to Cartagena was announced. During the
presence of the fleet there was bustling activity at
Cartagena; then came the long "dead time," broken
only by the occasional arrival of a small coasting
vessel from the islands or from Central America.[1]

Of much greater importance was the fair at Porto
Bello on the isthmus, which was the emporium of the
Peruvian trade. As the town was extremely unhealthy the fleet usually remained at Cartagena
until word was received of the arrival of the fleet
from Peru at Panama. During the fair, which, for
sanitary reasons, was limited to forty days, the
town was so crowded that a single shop would rent
for $1000 and large houses for $5000. While the
ships were unloading, long droves of mules loaded
with boxes of gold and silver, each drove numbering
over a hundred, were threading their way across the
isthmus. Bulkier goods like cacao, quinine, Vicuna
wool, would come down the Chagres River by boats.
Streets, squares, and houses were filled with bales
and boxes, and an enormous business was transacted
in the six weeks at the disposal of the merchants.[2]

Thomas Gage, the English friar, saw this fair in
1637, when the fleet was small and the sale lasted
only a fortnight. For a room which "was but as a

[1] Ulloa, *Voyage*, I., 79–84.   [2] *Ibid.*, 103 ff.

mouse-hole " he was charged $120. All prices of
food rose: fowls ordinarily selling for a rial (twelve
and one-half cents) now brought $1.50, "and a pound
of beef then was worth two Rialls, whereas I had
had in other places thirteen pound for half a Riall."
What he "most wondered at was to see the requas
(droves) of mules which came thither from Panama,
laden with wedges of silver; in one day I told two
hundred mules laden with nothing else, which were
laden in the publicke market place, so that there the
heapes of silver wedges lay like heaps of stones in
the street without any fear or suspition of being lost."

Gage calls Porto Bello an "open grave ready to
swallow in part of that numerous people, which at
that time resort unto it, as was seen the year that
I was there when about five hundred of the souldiers,
merchants, and mariners, what with Feavers, what
with the Flux caused by too much eating of fruit
and drinking of water, what with other disorders lost
their lives, finding it to be to them not Porto Bello,
but Porto malo." [1] The same dark cloud hung over
Vera Cruz during its fairs. In 1556 four out of the
eight members of the family of the merchant John
Field died in ten days,[2] and Cubero Sebastian says
that while he was there "it was a rare day in which he
did not bury three or four cachupins"[3] (Spaniards).

The system of fleets and fairs was perhaps the in-

[1] Gage, *New Survey of the West Indies*, 196–198.
[2] Hakluyt, *Voyages*, XIV., 145.
[3] Cubero Sebastian, *Peregrinacion del Mundo* (ed. 1688), 282.

evitable solution of the problem how to handle a commerce of relatively high value in small bulk with a region whose sea-approaches were in sickly tropical lowlands, at a time when corsairs and pirates swept the ocean.[1] With the development of more international respect for property on the sea, the improvement in ship-building, and the increase of colonial population, the fleet system became painfully inadequate; yet the vested interests were so strongly intrenched that changes were slow and reforms came only in response to outside pressure.

The gradual establishment of colonies by the other European states in the West Indies made an irreparable breach in the Spanish system. The English and Dutch islands in particular became the centres of wholesale smuggling.[2] From this illicit trade Venezuela, hitherto neglected in the Spanish system, profited greatly. Of momentous importance in breaking down the tight wall of commercial monopoly was the war of the Spanish Succession waged by Holland and England to prevent the establishment upon the throne of Spain of Louis XIV.'s grandson and the possible personal union of the two states at some subsequent time. Such a union, or even the close family alliance of the two powers, would give France a paramount interest in the Spanish-Amer-

[1] The fleet system was used by the Portuguese, the Dutch, and the English in their trade with the East Indies.

[2] Roscher, *Spanish Colonial System*, 37; Depons, *Voyage*, II., 268–270.

ican world. Soon after the war broke out Louis
XIV. authorized the merchants of St. Malo to trade
with Lima, which gave rise to a flourishing commerce
through the Straits of Magellan. The early comers
were reported to have made eight hundred per cent.,
but their privilege was cut off upon the restoration
of peace.[1]

The result of the contest secured to England by
the peace of Utrecht in 1713 the asiento or the
monopoly of the African slave-trade with the Spanish possessions, with the right of importing four
thousand eight hundred negroes per annum, and
also the right to send one registered ship of five hundred tons burden to Porto Bello. This breach was
widened by the factors of the English South Sea
Company, who secretly increased the capacity of
the single ship and accompanied her with transports
which kept out of sight by day and from which she
was reloaded in the night.[2]

After such a concession the monopoly of Seville
could hardly be maintained. First came the transfer
of the monopoly to Cadiz in 1717 to relieve ships of
the inconvenient voyage up the Guadalquivir, which
was growing shallow. In 1728 the commercial company of Guipuzcoa was chartered with the privilege
of despatching registered ships from San Sebastian
to Caracas. Six years later the company of Galicia

[1] Robertson, *America* (ed. 1831), 267; Colmeiro, *Hist. de la
Econ. Pol.*, II., 421.
[2] Ulloa, *Voyage*, I., 105, 106; Robertson, *America*, 267, 268.

was accorded the right to send two registered ships to Campeche and to sell any surplus at Vera Cruz.[1] The competition of smugglers and of the illegally swollen importations of the English through the authorized single ship sapped the commerce of the fleets, until hardly anything was left for them to carry except the king's royalty of one-fifth of the product of the silver-mines.[2]

To recover this loss of trade, the Spanish government authorized the merchants of Cadiz and Seville to send registered ships at more frequent intervals and to any ports where there might be a special demand; but in 1748 the fleets were finally discontinued. The Barcelona Company in 1755 undertook the revival of Spanish trade with the islands,[3] but it was at a perilous time, for Spain was ultimately drawn into the Seven Years' War.

It was from one of the apparent misfortunes of this struggle that Spain received a powerful object-lesson in the value of free commerce to colonies. When the English captured Havana in 1762 they opened the port to all English ships. The possibilities of Cuban commerce were immediately revealed, for in the short period they held the city—less than a year—seven hundred and twenty-seven merchant vessels entered the harbor.[4] The enlightened Charles III. of Spain, profiting by this example, opened the

[1] Saco, *Historia de la Esclavitud*, 324.
[2] Robertson, *America*, 268.
[3] Saco, *Historia de la Esclavitud*, 324.
[4] *Ibid.*, 325, on the authority of English periodicals.

trade of the islands in 1765 and of Louisiana in 1768[1] to eight Spanish ports besides Cadiz, and relaxed many of the regulations that had hampered the merchants.[2]   The prosperity of Cuba dates from the English capture of Havana.

In 1774 the prohibition of intercolonial commerce on the Pacific between Peru, New Spain, Guatemala, and New Granada was removed.[3]   Four years later Buenos Ayres, Peru, and Chili were opened to direct trade from the Spanish ports that were allowed to trade with the islands, and Palma, in Majorca, and Tenerife, in the Canaries, were added to the list.   On the American side twenty-three ports were opened in the Atlantic and Pacific, the only important exceptions being those of Venezuela, which were reserved for the Guipuzcoa Company.[4] In 1782 New Orleans and Pensacola were allowed to trade with French ports where there were Spanish consuls.[5]   It may be questioned whether in any other country such radical and extensive relaxations of the restrictions on colonial commerce were ever made in so short a time as those in Spain under Charles III.   It is one of many illustrations that whatever the drawbacks of despotic government it possesses a distinct advantage over more popular systems in the rapidity with which political, commercial, and social reforms may be brought about.

[1] Roscher, *Spanish Colonial System*, 39.
[2] Saco, *Historia de la Esclavitud*.
[3] *Ibid.*, 329.   [4] *Ibid.*, 337.   [5] *Ibid.*, 339.

The subject of Spanish colonial commerce has been treated in some detail because of its international bearings during the seventeenth and eighteenth centuries and its rather close relation to the colonial interests of England, and because comprehensive surveys of its various aspects from the historical point of view are not easily accessible. The internal economic life of Spanish America will now be reviewed much more briefly.

The principal pursuits in Spanish America were farming, grazing, and mining. The romance of the conquest and of the silver fleets has done much to give disproportionate prominence to the production of gold and silver in popular accounts of Spanish colonization. But in those days of small ships and costly land transportation it is obvious that the bulkier agricultural products could not profitably be raised for exportation.

Yet the vast majority of the population of Spanish America lived by farming and grazing, and the annual value of the products of the soil in New Spain at the beginning of the nineteenth century is estimated to have been $30,000,000,[1] or about one-third greater than the yield of the mines.[2] Of the distinctively farm products, corn or maize was the most important in New Spain, although it played

---

[1] Alaman, *Mejico*, I., 103.

[2] Humboldt estimated the annual yield of the mines in New Spain at $23,000,000, *Ensayo Politico sobre la Nueva España*, IV., 134. Bancroft's estimate is the same, *Mexico*, III., 599.

no part in the export trade. Next came maguey, the American agave. The more distinctly colonial products of sugar, cacao, vanilla, cochineal, cassia formed a large proportion of the cargo of the fleets.

The climate and soil of America proved favorable for European domestic animals—horses, horned cattle, sheep, and swine all multiplied with great rapidity, and stock-raising became one of the most profitable industries of the soil. It is a familiar fact that the cattle were slaughtered for their hides and hoofs and that beef was incredibly cheap; but the great wealth acquired by stock-raising even under such unfavorable circumstances is less familiar and presents a glaring contrast to the humble circumstances of the farmer in the English colonies.

The English friar Thomas Gage was amazed at the abundance in rural Mexico. Two days' journey south of the city there were "many rich townes of Spaniards and Indians." "Here live yeomen upon nothing but their farms, who are judged to be worth some twenty thousand, some thirty thousand, some forty thousand duckats." He found Indians living in this region "who traffique to Mexico and about the country witth twenty or thirty mules of their own, chopping and changing, buying and selling commodities, and some of them thought to be worth ten or twelve or fifteen thousand duckats." [1] In Guatemala, a great grazing district, he notes the price of beef as thirteen pounds and a half for threepence.

[1] Gage, *New Survey of the West Indies*, 85.

Gage mentions one farmer who owned forty thousand head of cattle and a public purveyor of meat who bought six thousand head from one man at one time for about $2.25 a head. In the city of Guatemala he knew, besides, many merchants worth from twenty thousand to one hundred thousand ducats—"five were judged of equal wealth and generally reported to be worth each of them five hundred thousand duckats." [1]   Citations like these might be multiplied. Making all necessary allowances for travellers' exaggerations or for Gage's special desire to magnify in English eyes the wealth of New Spain, there still remains enough to prove it to have been a country of private fortunes not equalled in English America until after the application of steam to industry.

Of manufacturing beyond the native arts [2] there was naturally not very much. Yet Gage reports that the cloth made in La Puebla de Los Angeles was thought to be as good as that of Segovia, that it was sent far and near, and that its production had much diminished the importation of Spanish cloths. Felt of high quality was also manufactured at Los Angeles, and glass, "which was a rarity," for it was not made elsewhere in New Spain. [3]

The mines were the source of vast private wealth

[1] Gage, *New Survey of the West Indies*, 125, 126.

[2] On the native arts, cf. Bancroft, *Mexico*, III., 617 ff.

[3] Gage, *New Survey of the West Indies*, 37.   On the cloth factories in Peru and the abuses arising from forced labor in them, see Ulloa, *Noticias Secretas*, 275.

and, as has been shown in another place, of the principal revenue of the crown derived from America.[1] Their number and productiveness steadily increased with the advance in methods and the additions to the number of mines worked. Humboldt estimated the average annual production from the discovery of America as follows:

YEARS	PESOS
1493–1500	250,000
1500–1545	3,000,000
1545–1600	11,000,000
1600–1700	16,000,000
1700–1750	22,500,000
1750–1803	35,300,000 [2]

The total yield from 1493 to 1803 he put at five billion seven hundred and six million seven hundred thousand pesos.[3] At the beginning of the nineteenth century the total annual production he calculated to be forty-three million five hundred thousand, or about ten times the known production of the rest of the world.[4]

[1] See above, p. 241.
[2] Humboldt, *Ensayo Politico*, III., 316.
[3] *Ibid.*, 304.   [4] *Ibid.*, 286, 288.

CHAPTER XX

THE TRANSMISSION OF EUROPEAN CULTURE

(1493–1821)

THE transmission of the heritage of European culture to the New World and its inhabitants, the great work of the colonial epoch, was the task undertaken by the church. From the beginning the conversion of the natives to Christianity was a dominant motive of the Spanish policy; yet this exaltation of religion was not at the sacrifice of the political interests of the crown. The church organization was a very perfect machine, thoroughly under the authority of the king, and a most effective agency in sustaining his rule in these distant dominions. Pope Julius II., in 1508, granted the king of Spain the right of patronage,[1] a concession of no great significance at the time when only the feeble settlements in Española were involved, but of enormous importance after the main-land conquests were completed. The right was broadly interpreted, and under it the king nominated to the pope all the high church dignitaries, prohibited the

[1] Icazbalceta, *Obras*, V., 217; Lowery, *Spanish Settlements*, 383.

circulation of any papal bulls in America without his consent, and required every priest and monk who proposed to go to the New World to obtain the royal license. No church, monastery, or hospital could be erected except in accordance with the king's ordinances.[1] One - ninth of the tithes was covered into the royal treasury,[2] and an even more important part of the king's revenue was derived from the sale of bulls of the Crusade or indulgences, the purchase of which was practically universal.[3]

The work of conversion in Mexico followed upon the heels of conquest, indefatigable friars devoting every moment to preaching, baptizing, and learning the native languages. The old religion withstood the assault as little as the old state: the destruction of the temples and the idols by the conquerors, the death of many of the old ruling caste and of the Aztec priesthood relaxed its bonds, and the masses were relieved from the dreadful burden of the earlier faith.[4] In the Old World the progress from actual to vicarious sacrifice for sin had been slow and painful through the ages; in the New it was accomplished within a single generation. The old re-

[1] Icazbalceta, *Obras*, V., 217. For details see *Recopilacion de Leyes*, lib. I., tit. VI., Del Real Patronazgo.

[2] Usually called the "two-ninths," because it was two-ninths of half the tithes, *Recopilacion de Leyes*, lib. I., tit. XVI., ley 23.

[3] Cf. Robertson, *America*, notes 195 and 196, for prices and income from the bulls.

[4] Cf. Icazbalceta, *Obras*, V., 155 ff.

ligion had inculcated a relatively high morality, but its dreadful rites overhung the present life like a black cloud, and for the future it offered little consolation. The adjustment to Christian morals of Indian customs, such as the polygamy of the chiefs, presented greater difficulties than mere conversion of the people.

The work of the church was rapidly adapted to the new field of labor. In the main it consisted of three distinct types—the parish work of the Spanish towns, in charge of a cura; the teaching and parish work in the Indian villages, or doctrina, in charge either of two or more friars or of a cura; and the mission among the wild Indians, in charge of misioneros. Every town, Indian as well as Spanish, was by law required to have its church, hospital, and school for teaching Indian children Spanish and the elements of religion.

As in Spain, the clergy consisted of the regulars, or members of the orders—the Franciscans, Dominicans, Augustinians, Mercenarians, and the Jesuits—and of the seculars, of all grades from the archbishops down to the simple cura. The regulars not only had large monasteries in the cities, but were scattered up and down through the country in little houses containing from two to five inmates.[1] The doctrinas of the Indian villages might be in charge of "religious," or monks, or of curas, but not of both together. No monastery could be es-

[1] Cf., *e.g.*, Velasco on Mexico, *Descripcion de las Indias*, 194 ff.

tablished in a pueblo where the doctrina was in charge of a cura.[1]

If the work among the wild Indians were successful they were gathered together in a village called a mission, where under the increasing supervision of the friars, they were taught the elements of letters and trained to peaceful, industrious, and religious lives. In fact, every mission was an industrial school, where the simple arts were taught by the friars, themselves in origin plain Spanish peasants. The discipline of the mission was as minute as that of a school: the unmarried youth and maidens were locked in at night; the day's work began and ended with prayers and the catechism; each Indian, besides cultivating his own plot of land, worked two hours a day on the farm belonging to the village, the produce of which went to the support of the church. The mission was recruited by inducing the wild Indians to join it, and also by kidnapping them.[2]

Spanish America from California and Texas to Paraguay and Chili was fringed with such establishments, the outposts of civilization, where many thousands of Indians went through a schooling which ended only with their lives. In the process of time a mission was slowly transformed into a

---

[1] *Recopilacion de Leyes*, lib. I., tit. XIII., ley 2.
[2] Cf. Garrison, *Texas*, 56; Depons, *Voyage*, II., 98 ff.; Humboldt, *Travels*, III., 40, 100, 211; Roscher, *Spanish Colonial System*, 11.

" pueblo de Indios," with its doctrina, and the mission frontier was pushed out a little farther. Then the white planters began to push in. "The whites, and the casts of mixed blood favored by the corregidors (provincial administrators of the tribute) establish themselves among the Indians. The missions become Spanish villages, and the natives lose even the remembrance of their natural idiom. Such is the progress of civilization from the coasts towards the interior—a slow progress shackled by the passions of man, but sure and uniform."[1]

Far different was the advancing frontier in English America with its clean sweep, its clash of elemental human forces. Our own method prepared a home for a more advanced civilization and a less variously mixed population, and its present fruits seem to justify it as the ruthless processes of nature are justified; but a comparison of the two systems does not warrant self-righteousness on the part of the English in America.

However great the work of the church in civilizing the Indians and in mitigating the conquest, one must not ignore the fact that, after the first flush of excitement over the vast field opened before it, there was a relaxation of discipline and of morals. Though not strange it scandalized European observers. In more ways than one the conditions of the Middle Ages were revived. The every-day familiarity and age-long contact with the Mohammedan life in old Spain

[1] Humboldt, *Travels*, III., 215.

had made the Spaniards as a people exceptionally tolerant of irregular relations of the sexes. In the centuries preceding the discoveries a qualified form of plural marriage among the laity was recognized by the laws, as were more or less permanent connections between single men and women, in some aspects a survival of the old Roman legalized concubinage.[1] The celibacy of the clergy in Spain had been more an ideal than a fact; indeed, the extraordinary efforts in the Middle Ages to enforce it against prevalent usage achieved less success in Spain than anywhere else in Europe; marriages of the clergy were not legal, yet a legal status was accorded their children.[2]

Queen Isabella had exerted much influence towards the improvement of the morals of the clergy, but when in the remote society of the New World the old-time conditions again presented themselves of the contact of a superior race with an inferior and compliant population, the clergy relapsed. Recruited as it was from the common people in Spain, concubinage became very general among both the friars and the curas.[3] Society in general seemed very lax and corrupt to foreign observers. Frézier remarks

---

[1] See art. "Barragan," in Escriche, *Diccionario Razonado de Legislacion*, Burke, *History of Spain*, I., 404.

[2] See Lea, *Sacerdotal Celibacy*, index art. Spain; Prescott, *Ferdinand and Isabella*, I., lxviii., II., 397.

[3] See Ulloa, *Noticias Secretas*, index under concubinas, frailes, curas, concubinato; Frézier, *Voyage*, II., 447. Frézier excepts the bishops and the Jesuits, *ibid.*, 433.

that the Spaniards are temperate in wine, but that continence has very little hold on them. The old-time quasi-legal concubinage was very general, and the duties and obligations of the more formal marriage bond were lightly borne by both husbands and wives.[1] The Peruvians, in addition, seem to have anticipated our own facilities for divorce and remarriage, a condition which scandalized the eighteenth-century Frenchman quite as much as the licentiousness of the clergy and their flocks.[2]

Both the crown and the church were solicitous for education in the colonies, and provisions were made for its promotion on a far greater scale than was possible or even attempted in the English colonies. The early Franciscan missionaries built a school beside each church,[3] and in their teaching abundant use was made of signs, drawings, and paintings.[4] The native languages were reduced to writing, and in a few years Indians were learning to read and write. Pedro de Gante, a Flemish lay brother and a relative of Charles V., founded and conducted in the Indian quarter in Mexico a great school attended by over a thousand Indian boys, which combined instruction in elementary and higher branches, the mechanical and the fine arts. In its workshops the boys were taught to be

[1] Frézier, *Voyage*, 446. Cf. also Captain Betagh's *Observations* on Peruvian life in the eighteenth century, Pinkerton, *Voyages*, XIV.   [2] Frézier, *Voyage*, II., 403.

[3] Icazbalceta, *Obras*, I., 171.

[4] Cf. Lowery, *Spanish Settlements*, 396–398.

tailors, carpenters, blacksmiths, shoemakers, and painters.[1]

Bishop Zumárraga wanted a college for Indians in each bishopric, and the first institution for higher education in the New World was founded in 1535, the college of Santa Cruz, in Tlaltelolco, a quarter in the Indian part of the city of Mexico. Besides the elementary branches, instruction was offered in Latin, philosophy, music, Mexican medicine, and the native languages. Among the faculty were graduates of the University of Paris and such eminent scholars as Bernardino de Sahagun, the founder of American anthropology, and Juan de Torquemada, himself a product of Mexican education, whose *Monarquia Indiana* is a great storehouse of knowledge of Mexican antiquities and history. Many of the graduates of this college became alcaldes and governors in the Indian towns.[2]

Nor was the education of the Indian girls neglected; and the increasing number of mestizo children led to the establishment of a college for them.[3] From 1536 dates the first royal provision for the teaching of the creole Spanish youth.[4] In 1551 Charles V. founded the universities of Mexico and Lima. Chairs of Indian languages were ordered to be established in both and in the more important of other institutions.[5] A year after the University of

---

[1] Icazbalceta, *Obras*, I., 176.
[2] *Ibid.*, 180–182; Alaman, *Disertaciones* (Havana ed., 1873), II., 110 ff.
[3] Icazbalceta, *Obras*, I., 182, 189.   [4] *Ibid.*, 193.
[5] *Recopilacion de Leyes*, lib. I., tit. XXII., leys 1 and 46.

Mexico opened in 1554, its professor of rhetoric, Dr. Cervantes Salazar, a graduate of Osuno, published three interesting Latin dialogues, the first describing the university, the other two taking up Mexico city and its environs, a work after the model of the more serious of Erasmus's colloquies.[1]

Not all the institutions of learning founded in Mexico in the sixteenth century can be enumerated here, but it is not too much to say that in number, range of studies, and standard of attainments by the officers they surpassed anything existing in English America until the nineteenth century. Mexican scholars made distinguished achievements in some branches of science, particularly medicine and surgery, but pre-eminently in linguistics, history, and anthropology. Dictionaries and grammars of the native languages and histories of the Mexican institutions are an imposing proof of their scholarly devotion and intellectual activity. Conspicuous are Toribio de Motolinia's *Historia de los Indios de Nueva España;* Duran's *Historia de las Indias de Nueva España;* but most important of all Sahagun's great work on Mexican life and religion.[2]

The most famous of the earlier Peruvian writers were Acosta, the historian, the author of the *Natural and Civil History of the Indies;* the mestizo Garcilasso de la Vega, who was educated in Spain and

---

[1] Reissued in 1875 with notes and Spanish version by Icazbalceta under the title *Mexico en 1554.*

[2] *Historia General de las Cosas de Nueva España.*

wrote of the Inca Empire and of De Soto's expedition; Sandoval, the author of the first work on Africa and the negro written in America;[1] Antonio Leon Pinelo, the first American bibliographer, and one of the greatest, as well as the indefatigable codifier of the legislation of the Indies. Pinelo was born in Peru and educated at the Jesuit college in Lima, but spent his literary life in Spain.

Early in the eighteenth century the Lima University counted nearly two thousand students, and numbered about one hundred and eighty doctors in theology, civil and canon law, medicine, and the arts. The French engineer Frézier reports that the training was good in scholasticism, but of little account in modern scientific subjects. Ulloa a generation later reports that "the university makes a stately appearance without, and its inside is decorated with suitable ornaments." There were chairs of all the sciences, and "some of the professors have, notwithstanding the vast distance, gained the applause of the literati of Europe."[2] The coming of the Jesuits contributed much to the real educational work in America. They established colleges, one of which, the little Jesuit college at Juli, on Lake Titicaca, became a seat of genuine learning.[3]

That the Spanish authorities in church and state did much to promote education is abundantly evi-

[1] *De Instauranda Æthiopum Salute; Historia de Æthiopia; Naturaleza, Policia Sacrada i Profana, Costumbres*, etc. (Madrid, 1647).   [2] Frézier, *Voyages*, II., 392; Ulloa, *Voyage*, II., 45.   [3] Cf. Markham, *Acosta*, v.

dent, and the modern sciences of anthropology, linguistics, geography, and history are profoundly indebted to the labors of the early Spanish-American scholars and missionaries. It is in these fields that their achievements shine, for in these fields they could work unhampered by the censorship of the press and the Inquisition. In philosophy and in politics the mind was less free. The part which the Inquisition played in confining intellectual work to the well-beaten track of traditional orthodoxy makes appropriate a brief consideration of its activities in America, about which great misconceptions have prevailed. The Holy Office was extended to America in 1569.[1] Earlier the bishops had been accorded inquisitorial powers. One occasionally meets with references to the cruelties practised by the Inquisition on the Indians, but that charge is without foundation, for the Indians were exempted from its jurisdiction as children in the faith not capable of heresy.[2] If they offended against the rules of the church they were punished, like children, with the whip. Foreign heretics, Portuguese or Spanish Jews, witches, and bigamists principally occupied its attention, but owing to the rigid exclusion of all emigrants tainted even with ancestral heresy this dreaded court ordinarily had little to do compared with its grewsome activities in the mother-country.

[1] *Recopilacion de Leyes*, lib. I., tit. XIX., ley 1.
[2] *Ibid.*, lib. VI., tit. I., ley 35.

The arrival of the Inquisition in Mexico in 1574 was signalized by pouncing on all of Hawkins's men who had been put ashore in 1568 that could be got hold of. Miles Philips gives a full account of its methods. Over fifty of them were condemned to be scourged and to serve in the galleys. Three "had their judgment to be burnt to ashes." [1] Frézier found the commissaries of the Inquisition in the villages in remote Chili, and remarks: " They busy themselves mainly about the visions of real or pretended sorcerers and certain crimes subject to the Inquisition, like polygamy, etc. For, as for heretics, I am sure they find none, there is so little study there." [2]

In its entire history in Peru the Inquisition celebrated twenty-nine autos da fe, the first burning taking place in 1581 and the last in 1776. Fifty-nine heretics in all suffered at the stake. [3] The list was shorter in Mexico. In two hundred and seventy-seven years, so far as has been learned, forty-one were burned as relapsed heretics and ninety-nine were burned in effigy. [4] The auto of 1659 is typical: the criminals were twenty-nine in number, twenty-three men and six women; twelve for blasphemy, two for bigamy, one for forgery, one for perjury, one for avisos de carceles, one for failure to complete a penance, one woman for

[1] Miles Philips, in Hakluyt, *Voyages*, XIV., 209–213.
[2] Frézier, *Voyages*, II., 182.   [3] Markham, *Peru*, 149.
[4] Icazbalceta, *Obras*, I., 316.

suspected Judaism, one for witchcraft, two, a father and daughter, for suspected connection with the heretics "illuminati." Seven relapsed were burned, five for heresy and two for Judaism.[1] Usually only a small proportion were executed as relapsed. In 1664 one offender was stripped to the waist and then "honeyed" and feathered.[2] In view of the witchcraft tragedy in Salem one notices with interest that executions for witchcraft were comparatively infrequent, the accused usually being subjected to some milder penalty or acquitted.[3]

With the intellectual awakening in the eighteenth century new perils beset these sheltered communities. The Inquisition redoubled its activity, and the catalogues of prohibited or expurgated books grew to include, according to Depons, the works of five thousand four hundred and twenty authors. On the lists were the names of the leading thinkers of the century.[4]

The early promoters of education and missions did not rely upon the distant European presses for the publication of their manuals. The printing-press was introduced into the New World probably as early as 1536, and it seems likely that the first book, an elementary Christian doctrine, called *La Escala Espiritual* (the ladder of the spirit), was

---

[1] Icazbalceta, *Obras*, I., 296.   [2] *Ibid.*, 300.
[3] Gage gives an interesting account of his experience with a witch, *New Survey of the West Indies*, 167.
[4] Depons, *Voyage*, II., 74 ff.   Cf. Alaman, *Mejico*, I., 121.

issued in 1537. No copy of it, however, is known to exist.[1] Seven different printers plied their craft in New Spain in the sixteenth century.[2] Among the notable issues of these presses, besides the religious works and church service books, were dictionaries and grammars of the Mexican languages; Puga's *Cedulario* in 1563, a compilation of royal ordinances; Farfán's *Tractado de Medicina*. In 1605 appeared the first text-book published in America for instruction in Latin, a manual of poetics with illustrative examples from heathen and Christian poets.[3]

Mexico was in a sense the mother-country of the Philippines, and the first general history and description of the islands in distinction from missionary narratives, Antonio de Morga's *Sucesos de las Islas Philipinas*, was printed in Mexico in 1609. Notwithstanding the efforts of the church and of missionaries in behalf of education it is not to be supposed that elementary education was anything like so generally diffused in the later days as in the English colonies, though Spanish America would have compared favorably with old Spain. If we compare Spanish America with the United States a hundred years ago, we must recognize that while in the north there was a sounder body politic, a purer social life, and a more general dissemination of elementary education, yet in Spanish

---

[1] Icazbalceta, *Obras*, I., 22.
[2] *Ibid.*, 36.   [3] *Ibid.*, 36.

America there were both vastly greater wealth and greater poverty, more imposing monuments of civilization, such as public buildings, institutions of learning, and hospitals, more populous and richer cities, a higher attainment in certain branches of science. No one can read Humboldt's account of the city of Mexico and its establishments for the promotion of science and the fine arts without realizing that, whatever may be the superiorities of the United States over Mexico in these respects they have been mostly the gains of the age of steam.

During the first half-century after the application of steam to transportation Mexico weltered in domestic turmoils arising out of the crash of the old régime. If the rule of Spain could have lasted half a century longer, being progressively liberalized as it was during the reign of Charles III.; if a succession of such viceroys as Revilla Gigedo, in Mexico, and De Croix and De Taboada y Lemos, in Peru, could have borne sway in America until railroads could have been built, intercolonial intercourse ramified, and a distinctly Spanish-American spirit developed—then a great Spanish-American federal state might possibly have been created, capable of self-defence against Europe and inviting co-operation rather than aggression from the neighbor in the north.

As it was, the English colonies, in the beginning more detached than the Spanish, yet contiguous, so that intercourse was easy, and enjoying the advantage of occupying a relatively small area, were able to join forces in the War for Independence. The Union became cemented by the acquisition first of half and then of the whole great central valley, an essential unit geographically, whose earlier lines of communication ran north and south, thus binding the two diverging sections by deep-lying ties. Then at just the right period came the steam-boat and the railroad to multiply the connecting links and unloose the great forces of economic interest and national pride to counteract the rising forces of disruption.

The Spanish colonies were more closely united administratively than the English, but at the time of their independence the physical and geographical obstacles to forming a United States of Spanish America were absolutely insuperable. Hence they tended to break up along lines roughly corresponding to the old administrative subdivisions. The Revolution consequently gave rise to a number of weak states whose peaceful progress under a clash of interests unknown in English America was impossible. The Spanish-American peoples have lacked the inspiration of united action, and their resources and powers have been frittered away in intestine quarrels. If the formidable apparition of the ever-extending United States draws them together for mutual defence; if the construction of railroads sufficiently overcomes the great geographical impediments to unity; if the Monroe Doctrine shall serve the temporary purpose of protecting them from foreign attack during this period of mutual approach—there may yet arise a great Spanish-American federal state, the counterpart of the United States, to become a wholesome check on its indefinite absorption of alien lands and peoples to the south, and the home of a great people which with the infusion of new blood will free itself from the evils of its earlier life while preserving the best of the heritage from Spain.

Society in Spanish America combines a great variety of more widely contrasting elements than are to be found in English America. In the old days, Europeans, Americans of European ancestry, African negroes, the descendants of the native stocks, all lived together as rulers and ruled, masters and slaves, "higher" and "lower" races, not entirely detached, not yet fused, rather a series of social layers, partly distinct and partly merged, with antagonisms and jealousies. Independence has not yet allayed those jealousies, but the continual reinforcement of the European stock by industrious immigrants from Spain, Italy, and Germany, relatively free from race and color prejudices, will in time give greater stability to social conditions, raise the average of intelligence, increase the production of wealth, and advance the progress of civilization, carrying on and not undoing the work of Spain. The Spanish language will still be the common tongue of the millions who live between the Rio Grande del Norte and the Straits of Magellan, and, with the advance in knowledge, national pride in the achievements of the Spaniards who explored a hemisphere and ineffaceably stamped upon its two continents their language and their religion will become an abiding inspiration.

CHAPTER XXI

CRITICAL ESSAY ON AUTHORITIES

BIBLIOGRAPHIES

THE most convenient guide to the sources and literature of the discoveries is in J. N. Larned, *Literature of American History, a Bibliographical Guide* (1902), 50–68. Justin Winsor, *Narrative and Critical History of America* (8 vols., 1888–1889), II., contains more titles, but comes down only to 1886. The bibliographical notes appended to some of the chapters in H. H. Bancroft, *History of Central America* and *History of Mexico* (3 vols., 1882), are very serviceable. Brief but exact references are provided in Channing and Hart, *Guide to the Study of American History* (1896), pp. 81–87, 92–94. In Winsor, *America*, I., i.–xviii., will be found an interesting historical sketch of the earlier and of the more elaborate bibliographies. The literature of the later history of the Spanish colonies is listed in detail in the notes to the appropriate chapters in Winsor, VIII. One can best keep abreast of the current European critical literature in this field by following the reviews published in *Petermann's Mitteilungen aus Justus Perthes' Geographischer Anstalt;* and in the two annuals: H. Wagner, *Geographisches Jahrbuch;* E. Berner, *Jahresbericht der Geschichtswissenschaft.*

GENERAL SECONDARY WORKS

An excellent general account of the progress of geographical knowledge and of the discoveries will be found in John Fiske, *Discovery of America* (2 vols., 1892). The second volume of Justin Winsor, *Narrative and Critical History of*

America, embraces the half-century extending from the first voyage of Columbus to the explorations of De Soto and Coronado; the critical chapters and the notes take account of a great mass of literature relating to the subject.

For the special student, Alexander von Humboldt, *Kritische Untersuchungen über die historische Entwickelung der geographischen Kenntnisse von der neuen Welt*, etc. (Ideler's translation from French to German, 3 vols., 1852), is still very valuable. The German translation is preferable to the French original, as it is provided with a complete index. K. Kretschmer, *Die Entdeckung Amerikas* (1 vol., with atlas, 1892), is a work of critical scholarship which registers the present state of knowledge of the history of geography. Pre-eminent among the recent general works relating to the discoveries for critical scholarship and wide research is H. Harrisse, *Discovery of North America: a Critical, Documentary, and Historic Investigation, with an Essay on the Early Cartography of the New World* (1892).

An earlier study of somewhat similar scope and still valuable is J. G. Kohl, *A History of the Discovery of the East Coast of North America*, in vol. I. of the *Documentary History of the State of Maine* (1869).

Among the general works, Oskar Peschel, *Geschichte des Zeitalters der Entdeckungen* (2d ed., 1877), is particularly serviceable to the student. The narrative is clear and accurate and the foot-notes are a running guide to the primary sources. Sophus Ruge, *Geschichte des Zeitalters der Entdeckungen* (1881), is an authoritative general account based on the sources and richly illustrated with portraits and maps. P. Gaffarel, *Histoire de la Découverte de l'Amérique, depuis les Origines jusqu'à la mort de Christophe Colomb* (2 vols., 1892), devotes his second volume to the career of Columbus and to the discoveries up to his death. It is a work of sound scholarship. S. Günther, *Das Zeitalter der Entdeckungen* (1901), is a very lucid short account, which admirably summarizes the present state of knowledge. The same is to be said of Carlo Errera, *L'Epoca delle Grandi Scoperte Geografiche* (1902), which has the additional merit of a full index and well-selected maps and portraits.   Luigi Hugues, *Cronologia delle Scoperte e delle Esplorazioni Geografiche dall'anno 1492 a Tutto il Secolo XIX.* (1903), is a very scholarly compendium, embodying the latest knowledge in the form of annals.   A similar conspectus with bibliographical notes is given in H. H. Bancroft, *Central America*, I. (1883), 68–152, coming down to 1540.   The most important repository of the facts of the first half-century of the Spanish discoveries is Antonio de Herrera, *Historia General de los Hechos de los Castellanos en las Islas y Tierra Firme del Mar Oceano* (1728–1730).   This work was based on official documents and reports of explorers, and in regard to the earlier period on the *Historia de las Indias* of Las Casas.   The index is very complete.   The English translation (incomplete) by John Stevens is not trustworthy. An epitome of Herrera is supplied in vol. I. of T. Southey, *Chronological History of the West Indies* (1827).

GENERAL COLLECTIONS OF SOURCES

The principal collection of documents relating to the discoveries of the Portuguese is J. Ramos-Coelho, *Alguns Documentos do Archivo Nacional da Torre do Tombo*, etc. (1892); it covers the period 1416 to 1529.   For the study of the Columbian and later Spanish voyages a new epoch was begun by the publication of M. F. Navarrete, *Coleccion de los Viages y Descubrimientos*, etc. (5 vols., 1825–1837). Later Spanish collections more comprehensive but by no means so well edited as Navarrete are: *Coleccion de Documentos Ineditos para la Historia de España* (112 vols., 1842–1895).   The material relating to America in the first 110 vols. is indexed by G. P. Winship in the Boston Public Library *Bulletin*, October, 1894.   Pacheco and Cardenas, *Coleccion de Documentos Ineditos Relativos al Descubrimiento, Conquista y Colonizacion de las Possessiones Españolas en America y Occeania*, etc. (42 vols., 1864 – 1884); vol. XXXIII. contains a chronological table of contents.   This collection is continued under the title *Coleccion de Docu-*

mentos Ineditos de Ultramar. Segunda serie (11 vols., 1885–1898), in which the contents are arranged topically. The most notable of recent documentary publications is that published by the Italian government, *Raccolta di Documenti e Studi* (6 parts in 14 vols., 1892–1896). Further details as to the contents of these collections and as to which of the documents are accessible in English translations will be found in Larned, *Literature of American History*.

Many interesting narratives of early voyages to America will be found in Hakluyt, *Principall Navigations, Voiages and Discoveries of the English Nation* (1589 and later eds.). A new edition is in process of publication. Many of the most important of the narrative sources for the history of the discoveries have been published in English translations under competent editors by the Hakluyt Society, London. For further details, see Larned, under index headings, "Eden," "Hakluyt," "Kerr," "Pinkerton," and "Purchas." Selected extracts from the early narratives are given in A. B. Hart, *American History Told by Contemporaries* (4 vols., 1897–1900), I., chaps. i.–v.

LIVES OF COLUMBUS

The earliest lives of Columbus are those by his fellow-townsmen Antonio Gallo, Bartolomeo Senarega, and Agostino Giustiniano, of which the first was largely copied by the other two. Their lives are most easily accessible in the original Latin and in English translation in the first volume of Thacher, *Christopher Columbus* (1903). Next in order of time comes the life by his son Ferdinand, *Historie del S. D. Fernando Colombo; nelle quali s'ha particolare e vera relatione della vita, e de fatti dell Ammiraglio D. Christoforo Colombo, suo padre*, etc. (1571 and later). The earlier part, prior to 1492, is of uncertain value and authenticity. From 1492 on it is founded on the journals and letters of Columbus. The Spanish original is no longer extant. An English translation was prepared for Churchill, *Voyages* (1744–1746), and is reprinted in Pinkerton, *Voyages*

(1808–1814). Bartolomé de Las Casas, *Historia de las Indias* (5 vols., 1875–1876), may be mentioned appropriately with the lives of Columbus, because through Herrera's extensive use of it it has constituted with Ferdinand's *Historie* the principal source from which later biographers drew until the publication of Navarrete's *Viages*. Las Casas had papers of Columbus and other explorers which have since been lost. He brings his history down to 1521.

The most famous of the biographies of Columbus is Washington Irving, *Life and Voyages of Christopher Columbus* (1828–1831), based on Navarrete's documents, Ferdinand's *Historie*, Las Casas, and Peter Martyr's *Decades*. His charm of style, his disposition to ignore Columbus's faults, and an occasional imaginative coloring to important scenes have unduly discredited Irving with certain modern scholars. No subsequent life, however, with the exception of Harrisse's, has been more conscientiously based on the primary sources for its narrative of facts. Henry Harrisse, in his *Christophe Colomb* (2 vols., 1884), greatly advanced Columbian studies by his publication of new documents and penetrating criticism of all sources of information. His work, however, is not so much a narrative of the life of Columbus as a series of "studies in historical criticism," as he entitles it. The next elaborate study of Columbus's life was that of José Maria Asensio, *Cristoval Colon, su Vida, sus Viajes, sus Descubrimientos* (2 vols., 1891). It is pronounced by Markham to be the best and most complete of the biographies.

The latest study of the discoverer's career is John Boyd Thacher, *Christopher Columbus* (3 vols., 1903–1904), in which many of the most important primary sources are reprinted with English translations, photographic facsimiles, etc. Special attention is given to the bibliography of Columbus's own writings, to supposed portraits, his autographs, and to the ultimate fate of his remains. Justin Winsor, *Christopher Columbus* (1892), puts before the reader the results of the investigations of Harrisse and other specialists touching the various aspects of

Columbus's career and the additions to geographical knowledge consequent to his discoveries. The work is richly illustrated.

Of the shorter lives in English the best by far is Clements R. Markham, *Life of Christopher Columbus* (1892). It is clear and accurate and is based on first-hand study of the sources. After enjoying the exceptional advantage of editing the writings of Columbus for the *Raccolta Colombiana*, Cesare de Lollis prepared his *Vita di Cristoforo Colombo narrata secondo gli ultimi documenti* (3d ed., 1895). It is not only a work of original scholarship, but is written with literary skill and feeling. The existing state of expert knowledge and opinion in regard to Columbus is presented in a clear and attractive fashion by Sophus Ruge, *Columbus* (2d ed., 1902). A bibliography and additional critical notes add to the value of the text. Further details as to the biographies of Columbus may be found in Harrisse, Winsor, Markham, and in Larned.

THE VOYAGES OF COLUMBUS

The principal source for the voyages of Columbus are his own writings so far as they have been preserved intact, in epitome, or embedded in historical narratives like the *Historie* of his son Ferdinand or the *Historia de las Indias* of Las Casas. The original texts of all the writings of Columbus that could be identified were published by Lollis in the *Raccolta Colombiana* (1892–1896). The most important of these writings were edited by Navarrete, in whose collection Las Casas' abridgment of the journal of the first voyage was first published. Translations of this have been published by Kettel, Markham, and Thacher. R. H. Major, *Select Letters of Columbus* (2d ed. 1890), contains the longer communications descriptive of his voyages. These, as well as a large number of his private letters, will be found in Thacher. Another translation of a considerable body of Columbus's private letters with some other documents was prepared by Dr. José Ignacio Rodriguez and published by the American Historical Association in its *Report* for 1894. The original texts of many of these private letters first saw the light in La Duquesa de Berwick y de Alba, *Autografos de Cristobal Colon* (1892). A new volume of these papers appeared in 1902, entitled *Nuevos Autografos de Cristobal Colon y Relaciones de Ultramar*.

Columbus's journal of the second voyage is not extant, but Lollis tentatively reconstructed its outlines by printing in parallel columns in the *Raccolta* the narratives in Las Casas and in the *Historie* of Ferdinand Columbus, both of which closely follow the original, but are in the main independently derived from it. Of these two accounts only Ferdinand's is accessible in English, except in so far as Stevens's translation of Herrera represents the Las Casas narrative.

An important account of the first part of the second voyage is that of Dr. Chanca, a physician on board, translated by Major and by Thacher. Chanca's narrative fell into the hands of Bernaldez, who embodied it in the one hundred and nineteenth and one hundred and twentieth chapters of his *Historia de los Reyes Catolicos* (unprinted till 1878), adding other information in regard to the later period of the expedition which he derived from Columbus himself. The chapters (cxviii.–cxxxi.) in Bernaldez have been translated into English and were published by the Massachusetts Historical Society, *Collections*, 3d series, vol. VIII. (1838).

For the other accounts derived from participants in the voyage, see H. Harrisse, *Christophe Colomb*, and Thacher. Of the third voyage outward Columbus gave an account in a letter to the king and queen, which is translated in Major. After his return in chains he wrote a letter to the former nurse of Prince Juan, dwelling upon his services and his misfortunes; translations of this letter are given by Major and Thacher. More detailed and much more satisfactory than these letters are the narratives of Las Casas and Ferdinand Columbus based on Columbus's own journal of the voyage. The Las Casas account appears unabridged in English for the first time in Thacher.

Las Casas and the *Historie* of Ferdinand Columbus are also of the first importance for the fourth voyage. We have in addition a letter of Columbus's describing its incidents, which is extant only in an Italian translation, of which Thacher reprints a fac-simile. English translations will be found in Major and Thacher. Other accounts of parts of the voyage are the Porras and Mendez narratives (in English in Thacher).

The most important source for the history of the diffusion of knowledge of the New World is Guglielmo Berchet, *Fonti Italiani per la Storia della Scoperta del Nuovo Mondo. I. Carteggi diplomatici. II. Narrazioni sincrone* (*Raccolta Colombiana*, pt. iii., vols., I., II., 1893). The first of these volumes contains every reference to the discovery of the New World in Italian diplomatic correspondence down to 1536; in the second are all the passages in books and manuscripts by Italian writers down to 1550 which refer to Columbus or the discovery of America, excepting Peter Martyr's *Decades*.

In the absence of the periodical press in the fifteenth and sixteenth centuries its place was in part supplied by the literary correspondent. The most noted of these correspondents in Spain was Peter Martyr, of Anghiera, in Italy, near Milan, who lived in Spain from 1488 to 1526, part of the time as apostolic protonotary at the court of Castile. In after life he collected his letters for publication, *Opus Epistolarum* (1530). The passages in the earlier ones relating to Columbus are excerpted by Thacher and translated into English. Whether they were originally written at the dates ascribed to them and in the exact form in which they were published is open to grave doubt. If certainty as to the date at which Peter Martyr put such and such a fact on record is required, recourse must be had to his narratives of the history of the discoveries, also written in the form of letters to various correspondents. So much of these as subsequently formed the first seven books of his *Decades* came into the hands of the Venetian Angelo Trivigiane, who translated them into Italian. They were subsequently printed in Venice as *Libretto de Tutta la Navigatione de Re de Spagna de le Isole et Terreni Novamente Trovati* (1504). Of this earliest history of America but one printed copy has survived to the present day. Thacher gives a fac-simile and also a translation of the text—both for the first time. The Latin original of the first *Decade* was first published in 1511. As finally completed, Peter Martyr's *Decades* constitute, as has been indicated, the first history of the New World. The narrative is brought down through the conquest of Mexico. The only complete edition is that edited by Hakluyt in 1587. The first three *Decades* were translated by Richard Eden, 1555, and the last five by Michael Lok. This English version is accessible in Hakluyt, *Voyages*, V. (ed. 1812). Peter Martyr utilized materials some of which are no longer extant, interviewed explorers and conquerors, and as a member in later life of the Council of the Indies had extraordinary facilities for getting at the truth. His history is an invaluable repository of facts relating to the explorations, and to the customs of the natives.

The next historian in order of time, and one whose wide acquaintance and extensive experience in the New World were supplemented by moderation of judgment, was Gonzalo Fernandez de Oviedo y Valde, *Historia General y Natural de las Indias* (first complete ed., 4 vols., 1851–1855).

THE VOYAGES OF OTHER NAVIGATORS

For the Cabot literature, G. P. Winship, *Cabot Bibliography* (1900), is a remarkably complete and thoroughly critical guide. The Cabot documentary material in the original and in English translation is most accessible in G. E. Weare, *Cabot's Discovery of North America* (1897). The same material is extracted in C. R. Beazley, *John and Sebastian Cabot* (1898). The contributions of H. Harrisse to the Cabot question are comparable to what he has done to elucidate the life of Columbus. His *Jean et Sébastien Cabot* (1882) greatly advanced knowledge of the material and its critical interpretation. His later *John Cabot the Discoverer of North America and Sebastian His Son*, etc. (1896), is invaluable to the student of Cabot problems, which have also received penetrating and critical treatment in his *Discovery of North America* (1892), and his most recent elaborate work, *Découverte et Évolution Cartographique de Terre-Neuve* (1900). The modern scientific study of the Cabot problem began with Richard Biddle, *Memoir of Sebastian Cabot* (1831), and the best critical survey of the question in English before the publication of Harrisse's work was Charles Deane's monograph, in Winsor, *Narrative and Critical History*, III. The principal Cabot documents are also to be found in translation in Markham, *The Journal of Christopher Columbus* (1893).

The documents relating to the Corte - Real voyages and the critical discussion of them will be found in Harrisse, *Les Corte-Real et leur Voyages au Nouveau-Monde* (1883). Harrisse makes a later survey of the same subject in his *Discovery of North America*. The documents are translated in C. R. Markham, *Journal of Columbus* (1893).

The documentary material on the voyage of Vasco da Gama has been critically edited by F. Hummereich, *Vasco da Gama und die Entdeckung des Seeweges nach Ostindien* (1898). The original material has been translated into English, with critical introduction and notes by E. G. Ravenstein, *A Journal of the First Voyage of Vasco da Gama, 1497–1499* (1898). The first great narrative history of the Portuguese discoveries was João de Barros, *Decadas da Asia* (1553, best ed., 24 vols., 1778–1788.) Barros's work, like that of Herrera, was founded upon documents and contemporary narratives. Barros has never been translated into English, but his history down to 1502 is accessible in a German version by E. Feust (1844).

An important contemporary account of Cabral's discovery of Brazil is that by Pero Vas de Caminha in *Alguns Documentos da Torre do Tombo*, 108. Chapter lxiv. of the

Paesi Novamente Retrovati (1507, reprinted in the *Raccolta Colombiana*, pt. iii.) contains the journal of a Portuguese sailor; and another account by the ship's surgeon, Maestre Juan, is noted by Peschel as in F. A. de Varnhagen, *Historia Geral do Brazil*, I., 423.

For the voyages of Pinzon and Niño the earliest account is that of Peter Martyr in the *Libretto* (in English in Thacher, *Columbus*, II.). These accounts reappear substantially unchanged in Peter Martyr's *Decades*. Hojeda's own testimony in regard to his voyage of 1499 and Navarrete's account are translated by Markham, *Letters of Amerigo Vespucci* (1894). Vespucci's narrative of his first voyage —dated by himself 1497—is now regarded as an account of this voyage. The fullest account in English of these early secondary voyages is that of Irving, *Voyages of the Companions of Columbus* (1831), based on Navarrete and Las Casas; the volume is usually published with his *Life of Columbus*. E. Channing has given a brief critical account in Winsor, *Narrative and Critical History*, II., chap. iii.

NAMING OF AMERICA AND THE VESPUCCI QUESTION

A complete bibliography of the Vespucci question and of the name America was prepared by G. Fumagalli for G. Uzielli's new edition of A. M. Bandini, *Vita di Amerigo Vespucci* (1893). The accepted and the questioned Vespucci letters are critically edited and interpreted by Francisco Adolpho de Varnhagen, *Amerigo Vespucci: son Caractère, ses Écrits, sa Vie et ses Navigations* (1865). Critical opinion, however, is not agreed in entirely rejecting some of the narratives that Varnhagen declared spurious. The best modern critical discussion of the Vespucci question is that by Hugues, in the *Raccolta Colombiana*. The earliest detailed hostile criticism of Vespucci's narrative of his first voyage was written by Las Casas. It became generally accessible in Herrera's incorporation of its substance in his history and deeply influenced opinion, although its real author was unknown until modern times. Las Casas' discussion is translated in Markham, *Letters of Amerigo Vespucci* (1894), which contains in translation the two accepted narratives of Vespucci. Markham's introduction is adverse to Vespucci's claims. Quaritch has published a convenient fac-simile reprint of the original edition of the Soderini letter published in Florence in 1505-1506 as *The First Four Voyages of Amerigo Vespucci* (1893). The English translation is more exact than Markham's. Of importance in the history of the Vespucci controversy are Humboldt, *Untersuchungen* (see index), and Santarem, *Recherches Historiques*, etc. (1842), accessible in English in E. V. Childe's translation (1850).

An excellent résumé of the diffusion of the name America is L. Hugues, *La Vicende del Nome "America"* (1898). Kretschmer's chapter, "Der Name des Neuen Weltteils," in his *Entdeckung Amerikas*, also traces the history of the name. Jules Marcou's arguments for a native origin of the name are fully presented in his *Nouvelles Recherches sur l'Origine du Nom d'Amérique* (1888). His view has won no adherents from among scholars of rank.

SEARCH FOR A STRAIT, AND MAGELLAN'S VOYAGE

The principal source for the Pinzon-Solis voyage of 1508 is Peter Martyr, *Decades*, II., lib. VII.

The sources for the attempts of Hojeda and Nicuesa to colonize the main-land are the cedula and the report of Colmenares, in Navarrete, *Viages*, III., 116, 386; the narrative of Las Casas, which he based upon a history in manuscript by one Cristobal de la Tovilla, entitled *La Barbarica* (Las Casas, III., 289); Peter Martyr, *Decades*, II., lib. I.–III.; and Oviedo, *Historia General*, book XXVII. Detailed modern narratives in Washington Irving, *Companions of Columbus;* H. H. Bancroft, *History of Central America*, I.; and Arthur Helps, *Spanish Conquest in America*, I.

Peter Martyr's account of Balboa and the discovery of

the Pacific is based on the contemporary reports of Colmenares and Caicedo and the letters of Balboa and others from the isthmus. Navarrete (III., 358, 375) prints two letters of Balboa to the king. Irving's account of Balboa, in his *Companions of Columbus*, is based on the sources, as is that of Helps, *Spanish Conquest in America*. The fullest recent narrative is that of H. H. Bancroft, *Central America*, I. Peter Martyr's account of the Solis voyage to the Rio de la Plata region is based on the reports of the survivors.

The original materials for Magellan's voyage occupy vol. IV. of Navarrete. The narratives are translated in Lord Stanley, *The First Voyage Round the World* (1874). The best modern account is F. H. H. Guillemard, *Life of Ferdinand Magellan and the First Circumnavigation of the Globe* (1891). For translations of the diplomatic negotiations between Spain and Portugal and of the account of the voyage by Maximilianus Transylvanus, see E. H. Blair and J. A. Robertson, *The Philippine Islands*, I. (1903).

EXPLORATION OF THE EAST COAST OF NORTH AMERICA

The primary sources for the Spanish explorations of the North-American coast and interior are indicated in the foot-notes to the text, see above, chaps. x.–xii. The following paragraphs are merely supplementary to that material. The best of the earlier accounts of the Spanish explorations and attempted colonization of North America is A. G. Barcia, *Ensayo Cronologico para la Historia General de la Florida*, etc. (1723), arranged in the form of annals covering the years 1512–1722. It was based in part on unpublished documents.

Among the modern critical accounts of the Spanish explorations of the Atlantic coast and of such Portuguese ones as occurred later than those mentioned in the text of the present work, Harrisse's *Discovery of North America* is pre-eminent. Next would be placed J. G. Shea's " Ancient Florida," in Winsor, *Narrative and Critical History*, II. The latest study of the Spaniards in North America is W. Lowery, *Spanish Settlements in North America* (1901), a work of sound scholarship based on the sources. Lowery's references also offer a useful clew to the monographic literature of his subject. Shea has based his account of Ayllon's attempted colony (Winsor, II.) on unpublished material.

For the voyage of Estevan Gomez, Harrisse published a previously unedited contemporary account by the Spanish geographer De Santa Cruz. Peter Martyr's account, too, is primary.

The best modern discussions of the Verrazano question are those of Hugues in the *Raccolta* and Harrisse in the *Discovery of North America*. Noteworthy, too, is K. Lechner, in the *Globus* (1890). The history of the discussion over the authenticity of Verrazano's voyage is narrated by George Dexter, in Winsor, *Narrative and Critical History*, IV., chap. i. Of the two texts of the Verrazano narrative the one first known was first published by Ramusio, *Navigationi*, 1556, and this text is the one which Hakluyt translated. The other text was first published by the New York Historical Society in 1841, accompanied by an English translation by Dr. J. G. Cogswell. A critical edition of this second text was included in the *Raccolta Colombiana*. H. C. Murphy's monograph, *The Voyage of Verrazzano* (1875), reprints Dr. Cogswell's translation of the narrative, and also translations from Portuguese documents relating to Verrazano, and from Spanish documents relating to the French pirate Jean Florin.

The original of the narrative of the first Cartier voyage was republished by Tross in Paris (1867); that of the second has survived in only one copy which was critically edited by D'Avezac in 1863. These early French ventures are vividly sketched in Francis Parkman, *Pioneers of France in the New World* (1865 and later).

By the side of Parkman's brilliant narrative of the clash between the French and Spaniards in Florida Shea's equally learned but less highly colored essay deserves to stand in the front rank of the secondary accounts. Paul Gaffarel, *La Floride Francaise* (1875), reprints the contemporary narratives. The primary sources are indicated in the footnotes to chap. xii.

EXPLORATION OF THE INTERIOR OF THE CONTINENT

The primary sources for De Soto's expedition will be found in the foot-notes to chap. xi. It is to be remarked in addition that Oviedo's account incorporates material from the diary of Rodrigo Ranjel (see his *Historia General*, I., 560), not elsewhere preserved. Buckingham Smith's translation of the narratives of the Gentleman of Elvas and of Biedma, together with an English translation of the Ranjel narrative, will be found in E. G. Bourne, *Narratives of Hernando de Soto* (1904). The Spanish text of the Biedma narrative is in B. Smith, *Documentos para la Historia de la Florida* (1857). W. Lowery and J. G. Shea in Winsor, *Narrative and Critical History*, II., are excellent guides to the interpretation of the route and to the literature relating to it.

In regard to the literature of southwestern exploration, G. P. Winship, *Bibliography of the Coronado Expedition*, is a very valuable guide. It was appended to his edition of all the Coronado documents in English translation, including the original Spanish text, not previously printed, of Castañeda's narrative, published by the United States Bureau of Ethnology, *Fourteenth Annual Report* (1896). The translations have been revised in G. P. Winship, *Journey of Coronado* (1904).

The wanderings of Cabeça de Vaca and the reconnoissance of Friar Marcos have been very carefully studied on the ground by A. F. Bandelier, *Contributions to the History of the Southwestern Portion of the United States* (1890). The chapters in Lowery's *Spanish Settlements* are furnished with abundant references to the literature. The whole field of southwestern exploration is covered in detail in H. H. Bancroft, *History of Mexico* (1883), *History*

of the North Mexican States (1884), *History of California*,
I. (1884), and *History of Arizona and New Mexico* (1889).

THE SPANISH COLONIAL SYSTEM

In addition to the two series of *Documentos Ineditos de
las Indias* and its continuation the *Documentos de Ultramar*, the *Recopilacion de Leyes de los Reynos de las Indias*
(last ed. 1841) is indispensable to an understanding of the
Spanish system. *The Politica Indiana* of Juan de Solorzano
Pereira (1703) is an elaborate treatise on colonial political
and religious institutions; it is very useful but trying, owing
to the author's rambling and discursive method. Other
valuable contemporary descriptions of Spanish colonial
organization are Juan Lopez de Velasco, *Geografia y
Descripcion Universal de las Indias* (1574, first published,
1894); and Antonio de Herrera, *Descripcion de las Indias
Occidentales* (1615). Bernard Moses, *The Establishment
of Spanish Rule in America* (1898), is a serviceable ex-
position of the governmental system. R. G. Watson,
Spanish and Portuguese South America (1884), is the
best general narrative of the history of colonial South
America. Somewhat more inclusive in scope, with a useful bibliography, is A. Zimmermann, *Die Kolonialpolitik
Portugals und Spaniens* (1896).

A. Fabié, *Ensayo Historico de la Legislacion Española en
sus Estados de Ultramar* (1896), is a compendious survey
of the colonial legislation for the first half-century. Among
the general accounts of the Spanish colonial system the following may be mentioned as particularly serviceable. As
an introduction, the fifth chapter of H. H. Bancroft, *History of Central America*, I.; W. Roscher, *The Spanish
Colonial System* (Bourne's ed., 1904); Konrad Häbler,
The Colonial Kingdom of Spain, in H. Helmolt, *History of
the World*, I.; and E. Armstrong, *The Emperor Charles
V.*, II., 90–113.

There is much that is still valuable in W. Robertson, *History of America*, book VIII. (1777). Of the accounts of the

system as it appeared in individual colonies, Alexander von Humboldt, *Personal Narrative of Travels* (1818–1829), is pre-eminent for northeastern South America and Cuba, and his *Political Essay on New Spain* (1811) for Mexico. One of the best pictures of Spanish colonial life is that in F. Depons, *Voyage to the Eastern Part of Terra-Firma* (1806); compare also R. M. Baralt's description of Venezuela at the end of the eighteenth century in his *Resumen de la Historia Antigua de Venezuela* (1841). Conditions in New Granada and Peru are described by Jorge Juan and Antonio de Ulloa, *Voyage to South America* (1758 and later). The dark side of life in Peru and the corruption of political and social life were set forth in strong colors in their confidential report to the king, published eventually as *Noticias Secretas de America* (1826). Much valuable information as to conditions in Peru early in the eighteenth century is contained in A. F. Frézier, *Voyage à la Mer de Sud* (1717).

Conditions in the Philippines in the seventeenth and eighteenth centuries are depicted in E. G. Bourne, "Historical Introduction" to *The Philippine Islands*, vol. I. (edited by E. H. Blair and J. A. Robertson, 1903).

The third volume of H. H. Bancroft, *History of Mexico* (1883), concludes with a detailed picture of Mexican life. and institutions at the end of the old régime. It is, on the whole, one of the best of the general descriptions.

Arthur Helps, *The Spanish Conquest in America* (1855–1861), devotes especial attention to the status of the Indians and the introduction of negro slaves. A new edition by M. Oppenheim (1900–) has valuable additional notes and references. One of the best single volumes on the economic side of the Spanish colonial system is A. de Saco, *Historia de la Esclavitud de la Raza Africana en el Nuevo Mundo* (1879), a work based upon contemporary materials often unprinted. Saco also published a valuable study of the encomienda system in the *Revista de Cuba*.

On the mission system, besides the references given above (p. 307), may be noted Lowery, *Spanish Settlements*, 181. Perhaps the most important account of the Jesuit mission work in Paraguay is M. Dobrizhoffer, *Account of the Abipones*, etc. (1822). E. Gothein, *Der Christlich-sociale Staat der Jesuiten in Paraguay* (1883), discusses the literature of the Paraguay mission, p. 32. The missions in California are described in La Pérouse, *Voyage autour du Monde* (1786), II., 260–275; in Beechy, *Voyage to the Pacific*, I., 353–371; Duflot de Mofras, *L'Orégon* (1844), I., 261–279; H. H. Bancroft, *California Pastoral* (1888).

The earlier regulations of the commerce between Spain and her colonies are set forth in Veitia Linage, *Norte de la Contratacion de las Indias Occidentales* (1672). Later usages and modifications are described in R. Antunez y Acevedo, *Memorias Historicas sobre la Legislacion y Gobierno del Comercio de los Españoles con sus Colonias en las Indias Occidentales* (1797), and J. G. Rubalcava, *Tratado Historico Politico y Legal del Comercio* (1750). The services of the Casa de Contratacion in advancing geographic knowledge and in developing the agricultural resources of the New World are described on the basis of its records by M. de la Puente y Olea, *Los Trabajos Geograficos de la Casa de Contratacion* (1900).

The relation of the colonial system to Spanish economic life is considered by M. Colmeiro, *Historia de la Economia Politica en España* (1863), II. The beginnings of the church in Mexico, as well as many other features of Spanish colonial policy, are treated in an illuminating way in J. G. Icazbalceta, "Don Fray Juan Zumárraga, Primer Obispo y Arzobispo de Mexico," *Obras*, I. (1896), and the monographs in the other volumes of his collected works. In addition, L. Alaman, *Disertaciones* (1844–1849).

NOTE

Read Casa de Contratacion instead of "Casa de Contractacion" wherever the latter occurs.

CHAPTER XXII

SUPPLEMENTARY BIBLIOGRAPHY

BY BENJAMIN KEEN

BIBLIOGRAPHIES

C. K. JONES, *A Bibliography of Latin American Bibliographies* (2nd rev. ed., 1942), offers a good point of departure for research, but is again in serious need of revision. The indispensable *Handbook of Latin American Studies,* published annually since 1936, attempts, with the aid of specialists in various disciplines, to digest the material published the preceding year. Oscar Handlin and others, *Harvard Guide to American History* (1954), replaces the old Channing, Hart, and Turner *Guide;* it is especially useful for the themes of discovery and exploration, but lacks annotation. R. A. Humphreys, *Latin American History: A Guide to the Literature in English* (1958), is an exemplary reference work; critical and occasionally pungent comments on entries enhance the book's value. Charles Gibson and Benjamin Keen, "Trends of United States Studies in Latin American History," *American Historical Review,* LXII, 4 (July, 1957), 855-77, "provides a useful survey with extensive bibliographical notes." The new American Historical Association *Guide to Historical Literature* (1961) replaces the old (1931) volume edited by Dutcher and others; the sections on "The Expansion of Europe" and Latin American history, edited by C. E. Nowell and H. F. Cline, respectively, are of special value. Among reference works in Spanish, B. Sanchez Alonso, *Fuentes de la historia española e hispanoamericana* (3rd ed., 3 vols., 1952), is the most comprehensive; it is an immense repository of titles, arranged according to subject and period, but without annotation. Since 1953 the quarterly *Índice Histórico Español*, published by the Centro de Estudios Internacionales, Universidad de Barcelona, has been giving brief critical notices of recently published materials on Spanish and Spanish American history. Note should also be taken of the series of historiographic studies in course of publication since 1953 by the Comisión de Historia of the Instituto Panamericano de Geografía e Historia; to date volumes dealing with Haiti, the British West Indies to 1900, Ecuador, Brazil in the sixteenth century, and Paraguay in the pre-Columbian and colonial periods have appeared.

Students can keep abreast of the most recent writing in the field by consulting the review sections in the *Hispanic American Historical Review* (1926–), the *American Historical Review* (1895–), the *Revista de Historia de América* (1938–), the *Review of Inter-American Bibliography* (1951–), and *The Americas, A Quarterly Review of Inter-American Cultural History* (1944–), published by the Academy of American Franciscan History.

GENERAL SECONDARY WORKS

All of the current college texts in Latin American history treat, in varying depth, the topics featured in Bourne's book. M. W. Williams, R. J. Bartlett, and R. E. Miller, *The People and Politics of Latin America* (4th ed., 1955), is an older work, repeatedly revised, but still very useful. A. Curtis Wilgus and Raul d'Eça, *Latin American History* (5th ed., 1962), is a guidebook in the Barnes & Noble College Outline Series. Three widely used recent texts are Hubert Herring, *A History of Latin America from the Beginnings to the Present* (1955); J. F. Rippy, *Latin America, A Modern History* (1958); and H. M. Bailey and A. P. Nasatir, *Latin America, The Development of Its Civilization, 1492 to the Present* (1960). Benjamin Keen, ed., *Readings in Latin American Civilization, 1492 to the Present* (1955), provides a comprehensive collection of translated sources.

R. B. Merriman, *The Rise of the Spanish Empire in the*

Old World and the New (4 vols., 1918–34), a work of vast scope and highest merit, views the process of discovery and colonization of America as a sequel to Spain's empire-building in the Mediterranean and Atlantic. For the background of this process, see J. H. Mariéjol, *The Spain of Ferdinand and Isabella,* tr. and ed. by Benjamin Keen (1961), a lively as well as learned book. B. W. Diffie, *Latin American Civilization: Colonial Period* (1945), reveals great erudition and intensive thought; influenced by Carlos Pereyra and other revisionists, Diffie emphasizes Spanish contributions to economy and culture and deprecates Indian pre-Columbian cultural achievements; on the other hand, he takes issue with those who claim that Spain imposed no restrictions on colonial culture. Diffie's positions are frequently debatable, but always command respect. Salvador de Madariaga, *The Rise of the Spanish American Empire* (1947), is readable but speculative. C. E. Chapman, *Colonial Hispanic America: A History* (1933), is written with the author's customary verve and is not altogether outdated. A. C. Wilgus, ed., *Colonial Hispanic America* (1936) is a collection of essays of uneven worth.

C. R. Beazley, *The Dawn of Modern Geography* (3 vols., 1897–1906; repr. 1949), traces in rich detail the gradual widening of medieval geographical horizons. G. A. T. Kimball, *Geography in the Middle Ages* (1938), summarizes geographical theory, ideas of the earth, and travel up to the beginning of the Renaissance. H. H. Hart, *Venetian Adventurer* (1942), is a sound yet readable account of Marco Polo; see also Leonardo Olschki, *Marco Polo's Precursors* (1943), for early travelers to the East. A. P. Newton, ed., *The Great Age of Discovery* (1932), is a series of essays by English authorities on the great explorers. C. E. Nowell, *The Great Discoveries and the First Empires* (1951), is a brief, informing account. See also Boies Penrose, *Travel and Discovery in the Renaissance, 1420–1620* (1952); and, among older works, J. A. Williamson, *Maritime Enterprise, 1485–1558* (1913). R. A. Skelton, *Explorers' Maps: Chapters in the Cartographic Record of Geographical Discovery* (1958), is a fascinating "pictorial companion to general histories of exploration."

B. W. Diffie, *Prelude to Empire: Portugal Overseas before Henry the Navigator* (1961), is a valuable background study. S. E. Morison, *Portuguese Voyages to America in the Fifteenth Century* (1940), subjects these voyages to careful scrutiny. Edgar Prestage, *The Portuguese Pioneers* (1933), is a well-written, reliable general account. J. P. Oliveira Martins, *The Golden Age of Prince Henry the Navigator* (1914), is very readable but partly outdated.

I. B. Richman, *The Spanish Conquerors* (1918); and F. A. Kirkpatrick, *The Spanish Conquistadores* (1934), cover the same ground with sound and well-written summaries. H. E. Bolton, *The Spanish Borderlands* (1921), is a model of good story-telling and sound scholarship; it opens with a series of chapters on sixteenth-century Spanish explorers in North America, then discusses individually the areas of Florida, New Mexico, Texas, Louisiana, and California, and concludes with a chapter on the Jesuits on the Pacific Coast. H. I. Priestley, *Coming of the White Man, 1492–1848* (1928), is a broad survey of the spread of Europeans over the continent and their cultural contributions. J. B. Brebner, *The Explorers of North America, 1492–1806* (1933; repr. 1955) is a comprehensive, well-written account. John Bakeless, *The Eyes of Discovery* (1950), interestingly weaves together the first explorers' descriptions of American flora, fauna, and geography.

The process of Spanish discovery, exploration, and colonization of America is traced in detail in successive volumes of Antonio Ballesteros y Beretta, ed., *Historia de América y de los pueblos americanos* (14 vols., 1936–56).

GENERAL COLLECTIONS OF SOURCES

The most important additional collection of sources on exploration in territory now possessed by the United States is J. F. Jameson, ed., *Original Narratives of Early American History* (19 vols., 1906–1917; repr. 1959 by Barnes & Noble, Inc.). Volumes touching topics treated by Bourne are J. E. Olson and E. G. Bourne, eds., *The Northmen, Columbus, and Cabot;* F. W. Hodge and T. H. Lewis, eds., *Spanish Explorers in the Southern United States;* H. S. Burrage, ed., *Early English and French Voyages;* W. L. Grant, ed., *Voyages of Champlain;* H. E. Bolton, ed., *Spanish Explorations in the Southwest.*

For some account of the publications of the Hakluyt Society, the Cortes Society, and the Quivira Society, all of which have issued translations of important early Spanish chronicles and documents relating to Spanish America, see Humphreys (cited above). Publication of the great *Colección de Documentos Inéditos Relativos al Descubrimiento,* etc., cited in Bourne's bibliography, was continued until 1932, when the collection numbered 67 volumes. It has been indexed by Ernst Schäfer, *Índice de la colección de documentos inéditos de Indias* (2 vols., 1946–47). Other important source collections for Spanish America include S. Montoto and Rafael Altamira, eds., *Colección de documentos inéditos para la historia de Hispano-América* (14 vols., 1928–32), most useful for institutional and social history; and L. C. Blanco and J. F. Guillén, *Colección de diarios y relaciones para la historia de los viajes y descubrimientos* (4 vols., 1943–46). Some of the most important early chronicles appear in M. Serrano y Sanz, ed., *Historiadores de Indias* (2 vols., 1919), and *Historiadores primitivos de Indias* (2 vols., 1925). For other pertinent collections, see entries under "printed sources" in the section on Latin American history edited by H. F. Cline in the new American Historical Association *Guide to Historical Literature.*

LIVES OF COLUMBUS

Two recent bibliographical aids are Donald Mugridge, *A Selected List of Books and Articles Published by American Authors or Published in America, 1892–1950* (1950); and C. E. Nowell, "The Columbus Question. A Survey of Recent Literature and Present Opinion," *American Historical Review,* XLIV (July, 1939), 802–22.

Ferdinand Columbus's biography of his father remains, in the words of Henry Vignaud, "the most important of our

sources of information on the life of the discoverer of America."
Bourne's statement (in his Critical Essay on Authorities) that
"the earlier part, prior to 1492, is of uncertain authenticity,"
may now be dismissed as unfounded. For the history of the
wearisome controversy concerning the book's authenticity, see
Rinaldo Caddeo's introduction to *Le Historie della vita e dei
fatti di Cristoforo Colombo per D. Fernando Colombo suo
figlio* (2 vols., 1930). Briefer accounts are found in Ramón
Iglesia's preface to his Spanish translation, *Vida del Almirante
Don Cristóbal Colón* (1947), and in my preface to *The Life
of the Admiral Christopher Columbus by His Son Ferdinand*
(1959), the first modern English translation, superseding the
archaic version cited by Bourne.

Bourne wrote when the process of re-evaluating Columbus
and the materials for his life by the methods of modern historical criticism, initiated by Henry Harrisse, was reaching
its climax. A major figure in this tradition was Henry Vignaud,
whose *Histoire de la grande entreprise de Christophe Colomb*
(2 vols., 1911) (summarized in his *The Columbian Tradition*
(1920), materially contributed to the reconstruction of
Columbus's early life by its meticulous sifting of sources.
Salvador de Madariaga, *Christopher Columbus* (1940), is a
vividly written but highly speculative work. S. E. Morison,
Admiral of the Ocean Sea: A Life of Christopher Columbus
(2 vols., 1942), supersedes all previous accounts; it is as close
to being the definitive life of the Discoverer as the mutability
of historical knowledge and opinion makes possible. Morison
based his account of Columbus's life on the researches of other
students, but brought to his work an admirable spirit of common sense lacking in some previous writers; his major contribution consisted in reconstruction of Columbus's voyages
through re-exploration of their routes with ships approximating those of Columbus in rig and burthen, combined with
careful study of Columbus's Journals and other sources. A
recent large Spanish work is Antonio Ballesteros y Beretta,
Cristóbal Colón y el descubrimiento de América (2 vols., 1945).
D. L. Molinari, *La empresa colombina* (1938), is an admirable
compact study.

THE VOYAGES OF COLUMBUS

The principal sources for the voyages of Columbus continue to be his own writings, some preserved intact, others abstracted or embedded in the biography by his son Ferdinand (see my translation, cited above), or in the monumental *Historia de las Indias* of Bartolomé de Las Casas. Of this work there are two recent editions; that of A. Millares Carlo, with an introduction by Lewis Hanke (3 vols., 1951), and that of Pérez de Tudela (2 vols., 1957).

Cecil Jane has translated and edited letters and journals of Columbus in *The Voyages of Christopher Columbus* (2 vols., 1930), and *Select Documents Illustrating the Four Voyages of Columbus* (2 vols., 1930–33). Using the Cecil Jane translation as his base, L. A. Vigneras has produced a new version of the Journal of the First Voyage, with critical annotations and a useful appendix by R. A. Skelton on "The Cartography of Columbus's First Voyage," *The Journal of Christopher Columbus* (1960). This is a very handsomely made and illustrated book.

The *Decades* of Peter Martyr d'Anghera, cited by Bourne as the first history of the New World, is now available in a modern English translation by F. A. MacNutt, *De Orbe Novo, The Eight Decades of Peter Martyr d'Anghera* (2 vols., 1912). The word *Decades* in the title has no chronological denotation. The work originally consisted of a succession of Latin letters; hence the name *Decades* (groups of ten letters).

Recent monographs have enlarged our knowledge and understanding of the Columbian enterprise at various points. G. E. Nunn has shed light on *The Geographical Conceptions of Columbus* (1924). For ship construction see J. F. Guillén Tato, *La caravela Santa María* (1927) and Heinrich Winter, *Die Kolumbusschiffe* (1944). Columbus's language and vocabulary have been studied by Ramon Menéndez Pidal, *La lengua de Cristóbal Colón* (1942); Rodrigo de Sa Nogueira, "Portuguesismos en Cristovão Colombo," *Miscelanea de Filologia, Literatura, e Historia Cultural a Memoria de Francisco Adolfo Coelho* (1950), pp. 81–107; and J. F. Guillén Tato, *La*

*parla marinera en el diario del primer viaje de Cristóbal
Colón* (1951). Alice Gould has provided a biographical dic-
tionary of Columbus's shipmates in her "Nueva lista docu-
mentada de los tripulantes de Colón en 1492," *Boletín de la
Real Academia de la Historia* (Madrid), LXXXV–CXV
(1924-44). The problem of the site of Columbus's landfall has
recently come up for renewed discussion. E. A. and M. C.
Links, "A New Theory on Columbus' Voyage Through the
Bahamas," *Smithsonian Miscellaneous Collections* (Washington), CXXXV, 4 (1958), 1–32, argue that Columbus first
landed on Caicos; E. Roukema, "Columbus Landed on Wat-
lings Island," *The American Neptune,* II, ii (April, 1959),
pp. 79–113, restates the traditional position.

THE VOYAGES OF OTHER NAVIGATORS

On the Cabot voyages, the material cited by Bourne should
be supplemented by J. A. Williamson, *The Voyages of the
Cabots and the English Discovery of North America under
Henry VII and Henry VIII* (1929), "a definitive study," according to C. M. Andrews, "which for the first time treats
the subject dispassionately and with an historian's regard for
evidence." L. A. Vigneras has two interesting notes based on
a recently unearthed letter, "New Light on the 1497 Cabot
Voyage to America," *Hispanic American Historical Review,*
XXXVI (November, 1956), 503–509; and "The Cape Breton
Landfall: 1494 or 1497; Note on A Letter from John Day,"
Canadian Historical Review, XXXVIII (September, 1957),
219–28. For Sebastian Cabot's activity under the Spanish flag,
see the heavily documented work of J. T. Medina, *El veneciano
Sebastian Caboto al servicio de España* (2 vols., 1908).

For general accounts of the Portuguese explorations, see
Prestage, *The Portuguese Pioneers,* and other relevant entries
under "General Secondary Works."

H. H. Hart has told the story of Vasco da Gama and his
exploit in a sound yet readable work, *Sea Road to the Indies*
(1950). Jaime Cortesão, *A expedicão de Pedro Alvares Cabral
e o descobrimento do Brasil* (1922), is a standard work. On

Cabral's intentions, see C. E. Nowell, "The Discovery of Brazil—Accidental or Intentional?," *Hispanic American Historical Review,* XVI (1936), 311–38, but compare Prestage, *The Portuguese Pioneers,* Morison, *The Portuguese Voyages,* and W. B. Greenlee, ed., *The Voyage of Pedro Alvares Cabral to Brazil and India, from Contemporary Narratives and Documents* (1938).

For the secondary voyages of Pinzón, Niño, and Hojeda, see Amando Melón y Ruiz de Gordejuela, *Los primeros tiempos de la colonización, Cuba y las Antillas, y la primera vuelta al mundo* (1952), Vol. VI of Ballesteros y Beretta, ed., *Historia de América y los pueblos americanos.* D. L. Molinari, *El nacimiento del nuevo mundo (1492–1534)* (1942), is an admirable summary of the Columbian enterprise and its sequel of exploration and conquest.

NAMING OF AMERICA AND THE VESPUCCI QUESTION

The most significant development in the Vespucci controversy is the notable effort made by Alberto Magnaghi in his *Amerigo Vespucci: Studio critico* (1926) to rehabilitate the Florentine navigator by declaring spurious the two letters attributed to Vespucci describing four voyages to America, while accepting as genuine the three letters describing only two voyages. Magnaghi thus absolves Vespucci of having foisted his name upon the New World by publishing accounts of a fictitious voyage in which he claimed to have reached the American mainland before Columbus. F. J. Pohl, *Amerigo Vespucci, Pilot Major* (1944), adopts the Magnaghi position, and rates Vespucci highly as an explorer and cartographer. Not content with Magnaghi's compromise formula, Roberto Levillier, *América la bien llamada* (2 vols., 1948), claims the utmost for Vespucci, arguing for the authenticity of all the voyages on the basis of cartographic evidence. Stefan Zweig, *Amerigo, A Comedy of Errors in History* (1942), is a delightful literary version of the Magnaghi interpretation; German Arciniegas, *Amerigo and the New World; The Life and Times of Amerigo Vespucci* (1955), is an equally readable

presentation of the Levillier thesis. For source materials, see
G. T. Northrup, ed., *Vespucci Reprints* (7 vols., 1916).

SEARCH FOR A STRAIT, AND MAGELLAN'S VOYAGE

For recent surveys of these topics, see the works of Melón
y Ruiz de Gordejuela, *Los primeros tiempos de la colonización,*
and Molinari, *El nacimiento del nuevo mundo* (cited above).
On Balboa and Magellan, see the works of the eminent Chilean
scholar J. T. Medina, *El descubrimiento del océano pacífico.*
Vasco Núñez de Balboa, Hernando de Magallanes y sus com-
pañeros (2 vols., 1913–14) ; and *El descubrimiento del océano*
pacífico. Hernando de Magallanes y sus compañeros (2 vols.,
1920). C. L. G. Anderson, *Life and Letters of Vasco Núñez*
de Balboa (1941), is a semipopular treatment. C. M. Parr,
So Noble A Captain: The Life and Times of Ferdinand
Magellan (1953), is both scholarly and readable. An older life
of value is Jean Denucé, *Magellan, la question des Moluques*
et la premiere circumnavigation du globe (1911). See also
Antonio Pigafetta, *Magellan's Voyage Around the World,* tr.
and ed. by J. A. Robertson (2 vols., 1906), the journal of
Magellan's secretary.

EXPLORATION OF THE EAST COAST OF NORTH AMERICA

For convenient summaries of Spanish exploration of the
Gulf and Atlantic Coasts, see Bolton, *The Spanish Border-*
lands; H. I. Priestley, *The Coming of the White Man;* and
J. B. Brebner, *The Explorers of North America.*

Vicente Murga Sanz, *Juan Ponce de León* (1959), is an
important new work based on Spanish manuscript sources and
offers a positive assessment of Ponce as a constructive figure
in Spanish empire-building. Barcia's chronicle, cited by
Bourne, is now available in a translation by Anthony Kerrigan,
Barcia's Chronological History of the Continent of Florida
(1951).

On early French explorations, Parkman's classic *Pioneers*
of France in the New World, cited by Bourne, should be

supplemented by the opening chapters of G. M. Wrong, *The Rise and Fall of New France* (2 vols., 1928). C. G. M. B. de la Ronciere, *Jacques Cartier* (1931), and Gaston Martin, *Jacques Cartier et la découverte de l'Amérique* (1938), are two modern lives. For source materials, see the collections of documents edited by H. P. Biggar, *The Precursors of Jacques Cartier* (1911); and *The Voyages of Cartier* (1924).

EXPLORATION OF THE INTERIOR OF THE CONTINENT

William H. Prescott's classic *History of the Conquest of Mexico* (1843) remains unsurpassed for breadth of conception and literary charm, but its romantic attitudes clearly reveal the book's age. F. A. MacNutt, *Fernando Cortes and the Conquest of Mexico* (1908), is a semipopular account very favorable to its hero. H. R. Wagner, *The Rise of Fernando Cortes* (1944), is a scholarly biography. Salvador de Madariaga, *Hernan Cortes, Conqueror of Mexico* (2nd ed., 1955), features a dubious psychological interpretation; quite unreliable. Maurice Collis, *Cortes and Montezuma* (1955), is a well-written account of the conflict between two worlds of culture. Studies of the military aspects of the Conquest include C. H. Gardiner, *Naval Power in the Conquest of Mexico* (1956); Mario Alberto Salas, *Las armas de la conquista* (1950); and R. M. Denhardt, "The Equine Strategy of Cortes," *Hispanic American Historical Review,* XVIII (1937), 550–55.

Among the considerable number of sources turned into English since the appearance of Bourne's book, two of the most important are *The Letters of Cortes,* tr. and ed. by F. A. MacNutt (2 vols., 1908); and Bernal Díaz del Castillo, *The True History of the Conquest of New Spain,* tr. by A. P. Maudslay (5 vols., 1908–16).

On the subject of northern explorations, H. E. Bolton, *The Spanish Borderlands;* J. E. Brebner, *The Explorers of North America,* and H. I. Priestley, *The Coming of the White Man,* all offer sound, concise surveys. The dramatic story of Cabeza de Vaca is told in detail in Cleve Hallenbeck, *Alvar Núñez*

Cabeza de Vaca (1940). Morris Bishop, *The Odyssey of Cabeza de Vaca* (1933), is a pleasantly written biography. Newly available sources on De Soto include Garcilaso de la Vega, *The Florida of the Inca. A History of the Adelantado, Hernando de Soto,* ed. by J. G. and J. J. Varner (1951), and a new translation by J. A. Robertson of the Gentleman of Elvas, *True Relation of the Hardships suffered by Governor Fernando de Soto and certain Portuguese Gentlemen during the Discovery of the Province of Florida* (2 vols., 1932–33). For the exploits of Fray Marcos de Niza, who sighted "the Seven Cities of Cibola," see Cleve Hallenbeck, *The Journal of Fray Marcos* (1949). Recent studies of the Coronado expedition include H. E. Bolton, *Coronado on the Turquoise Trail: Knight of Pueblos and Plains* (1949), and A. G. Day, *Coronado's Quest. The Discovery of the South-Western States* (1940). For documentary material, see G. P. Hammond and Agapito Rey, eds., *Narratives of the Coronado Expedition, 1540–1542* (1940).

On Spanish explorations along the Pacific Coast, see H. R. Wagner, *Spanish Voyages to the Northwest Coast of America in the Sixteenth Century* (1929).

On the subject of Bourne's Chapter XII, "French and Spaniards in Florida," Bourne's references should be supplemented by Woodbury Lowery, *The Spanish Settlements in Florida, 1562–1574* (1911), especially for the Menéndez episode. On the general subject of Franco-Spanish conflict, see Henry Folmer, *Franco-Spanish Rivalry in North America* (1953).

THE SPANISH COLONIAL SYSTEM

C. H. Haring, *The Spanish Empire in America* (2nd ed., 1952), is an authoritative study of colonial institutions; it is particularly good on political administration. B. W. Diffie, *Latin American Civilization: Colonial Period,* is a work of formidable scholarship and sharply defined viewpoints on many topics. Bernard Moses, *The Spanish Dependencies in South America* (2 vols., 1914), is pedestrian in style and uninspired in approach, but faithfully digests available printed sources. Outstanding general works in Spanish include Carlos Pereyra, Vol. II, *El Imperio Español,* of his *Historia de la América Española* (8 vols., 1924–25), and J. M. Ots Capdequi, *El estado español en las Indias* (2nd ed., 1946).

In recent decades the political institutions of the Indies have been explored in monographic detail. Ernst Schäfer, *El Consejo Real y Supremo de las Indias* (2 vols., 1935–47), is a definitive study of the fountainhead of Spanish colonial policy. J. H. Parry, *The Spanish Theory of Empire in the Sixteenth Century* (1940), is a useful background study. Typical monographs on administrative structure include L. E. Fisher, *Viceregal Administration in the Spanish American Colonies* (1926), and her *The Intendant System in Spanish America* (1929); John Lynch, *Spanish Colonial Administration, 1782–1810: The Intendant System in the Viceroyalty of the Rio de la Plata* (1958), a study in Bourbon efforts at political reform; and J. P. Moore, *The Cabildo in Peru under the Hapsburgs* (1954). Important political biographies include A. S. Aiton, *Antonio de Mendoza, First Viceroy of New Spain* (1927), Roberto Levillier, *Don Francisco de Toledo, Supremo Organizador del Peru* (5 vols., 1935–1947), and Ursula Lamb, *Fray Nicolas de Ovando, gobernador de la Indias, 1501–1509* (1958).

An extensive literature has arisen on the juridical and moral problems created by the Conquest and on the development of Spain's Indian policy. Silvio Zavala ably summarizes modern insights into the evolution of political, social, and economic institutions in the Indies in his *New Viewpoints on the Spanish Colonization of America* (1943). He has also written on *Las instituciones jurídicas de la conquista de America* (1933), on *The Political Philosophy of the Conquest of America* (1953; orig. pub. in 1947), and on Utopian elements in the ideology of the Conquest, in *La 'Utopia' de Tomás Moro en la Nueva España* (1937) and *Ideario de Vasco de Quiroga* (1941). See also, for Messianic and Utopian influences in the Conquest, Lewis Hanke, *The First Social Experiments in America* (1933), and J. L. Phelan, *The Millenial Kingdom of the Franciscans in the New World* (1956).

On Las Casas, who played so large a part in the debate on Spain's Indian policy, see the writings of Lewis Hanke, especially *The Spanish Struggle for Justice in the Conquest of America* (1948), *Bartolomé de las Casas. An Interpretation of His Life and Writings* (1951), and *Aristotle and the American Indians* (1959), a study of the controversy between Las Casas and Juan Ginés de Sepúlveda over the nature and capacities of the Indians.

A considerable literature now exists on the economic life of the Spanish colonies. C. H. Haring, *Trade and Navigation between Spain and the Indies in the Time of the Hapsburgs* (1918), remains a standard work. Huguette and Pierre Chaunu are exploring Spain's commerce with the Indies on an archival base in *Seville et l'Atlantique* (8 vols. planned, 1955–). William Schurz, *The Manila Galleon* (1939), studies the colorful Chinese silk trade between Manila and Acapulco. On mining, see Modesto Bargallo, *La minería y la metalurgía en la América Española durante la epoca colonial* (1955), for a general survey; and, for special studies, R. C. West, *The Mining Community of Northern New Spain: The Parral Mining District* (1942) and *Colonial Placer Mining in Colombia* (1942), A. P. Whitaker, *The Huancavelica Mine* (1941), C. G. Motten, *Mexican Silver and the Enlightenment* (1950), and Walter Howe, *The Mining Guild of New Spain and Its Tribunal General, 1770–1821* (1949).

J. M. Ots Capdequi, *España en América: El régimen de tierras en la época colonial* (1959), surveys the juridical foundations of colonial land tenure. François Chevalier, *La formation des grands domaines au Mexique: terre et société aux XVIe–XVIIe siècles* (1952), a landmark in the study of colonial land systems, traces the interplay of demographic and economic trends in the development of the hacienda. L. B. Simpson has studied *Exploitation of Land in Central Mexico in the 16th century* (1956), showing, among other conclusions, the replacement of men by sheep.

The encomienda has been the subject of careful scrutiny in recent decades. A pioneer work in the field is L. B. Simpson, *The Encomienda in New Spain* (rev. ed., 1950). See also, among other studies, Silvio Zavala, *La encomienda indiana* (1935), E. R. Service, *Spanish-Guarani Relations in Early Colonial Paraguay* (1954), and E. Arcila Farias, *El régimen de la encomienda en Venezuela* (1957). José Miranda, *El tributo indigena en la Nueva España durante el siglo XVI* (1952) is a technical study for the advanced student.

On the closely related subject of population and demographic trends, see, for a general survey of nonwhite groups, Angel Rosenblatt, *La población indígena y el mestizaje en América* (2 vols., 1954). S. F. Cook and Woodrow Borah have made an extraordinarily illuminating series of studies of post-Conquest Indian population trends in Mexico; they have consolidated and revised their findings in *The Indian Population of Central Mexico, 1531–1610* (1960). Woodrow Borah's *New Spain's Century of Depression* (1951), is a fundamental work that links the decline in population to a drop in mining and food production, to the rise of Spanish latifundia, and to the growth of repartimiento labor and debt peonage. On the rise of peonage, see also Silvio Zavala's *New Viewpoints,* and his "Orígenes coloniales del peonaje en Mexico," *Trimestre Económico* (Mexico), X (1944), 711–48.

On the Negro in the Spanish colonies, see, for a general survey, Arturo Ramos, *Las culturas negras en el Nuevo Mundo* (1943), and, for a special study, G. Aguirre Beltrán, *La población negra de México, 1519–1810* (1946). Frank Tannenbaum, *The Negro in the Americas* (1946), is a comparative study of the status of the Negro in Latin America and the United States. On the slave trade, see G. Aguirre Beltrán, "The Slave Trade in Mexico," *Hispanic American Historical Review,* XXIV (1944), 402–31; and Fernando Romero, "The Slave Trade and the Negro in South America," *ibid.,* XXIV (1944), 368–86.

On immigration to the Indies, see L. Rubio y Moreno, *Pasajeros a Indias. Siglo primero de la colonización de América, 1492–1592* (2 vols., 1932). V. A. Neasham, "Spain's Emigrants to the New World, 1492–1592," *Hispanic American Historical Review,* XIX (1939), 147–60, is a slight summary article.

For summaries of Spain's Indian policy in the two great colonial centers, see Silvio Zavala and José Miranda, "Instituciones indígenas en la colonia," in Alfonso Caso, ed., *Métodos y resultados de la política indigenista en Mexico* (1954), pp. 29–112, and J. H. Rowe, "The Incas under Spanish Colonial Institutions," *Hispanic American Historical Review*, XXXVII (1957), 155–99. Charles Gibson, *Tlaxcala in the Sixteenth Century* (1955), is a careful study of Indian adaptation to the ways of their conquerors; see also Gibson's "The Transformation of the Indian Community in New Spain, 1500–1810," *Journal of World History*, II (1955), 581–607. E. R. Wolf, *Sons of the Shaking Earth* (1959), contains much provocative discussion on Mexican cultural evolution under the impact of Spanish conquest, and is provided with a very useful bibliography.

J. L. Mecham, *Church and State in Latin America* (1934), contains introductory chapters covering the colonial era. The best work on the process of conversion is Robert Ricard, *La "Conquete spirituelle" du Mexique* (1933); but see also C. S. Braden, *Religious Aspects of the Conquest of Mexico* (1930). H. C. Lea, *The Inquisition in the Spanish Dependencies* (1908), remains a standard work on the Holy Office in the Spanish colonies; for special studies, see J. T. Medina, *Historia del tribunal del santo oficio de la Inquisición en Lima, 1569–1820* (2 vols., 1887), and *La primitiva inquisición americana, 1493–1569* (2 vols., 1914). J. F. Rippy and J. T. Nelson, *Crusaders of the Jungle* (1936), is a slight semipopular treatment.

V. G. Quesada, *La vida intelectual en la América española durante los siglos XVI, XVII y XVIII* (1917), is still a useful introductory sketch. Bernard Moses, *Spanish Colonial Literature in South America* (1922), is pedestrian in style and tone, but presents basic information. Pedro Henríquez Ureña, *Literary Currents in Hispanic America* (1945), contains brilliant discussion of the colonial literary achievement. For the culture of colonial Mexico, see Julio Jimenez Rueda, *Historia de la cultura en México: El Virreinato* (1950), a work that richly merits translation; for that of Peru, Felipe Barreda

Laos, *Vida intelectual del virreinato del Perú* (1937); for that of Argentina, José Ingenieros, *Evolución de las ideas argentinas* (1937), a penetrating work written from a Marxist point of view. I. A. Leonard is a leading authority on the literary culture of the Spanish colonies; his *Books of the Brave* (1949), is "an account of books and of men in the Spanish conquest and settlement of the . . . new world"; his *Baroque Times in Old Mexico* (1960), is an elegant and sensitive recreation of the literary and social climate of seventeenth-century Mexico. J. T. Lanning is the author of a standard work on *Academic Culture in the Spanish Colonies* (1940); see also his *The University in the Kingdom of Guatemala* (1955) and *The Eighteenth-Century Enlightenment in the University of San Carlos de Guatemala* (1956). Among the substantial contributions to the history of colonial art are Pal Kelemen, *Baroque and Rococo in Latin America* (1951), G. A. Kubler, *Mexican Architecture of the Sixteenth Century* (2 vols., 1948), and H. E. Wethey, *Colonial Architecture and Sculpture in Peru* (1949).

INDEX

ABREU, ANTONIO D', at Spice Islands, 114.
Administration. *See* Colonies.
Africa, voyages on west coast, 4–7; Mauro's map, 5.
Agents. *See* Proctors.
Agriculture in Spanish colonies, royal encouragement, 215–217; value, 298; products, 298; grazing, 299, 300.
Alaminos, with Cordova, 150.
Alarcon, exploration, 171.
Albuquerque, Alfonso d', conquers Malacca, 114.
Alcaldias mayores, 234, 235 *n.*
Alexander VI., and Columbus's discovery, 29; bulls of demarcation, 31.
Alfonso V., explorations, 6; Toscanelli's letter, 12.
Almagro, exploration, 193.
Alvarado, in Mexico, 156; in Guatemala, 158; at Quito, 191.
Amazon River, discovered, 70; explored, 192.
America, discovery inevitable, 75; and Asia, 97, 104; origin of name, 90–102; supposed strait, 104; effect of Magellan's voyage, 132; character of Spanish interest, 142; bibliography on naming, 330, 346. *See also* North America, South America, and subdivisions by name.
Anticosti discovered, 146.
Antilia on Benincasa's map, 6.

Arriaga, Luis de, colony, 216.
Asia, and Columbus's objective and land-fall, 10, 11, 17, 18, 23, 24, 30; and New World, 97, 104.
Asshehurste, Thomas, charter, 62.
Audiencias, colonial, nucleus, 227; districts, 229, 232; functions, 232; court officials, 233; council, 233; appeal, 234; tour of inspection, 234; subdivisions, 234.
Ayllon, L. V. de, exploration and colony, 138–140; death, 140; location of colony, 140 *n.*
Ayolas, Juan de, exploration, 192.

BADAJOS Junta, 131.
Balboa, V. N. de, in Darien, 108; and Indians, 109; hears of Peru, 109; discovers Pacific, 109–111; fall, 111; character, 111; bibliography, 331, 347.
Bastidas, Rodrigo de, voyage, 71.
Benalcazar, at Quito, 192.
Benincasa, Graciosus, map, 6.
Bering, Vitus, voyage, 132.
Bibliographies, of Spanish America, 320, 338; of Cabot, 328, 345; of naming of America, 330, 345; of Coronado, 334, 346.
Bimine, Ponce's search, 134.